NEW EAST ASIAN
ECONOMIC
DEVELOPMENT———

NEW EAST ASIAN ECONOMIC DEVELOPMENT——

Interacting Capitalism and Socialism

————KEUN LEE————

An East Gate Book

M.E. Sharpe
Armonk, New York
London, England

An East Gate Book

The following articles are used with permission:

For chapter 1: Lee, Keun, and Hong Yong Lee, "States, Markets, and Economic Development in East Asian Capitalism and Socialism," *Development Policy Review* (London: Sage Publications) 10, no. 2, pp. 107–30 (June 1992).

For chapter 3: Lee, Keun, and Chung H. Lee, "Sustaining Economic Development in Korea: Lessons from Japan," *Pacific Review* (Oxford Univ. Press) 5, no. 1, pp. 13–24 (March 1992).

For chapter 5: Kang, Myoung-Kyu, and Keun Lee, "Industrial Systems and Reform in North Korea: A Comparison with the Case of China," *World Development* 20, no. 7, pp. 947–58 (July 1992). Pergamon Press Ltd., Headington Hill Hall, Oxford OX 3 OBW, UK.

For chapter 7: Lee, Keun, Chung H. Lee, and Won B. Kim, "Problems and Profitability of Direct Foreign Investment in China," *Journal of Northeast Asian Studies* (Gaston Sigur Center for East Asian Studies) 9, no. 4 (Winter 1991): 36–52.

For chapter 8: Lee, Keun, and Chung H. Lee, "Trade between Korea and China and Its Bohai Region: An International Perspective," *Journal of Northeast Asian Studies* (Gaston Sigur Center for East Asian Studies) 9, no. 4 (Winter 1991): 15–35.

For chapter 9: Lee, Keun, and Michael Plummer, "Competitive Advantages, Two-Way Foreign Investment, and Capital Accumulation in Korea," *Asian Economic Journal* (East Asian Economic Association) 4, no. 2 (July 1992): 93–114.

Library of Congress Cataloging-in-Publication Data

Lee, Keun, 1960–
New East Asian economic development: interacting capitalism and socialism / Keun Lee.
p. cm.
Includes bibliographical references and index.
ISBN 1–56324–218–4. — ISBN 1–56324–219–2 (pbk.)
1. East Asia—Economic conditions. 2. East Asia—Commerce.
3. Investment, Foreign—East Asia. 4. Investment, Foreign—China.
5. International division of labor. I. Title.
HC460.5.L43 1993   93–19555
338.95—dc20   CIP

Printed in the United States of America

The paper used in this publication meets the minimum requirements of American National Standard for Information Sciences— Permanence of Paper for Printed Library Materials, ANSI Z 39.48–1984.

∞

BM (c) 10 9 8 7 6 5 4 3 2 1
BM (p) 10 9 8 7 6 5 4 3 2 1

Dedicated to
So-yeon, my wife,
and
Hyung-seok, my son,
for their support

Contents

List of Tables

Acknowledgments

The two most important economic phenomena in East Asia in the 1980s and 1990s were, first, accelerating interaction among China, Taiwan, and North and South Korea, and, second, structural changes in Taiwan and South Korea. The collected essays in this volume address these two developments in an effort to highlight the newly emerging East Asian economic dynamism.

Because of the broad and current nature of the issues, I have become greatly indebted to many other scholars in compiling this volume. Some of the essays are coauthored with others, although I am the primary author of all except one article. For allowing their coauthored articles to appear in this volume, I would like to thank professors Hong Yong Lee (Chapter 2), Chung H. Lee (Chapters 3, 7, and 8), Myoung-kyu Kang (Chapter 5), Won-Bae Kim (Chapter 8), and Michael Plummer (Chapter 9).

My field work and data collection in China, Taiwan, and Korea would have been impossible or, at least, very difficult if there had not been help from Byung-gap Ahn, Wuyue Chang, Jungang Geng, Guogong Gan, Kyong-koo Kim, my elder brother Seok-keun Lee, Kesi Li, Yeong Sang Park, Yong-hee Park, Soo-Yong Shin, Keun-yi Suh, Sungshou Wei, Huimei Tzai, Gang Wang, Yuduan Wu, Xuejun Ye, Tzongshian Yu, and Teh-pei Yu.

Many other people provided me with useful comments, information, and encouragement while I wrote the essays collected in this book. For this, many thanks go to Robert Dernberger, James Dorian, Roberto

Hong, William James, Yong-wook Jun, Hagen Koo, Joon-koo Lee, Shelley Mark, Robert McCleery, Manuel Montes, Charles Morrison, Seiji Naya, Gustav Ranis, Dai-sook Suh, and Ippei Yamazawa.

The manuscript for this book was completed while I was a research fellow at the East-West Center, and I received generous support from the Institute for Economic Development and Policy and the Population Institute of the center and the two institute directors, Bruce Koppel and Lee-Jay Cho, as well as program coordinators William James and Won-Bae Kim. This work was also supported by a research grant from the Pacific Cultural Foundation in Taipei and by the University Development Funds of Seoul National University.

Finally, I would like to thank the publisher, M. E. Sharpe, Inc., and Douglas Merwin, the editor who supported this work, and I am most grateful for the editorial or research assistance of Janis Togashi, Karen Eggleston, copy editor Debra Soled, Mark Schumacher, Shung-Cho Hwu, and An-sing Chen.

NEW EAST ASIAN ECONOMIC DEVELOPMENT——

Chapter 1

Introduction

East Asia is the most dynamic economic region in the world, home to the fastest growing economies. Only in this region have we seen countries that have already joined, or are in the process of joining, the group of advanced industrialized economies, and thus graduating from the category of developing economies. If the growth decades of the 1960s and 1970s were led by East Asian variants of capitalist economies, that is, Japan, South Korea, and Taiwan, then the 1980s and 1990s have seen the increasing participation in East Asian economic development of the East Asian socialist economies of China, North Korea, Mongolia, and the Russian Far East. Furthermore, East Asian socialist regimes are expected to survive for the foreseeable future, despite the collapse of socialism in Eastern Europe, although they are also undergoing substantial political and economic changes.

The greater participation of socialist economies began with China's open-door policy and economic reforms since 1978, and then gained a second wind from the so-called end of the cold war in 1990. Postwar economic history in East Asia and radical political economic change since the 1980s in this region and the surrounding world have raised two important questions that form the themes of this book.

First, what can East Asian economies learn from one another's growth experiences? In other words, what can Taiwan and South Korea learn from Japan? What can China learn from its capitalist neighbors? What can more conservative North Korea learn from more liberal China in terms of reform strategies? And why has China shown better economic performance, compared with the former Soviet Union, despite its apparently conservative political leadership?

Second, if the current and coming decades are expected to see more economic interaction among East Asian capitalist and socialist economies, what will be the emerging or desirable mode of interdependence and international division of labor among these economies? We have already seen greater economic interaction between China and Japan, followed by emerging economic interaction among China, South Korea, and Taiwan in the last decade. In the 1990s, greater economic transactions are predicted among North Korea, South Korea, and Taiwan, and among the Russian Far East, South Korea, and Taiwan.

The mutual lessons for development and reform and the emerging mode of international division of labor in East Asia—these are the two main issues addressed by the chapters in Part 1 and Part 2, respectively, of this volume.

Chapter 2 sets the background for subsequent chapters in Part 1, focusing on strategies for economic development and reform, by providing a somewhat historical analysis of the development experiences in the region, comparing those of capitalist Japan, South Korea, and Taiwan with socialist China and North Korea. The central question addressed is how the different mechanisms of state activism in these economies led to different economic outcomes, in spite of the common initial conditions of the "hard" Confucian state in East Asia. Chapter 2 tries to characterize the unique capitalistic developmental economic systems in East Asia, where we have seen varying mixes of plans and markets. Such an effort is particularly interesting since reform-oriented China and the formerly centrally planned socialist economies of Russia and Eastern Europe are looking at the East Asian mixed capitalist economies in their search for an optimal mix of plans and markets in their economies.

Chapter 3 addresses the question of what the South Korean economy should do to sustain its development until it joins the ranks of the world's advanced industrialized countries. As a result of the rapid economic growth it has achieved in the past three decades, South Korea is now called a new giant in Asia and has become the envy of and a model for other developing countries in the world. There are now some doubts, however, about South Korea's ability to maintain sustained economic growth and eventually catch up with the industrialized countries, given its slow growth during the early 1990s.

Because Japan's development strategies have served as a model for Korean policymakers and because Japan has succeeded in achieving sustainable economic growth, this chapter compares the Japanese and South Korean economies in order to find useful lessons for the latter. The comparison focuses on the following four aspects of the two economies: state–enterprise relations, the structure of enterprise ownership and owner–manager relations, time horizon and productivity, and management and labor relations. The industrial system that supported rapid growth in the past decades in South Korea is characterized by having closed or concentrated ownership, a unified owner–manager structure, forced cooperation or confrontation between management and workers, and a conflicting time horizon between the long-term–oriented owner–manager and short-run–oriented workers. It will be argued that what South Korea needs now is a change in its industrial system such that it will become more like the Japanese system, which has open and dispersed ownership, professional management, and long-term–oriented, cooperative shareholder–management–labor relations.

Chapter 4 tries to solve the "puzzle" of contrasting postreform economic performance in China and the former Soviet Union. Why did China achieve at least mixed success, compared with the economic crisis in the former Soviet Union? This puzzle is even more interesting, considering that the Chinese leadership used to be even more conservative than the Gorbachev leadership, and seems to be more constrained by socialist ideology. Even before the aborted August 1991 coup to oust Mikhail Gorbachev from power, he was seriously losing popularity among his own population, including the intelligentsia, which once vigorously supported him, because of domestic economic crisis. For the first time in the postwar period, official Soviet sources reported negative economic growth in 1990 and 1991. In contrast, China has maintained an average 9.6 percent real growth during the reform decade from 1978 to 1988.

This chapter argues that Chinese leaders were more cautious but radical than the Soviet leaders, and that the initial conditions for success of reform were more favorable for China. Despite the failure of state-sector reform in both countries, China alone has succeeded in creating many new nonstate economic entities as the "engine" of growth whereas the former Soviet Union failed to do so.

Chapter 5 evaluates the effectiveness of recent North Korean reform measures through comparison with the Chinese reform experience. It first describes the North Korean economic system and identifies recent reform efforts, which were motivated by the increasing seriousness of the problems typical of centrally planned socialist economies. The comparative analysis focuses on the following four aspects of the industrial systems in North Korea and China: state–enterprise relations and the soft budget constraint problem; the decision-making structure in enterprises; intraenterprise income distribution and the problem of incentives; and changes in the planning system and the associated enterprises.

It will be shown that there is nothing innovative about North Korean reform measures, most of which were tried in other socialist economies, in particular, China. Thus it is expected that the impact of state-sector reform will be quite limited. It will be easier for North Koreans to try to allow nonstate sector and foreign joint ventures to grow than to try radical reform of the state sector. Only in such areas will reform be successful, as the Chinese experience suggests.

As the first chapter of Part 2 on the international division of labor and interdependence in East Asia, Chapter 6 provides an overview of China's open-door policy, which signaled the beginning of a new era in the Asian-Pacific economy, moving toward more interaction among diverse economies based on different economic systems and ideologies.

The overview first describes the country composition of China's foreign trade, investment, and borrowing in the Asian-Pacific region. Next, it addresses the issue of international economic complementarity and competition among China, Japan, the newly industrializing economies (NIEs), and the members of the Association of Southeast Asian Nations (ASEAN). The rise of South Korea and Taiwan as China's major trading and investment partners will be discussed, as well as less complementarity between China and the ASEAN–4 (Indonesia, Thailand, Malaysia, and the Philippines) than between China and the four NIEs (South Korea, Taiwan, Hong Kong, and Singapore).

It will be argued, in view of China's very low debt–service ratio, that Chinese policymakers have too conservative a perception of the appropriate level of foreign debt, and that China can and should borrow more for rapid modernization, which would also ease domestic capital shortages. Aggressive foreign borrowing will be important since the competition for labor-intensive direct foreign investment will be stiff between China and the ASEAN–4, whereas the NIEs will attract skill- or technology-oriented investment.

If Chapter 6 is a macroeconomic overview of China's open-door policy, Chapter 7 provides a microeconomic assessment of it, with statistical analysis of survey data of foreign ventures in the Tianjin area. This chapter first explains briefly the three major forms of direct foreign investment in China and the situation in the Special Economic Zones (SEZs). Then it uses the survey data to investigate the problems and profitability of direct foreign investment in China and to draw some policy implications.

The empirical analysis finds that there are several systemic constraints on the profitability of foreign investment in China, such as input and foreign exchange shortages, rigid labor policies, conflicts between business partners, and uneasy relations with state authorities. The derived policy implication is that unless the investment environment is further improved, China will not succeed in competing with other developing countries to attract enough foreign capital for its modernization.

Although South Korea's so-called Northern Economic Policy coincided with China's open-door policy, it has been on the top of the South Korean government's policy agenda since the 1980s. The Northern Economic Policy aimed to expand South Korea's economic interaction with the economies of China, the former Soviet Union, Mongolia, Vietnam, and the East European economies. Among those (currently or formerly) socialist economies, China is still the biggest economic partner for South Korea. In particular, South Korean economic transactions with China tend to be heavier with China's northeast provinces and the Bohai region (Beijing and Tianjin and Hebei, Shandong, and Liaoning provinces). Chapter 8 investigates the current state and future prospects of trade between South Korea and China and Bohai.

First, the chapter compares the basic economic profiles, including trade patterns, of China, Bohai, and South Korea. Then it explores the trade prospects between these economies using one index of export similarity and another of trade complementarity. Also examined are the trade creation and diversion effects of the trade opening between South Korea and China and Bohai during the last decade, and alternative future trade projections are presented.

Another important economic change happening in East Asia is the industrial restructuring and economic transition in two NIEs, South Korea and Taiwan. These two countries are facing one of the most critical stages in their economic development, which will determine whether they can smoothly join the group of the advanced industrialized economies or remain semi-industrialized economies.

In South Korea and Taiwan, substantial increases in domestic wage rates and previous accumulation of capital have raised the issue of transition into more skilled labor- or technology-intensive industries and restructuring or foreign reallocation of old labor-intensive industries in accordance with changing comparative advantage. Taiwan and South Korea have emerged as important sources of outward direct foreign investment (DFI) flows since the mid-1980s. The last two chapters in this volume take up these issues from an international perspective, focusing on DFI flows.

Chapter 9 provides a simple theoretical framework and an empirical analysis of the relationship among competitive advantages, inward and outward DFI, and domestic capital accumulation, applied to the case of South Korea. Outward DFI in Korea is found to originate largely in those sectors where Korea has proved its competitive advantages in world markets and Korea has received a large amount of inward DFI. In other words, inward DFI flows seem to have contributed to enhancing the competitive advantages of Korean manufacturing in certain sectors, although it does not seem to have led to a more rapid domestic capital accumulation of the recipient sector, which is determined largely by profit rates. The analysis in this chapter also identifies the three types of outward DFI in Korea: outward DFI seeking cheap labor in foreign countries to maintain competitiveness or profitability of production; outward DFI defending market shares, mostly in markets of members of the Organization for Economic Cooperation and Development (OECD), given the increasing protectionistic trade barriers; and outward DFI seeking advanced technology in developed countries.

Chapter 10 investigates structural changes in Taiwan's economy and related outward DFI flows into China and other Asian countries. It addresses the issue of what roles outward DFI can play in Taiwan's industrial restructuring and transition. Regarding investment relations with China, the following questions will be addressed: What motivates Taiwanese businessmen to invest in China? What difficulties do they face? And what are the responses and policies by state authorities in Taiwan and China? These questions are asked to determine the typical and most suitable model of Taiwanese investment in China. Information from case studies of several Taiwanese companies in China will be used to address this issue.

Part I

Strategies for Economic Development and Reform

Chapter 2

States, Markets, and Economic Development in East Asia

Many economists now openly admit that where market signals alone are not effective guides to desirable action, appropriate nonmarket institutions should be created, and that the market-versus-government dichotomy is deceptive. If this is so, then the difficult question is how the state should intervene. The numerous cases of state failure in capitalist developing economies as well as in socialist planned economies show how difficult this problem can be. In this light, the rapid economic growth achieved in Japan, South Korea, and Taiwan—which all had a substantial degree of state intervention—should be considered as remarkable.[1]

This chapter analyzes state activism under the different economic systems of capitalism and socialism in East Asia. Such a comparison is interesting because East Asian capitalism grew with several socialist-like elements in it, including a state-owned or state-controlled banking sector, a relatively large number of state-owned enterprises (especially in Taiwan), and direct state intrusion in private enterprise operation. Thus China, South Korea, Japan, and Taiwan can be considered along a continuum ranging from a centrally planned socialist economy to a purely capitalist market economy. Furthermore, a strong trend in China from a centrally planned economy toward market socialism is reducing the distance between China and East Asian "state capitalism," though the latter is undergoing liberalization. Many policymakers in China, and in the formerly centrally planned economies of Eastern Europe as well, openly say that the coexistence of plans and markets in East Asian capitalism can be a useful guide in their transition efforts.

Our analysis focuses on the nature of state control, the mix of public goals and private business, and the discipline mechanism, and thereby tries to characterize an East Asian economic system that is neither capitalist free market nor (centrally planned or market) socialist. While our attention will be on the relationship between economic performance and state activism, this does not mean that other factors are ignored. In fact, the state is conceptualized as a goal-oriented institution operating as an intervening variable between a country's given historical, economic, political, and natural conditions and economic outcomes. Obviously, these are interrelated and influence each other. Performance of any institution, including the state, which is basically a historical product, depends on the cultural setting, among other factors. The acceptable scope of state activities is determined largely by the cultural and traditional expectations of the rulers and the ruled. Markets also operate within a specific context of existing political and cultural institutions.

In this light, comparing Japan, South Korea, and Taiwan with China is worthwhile since all four countries have similar cultural and historical traditions, which differ from those of the West. We first identify the common initial condition as the tradition of a hard Confucian state in East Asia. Then we investigate the different mechanisms of state activism in these economies, which we believe are responsible for the differences in the economic outcomes. In the next section, theoretical discussion on the nature of states is presented with particular focus on the relationship between political authority and economic activity.

States, Markets, and Economic Development

Broadly speaking, there are three ways to induce selfish and individualistic human beings to cooperate with one another in society: coercion based on power, persuasion based on shared beliefs, and exchange based on self-interest (Lindblom 1977). Politics largely involves authority relations, which use a mixture of coercion and voluntarism (depending on the degree of its legitimacy) to command compliance; in contrast, economic activities are fundamentally driven by exchange relations, which are supposedly voluntary insofar as the exchange satisfies the utility of the actors involved in the transactions.

Diverse combinations of authority and exchange relations can be used by states to regulate political and economic activities in various concrete systems. The minimal noninterventionist state intervenes in the economy only to correct narrowly defined instances of market failure, such as failing to provide public goods.[2] Thus economic activities are independent from political authority. In maximal states, authority relations are predominant not only in the polity but also in the economy, and thus replace voluntary exchange relations based on self-interest. In the socialist maximal state, the state's political authority in the economy is reinforced by state ownership of the means of production. Between noninterventionist minimal and maximal states, there can be diverse medium states. In other words, everything that does not qualify as one of the two extreme types can be considered a medium state. A medium state's intervention goes beyond correcting market failure or simply setting the rules of the game; at the same time, a medium state does not allow complete control of the economy through political authority. Japan, South Korea, and Taiwan can be considered medium capitalist states, while many socialist states now undergoing marketizing and privatizing reform would qualify as medium socialist states. In view of our research plan, the nebulous definition of a medium state is sufficient at this stage. Any effort to define the medium activist states more precisely may lead to omission or oversight of key factors. Eventually, our investigation of the East Asian medium states will identify several important elements of medium states' intervention in these economies.

It is also useful to distinguish between hard states and soft states. Hard states are autonomous from partisan interests of social groups and foreign interests, while soft states are not.[3] If autonomy from partisan interest is a definition of the hard state in its passive meaning, the hard state in its more active meaning can be defined as one that is ready to place an obligation on people in all social strata and to require rigorous enforcement of the obligation, in which compulsion plays a strategic role.[4] In soft states, as Myrdal (1968, 277) refers to South Asian societies, with their low level of social discipline, the leaders are unwilling to impose obligations on the people.

By combining minimal, medium, and maximal states with a hard or soft state, we can generate diverse types. The relative effectiveness of the various types of states can be assessed in terms of their capacity to fulfill different tasks, such as development, war, postwar reconstruction, and so forth.[5] An economy whose goal is to catch up in terms of economic development would require a hard state because development requires a well-coordinated, nationwide effort. Soft states would not be effective for the purpose, since soft states impose few obligations on individuals either to do things in the interest of the whole society or to avoid actions opposed to that interest. Furthermore, the developmental state should be hard enough to resist pressures from social groups and partisan interests because these distributional coalitions tend to bring about institutional paralysis and thereby slow down a society's innovational and adaptational capacity (Olson 1982).

The hard or soft nature of the state is important because the possibility for the state to promote economic growth for the benefit of all its members is logically predicated on the state's internal autonomy from a particular social class or group and on the state's external autonomy from foreign interests. In our opinion, a common initial condition that was shared by all the East Asian states was the tradition of the hard Confucian state. Thus, in what follows, we first examine the hard Confucian state in East Asia, which sets the basic background for the peculiar role of the state in East Asian economic development.

Capacity and Autonomy of the Hard Confucian State

Several factors have determined the capacity and autonomy of the states in East Asia, including the historical role of the state, the state's autonomy from domestic partisan interests, and the state's external autonomy from foreign interests. The state as an institution and its domination of society have long been part of East Asia both intellectually and culturally. In East Asia, the origin of the state, regardless of how one defines it, can be traced back to the beginning of the societies. Since the Qin dynasty established a centralized state almost two thousand years ago, the states in China, Korea, and, to a lesser extent, Japan, have developed elaborate and complex structures with an absolute (or symbolic) emperor and elaborate bureaucracy that wielded not only political but cultural and economic power over society. States in East Asia are historically expected to be militarily creative, spiritually impressive, and economically productive. East Asians expect the state to foster economic growth not only to benefit the public but to build the country's military potential (Hofheinz and Calder 1982).

The capacity of the East Asian states has been determined by the strong elitist orientation, which allowed the Confucian paternalistic state to be staffed by the best educated elites. Japan, Korea, and Taiwan followed the Chinese tradition of recruiting civil servants from the best-educated individuals through a competitive civil service examination. The state examination system kept the channel to political power open for talented and ambitious individuals. Such a tradition enabled the existence of a highly trained bureaucracy whose autonomy from society is usually discussed with reference to the social class from which they were recruited and to their personal relations with the dominant class after assuming official positions.[6] Despite the expansion of employment opportunities in the private sector in the modern era, the most able and talented young people in these countries preferred to be government officials selected through the civil service examination, and they are supposed to act as the guardians of the public interest.

Another factor that has influenced the role of the state in East Asia is the contact and sometimes humiliating experiences of East Asian states with the Western powers in the modern era. Unable to defend themselves from external pressure, the old feudal regimes in China and Korea collapsed; the one became a semicolony, and the other a colony. As they recognized their backwardness and were subjected to Western imperialist aggression, the East Asians came to believe that they needed a powerful state that would use its overwhelming political power to resolve their problems at once. Western pressure on Japan to open itself to the outside world led some elements of the Tokugawa ruling class to seize state power. After the successful "revolution from above" in the Meiji restoration, Japan became the first Asian country to hold status equal to that of the Western powers.[7]

The modern experiences with foreign powers nurtured the East Asian proclivity to view existing world markets as favoring economically strong actors—who at least have more choice than economically poor ones, even in an ideal free-trade regime—and to regard power relations as having a crucial bearing even on economic comparative advantage. Thus from the beginning, the East Asian states tended to show a strong nationalist attitude. In the extreme, China and North Korea adopted a stance of self-reliance and closed their economy to any foreign influence. Even for the followers of an outward-oriented development strategy, such as South Korea and Taiwan, self-reliance or economic independence had great appeal, and the outward orientation was accepted only as a means of attaining self-reliance.

Although both South Korea and Taiwan have increased their economic dependence on the world market, they managed to remain autonomous from international capital. While their national economies became increasingly competitive in the world market, they successfully resisted excessive penetration by multinational corporations. To a certain extent, this success derived from the cultural tradition of a strong state and nationalism. These two factors, among others, dissuaded domestic capitalists from colluding with foreign interests against the national government. Consequently, it was the national state rather than foreign capital that determined what role transnational capital would play in the domestic division of labor.[8] Of course, nationalism supported the Japanese rise as a late imperialist power in Asia during the prewar period. Japanese nationalism continued after the war, though with a more economic connotation. In fact, according to one Ministry of International Trade and Investment (MITI) official, Japanese industrial policy is a reflection of economic nationalism, with nationalism understood to mean giving priority to the interests of one's own nation (Johnson 1982, 26).

While their modern experiences with foreign powers led East Asian states to develop a strong nationalistic tendency, their turbulent sociopolitical experiences more recently have further contributed to the strong internal autonomy of the states. The dominant class had less political influence in East Asian countries than in Western Europe—which allowed for greater state autonomy.

In China, the Communist revolution overthrew the preliberation class structures.[9] Land reform ended the political influence of the landlord class, which had frequently acted as the guardian of society when the traditional state adopted policies adverse to its interests. The collectivization of agriculture shifted control over economic resources from individual peasants to the state, thus depriving society of resources with which to challenge the state's authority. Similarly, the nationalization of industry deprived the capitalist class, which had never developed much political influence, of any control over those resources. The introduction of the materials allocation system through the state plan politically emasculated the urban population, making it completely dependent on the state for its income. A series of campaigns after 1949 undermined the social prestige and political influence of intellectuals. Consequently, the socialist state in China became totally autonomous, even with regard to the interests of the working class.

In Korea, Japanese colonialism had substantially weakened the legitimacy of the traditional ruling class, even though the policy was to co-opt rather than to destroy them. Although compromising in nature, land reform after liberation reduced the political influence of the landlord class (H. Lim 1985, 47). Thereafter, it was the state—by means of its authority over domestic and imported foreign resources, including the formerly Japanese-owned properties—that created a new capitalist class. Therefore, the state has retained strong leverage over the capitalist class; with recent limited political democratization, however, the capitalist class's political influence over the state has been increasing.

In Taiwan, the Nationalist party elite, who fled to the island after losing in mainland China, did not control much of the economic interests in Taiwan. However, they carried out a successful land reform, thereby reducing the political clout of the traditional landlords. The mainland-origin political elites, mainly concerned with recovering the mainland, allowed the native Taiwanese to pursue their interests in the economic arena. Although the state initiated many large-scale state-owned enterprises, many small firms have sprung up since then. However, the capitalist class continues to have only limited political influence (Haggard 1990). Although the Japanese case is complicated, one can stress that the U.S. occupation reduced the political clout of the dominant class by dismantling the prewar zaibatsus (large conglomerates owned by rich families) and the military machine, while leaving the prewar bureaucratic structure largely intact (Johnson 1982).

Thus in the authoritarian regimes of South Korea and Taiwan, strong leaders, backed by the military, did not allow any challenge to the state's authority; at the same time, they tried to keep most of the population politically demobilized. Stressing political stability and social order as prerequisites for economic growth, the authoritarian regimes tried to prevent the formation of distributional coalitions, which are often not conducive to economic growth. In a slightly different political context, postwar Japanese "soft authoritarianism" (Johnson 1982) allowed the extremely strong and comparatively unsupervised state administration to be ruled by one party for more than three decades and permitted the state to regulate social conflict for economic purposes.

In sum, the hard state nurtured through the tradition of Confucian Chinese culture and strong nationalism made it possible for China, Japan, Korea, and Taiwan to view the state as a mobilizer for economic development—a goal accepted as a common good, beneficial to all members. Although explicit coercion was, in reality, frequently employed, the Confucian tradition helped to justify, and, to a certain extent, actually moralize, political authority by stressing the collective interest and the ruler's responsibility to take care of the needs of the ruled. Furthermore, some of the Confucian values must have worked positively with the economic development process. For example, the stress on worldly achievement, working hard, frugality, discipline, and a commitment to education in the Confucian tradition are also qualities that Max Weber found in the Protestant ethic; these qualities played a decisive role in developing Western capitalism.[10] However, the mode of state involvement in the development process was diverse in various countries, which resulted in correspondingly different economic outcomes today.

Intersection of States and Markets in East Asia

Market-Suppressing State Activism in China

In the socialist maximal state of China, the state used its political authority to socialize all means of production and directly manage the economy, and rejected exchange relations as a principle by which to guide economic activities. Communist party authority penetrated every formal organization and institution, leaving little room for exchange relations to operate. Thus the state was a highly inclusive structure, outside which no autonomous social group or organization existed. All individual Chinese are frozen to a work unit (*danwei*), which was organized to be as self-sufficient as possible, that made authoritative decisions affecting one person's entire life (Tsou 1986).

The strength of the socialist maximal state in China was in its extensive mobilization of human and physical resources, which enabled it to solve the problem of absolute poverty and to provide basic living requirements to the world's largest population. Mobilization capability is important at the initial phase of development, when capital formation is critical. However, as the economy matures, mobilization becomes less important, and the state's ability to mobilize resources tends to decrease with time. The long-run sustainability of the socialist maximal state strategy is problematic for various reasons.

First, the state administration severs voluntary exchange relations between economic actors and instead imposes a vertical authority structure similar to a government hierarchy. In other words, authority relations are used inappropriately, namely, to run the economy, which requires a different kind of treatment. This tends to nurture corruption as well as inefficiency, as the need to obtain stamps of approval from various state authorities becomes more important in running the economy than any economic criteria. The state apparatus itself is contaminated by commercialism because of its direct involvement in running the economy (Y. Wang 1987). Features of the economy, such as bargaining and exchange for the pursuit of private economic gains, invade the state apparatus.

Moreover, a critical tension emerges in the socialist hard maximal state—namely, the tension between the hardness and socialism—which originates from the contradiction between socialist values, such as economic security and equality, on the one hand, and the requirements of the hard state, such as an individual's obligation to society and social discipline of individuals, on the other. As the initial revolutionary passion loses its intensity over time, individuals' feelings about their obligations to society weaken. In addition, because socialism guarantees basic living conditions to all individuals and continuation of operation to all enterprises regardless of their performance, socialism is bound to face the problem of weakening social discipline. If we borrow Kornai's terms, all economic actors in socialism, whether they are enterprises or individuals, tend to be under a "soft budget constraint," which implies low motivational efficiency (Kornai 1986).[11]

While all hard states face the potential danger of degenerating into soft states, the existence of the aforementioned two problems in socialism makes the possibility much higher in the case of the socialist hard state. One symptom of the soft state is the gradual decrease of socialist states' implementation capability. This is also related to the increasingly high cost of implementation based on coercion and the ineffectiveness of persuasion based on shared beliefs (that is, socialism losing its power as a mobilizing ideology). Obviously, the soft maximal state is the worst combination as compared with the soft minimal state, where the impacts of the state on the economy are relatively limited.

Unless future growth is supported by improvements in productivity, innovation, and voluntary initiatives, and unless state policy implementation can base exchange relations on self-interest rather than on compulsory mobilization, modernization at a pace that is sufficient for China to catch up with more advanced countries or even the NIEs will remain a distant goal. Recognition of this point led the Chinese leadership to initiate economic reform in the late 1970s. However, the danger of the reform is that it is, at least in the short run, more likely to contribute further to turning the hard maximal state into a soft chaotic one. While the reform substantially loosened the former vertical control of the economy, no alternative mechanism for horizontal or autonomous discipline, such as a full-fledged market mechanism, was institutionalized. Given the distorted resource allocation mechanism and unfair economic competition, the emphasis on voluntary material incentives resulted in the pursuit of pecuniary gains by local bureaucrats, private entrepreneurs, and ordinary workers, often through rent-seeking activities rather than through production or economic efficiency–improving activities (Keun Lee 1991).

Therefore, even after a decade of reform, the Chinese are still trying to find out what the most suitable form of new economic management is for them, namely, a proper balance between authority and exchange relations, and what is a workable mixed economy of plans and markets (*shangpin jihua jingji*, commodity planned economy). The Chinese are now trying to learn from the experiences of their NIE neighbors, where authoritarianism and markets have coexisted.

Market-Conforming State Activism in Japan, Korea, and Taiwan

The tradition of the hard nationalistic Confucian state designated the state as mobilizer for a common goal in East Asia. The political leadership viewed economic development as a national imperative and persuaded the society that a strong modern economy was a public good that would benefit everyone (although in reality the sacrifice of the many might have created disproportionate opportunities for the few). Such a consensus on basic goals—regardless of whether it is created in a deceitful manner through false persuasion, through coercion, or is genuinely based on shared beliefs—is one of the most important requirements for the success of state intervention (Eads and Yamamura 1987).[12] Such a national consensus on the basic goals and the role of state activism to attain these goals did exist in China. The differences between China and the three East Asian countries of Japan, South Korea, and Taiwan thus lie in terms of the nature of the state activism.

The Nature of State Control

The serious scarcity of capital across the three countries forced firms to depend heavily on credit for raising finance beyond retained earnings.[13] In the absence of effective capital markets, the state used its control over the banking system to channel domestic and foreign savings to selected industries or firms. Virtually all banks are owned by the government in Taiwan, and this was also true in South Korea until recently. Although many banks have been privatized, the South Korean government still remains the biggest shareholder or maintains effective control over the banking institutions through its personnel policies. In Japan, the banks are largely privately owned, but they depend on the central bank for access to supplementary deposits on which to expand their lending (Johnson 1982; Wade 1988). Their enormous levels of borrowing from the central bank are permitted so long as they respect the central bank's conditions for allocation of the funds.

In Japan and South Korea, the government exercised almost direct control over private sectors through their control of credits. In contrast, the Taiwanese government did not exercise such direct control over small business-oriented private sectors through bank credits, although it maintained certain control over them through its control of imports and foreign exchange.[14] However, small private firms were heavily affected through production linkages by the surrounding large-scale firms (Wade 1990, 249), and the Taiwanese government had direct control over these mostly state-owned, large enterprises, which had a more significant impact on the economy in the 1950s and 1960s than the large number of small and medium-size private enterprises.[15] Thus it can be said that to the extent that government interference was effective toward the large-scale sector, the government was able to influence indirectly the investment decisions of the private sector. Although Taiwan's industrial policies have not been so aggressive as those in South Korea and Japan, the argument that Taiwan is a good example of a free-market economy is misleading.[16]

For state activism to be effective, state ability for financial control is critical. One often does not notice the critical difference between state's financial control through credit allocation and other control instruments, such as tariffs, import quotas, tax incentives, and entry or trade licenses. First, financial control implies more discretionary control. In credit allocation, the state can not only control the financial ability of firms, but can also force the firm's compliance in other matters. Second, a qualitative difference is that the state's financial control is not based on its political authority, as it is for other instruments supported by legislation or regulations; rather, the state's financial control is based on the state's economic power, which is associated with its ownership of either banks (in South Korea and Taiwan) or funds themselves (in Japan, city banks owe money to the central bank). Third, whereas most other controls, except licensing, are aimed at specific industries or sectors, and thus affect firms only indirectly, financial control is directly aimed at individual firms. For these three reasons, the nature of financial control in Japan, South Korea, and Taiwan is similar to the control mechanism in socialist economies, which have no macroeconomic policies, only microeconomic firm-level control that is discretionary, ownership based, and direct.

In this regard, a simple but fundamental fact should be noted: the state's financial leverage over firms translates into control because firms have a strong motivation to improve their performance and because firms believe that credit supply is critical. In these three countries, the firms' motivation for success derives from private ownership and the expectation that they will be the beneficiaries of their good performance.[17] Thus even if big business is subject to a so-called soft budget constraint because of special connections with state agencies, that does not necessarily lead to weak motivational efficiency, as it does in socialist firms, but can, in fact, lead to exactly the opposite behavior, that is, excessive risk taking.[18]

Exercise of financial control over firms by the state in Japan, South Korea, and Taiwan placed the firms in a condition of dual dependence on both the state and markets. This dual dependence is also found in the socialist medium states undergoing marketizing reform, where state enterprises are dependent on both the state and markets (Kornai 1987). Apart from ownership, the difference between the two groups lies in the direction of state control, which originates from the different nature of the state agencies involved.

State agencies that oversee socialist firms are industrial ministries or local supervisory agencies, which used to have complete control over every aspect of firm management in the pre-reform period. Newly introduced market forces are generally viewed as threatening the authority and control of the state agencies, and thereby their defined interests. These state agencies are not the central planning agency interested in overall economic rationality; rather, they want to maintain their control over firms for the sake of control, so their control is "market defying." In contrast, state agencies that utilize the state's financial leverage over firms in the three countries are central ministries, and their control is "market conforming" in the sense that their aim is to foster competitiveness of specific sectors or firms, which would otherwise be difficult to attain by market forces alone within a short period of time (Eads and Yamamura 1987, 435). Their purpose is to buffer market swings and to anticipate market developments, not to go against the market.

The Mix of Public Goals and Private Business

State intervention in the three countries has often been described by the term *industrial policy* (*sangyo seisaku* in Japanese; *chanye zhengci* in Chinese), which is aimed at affecting specific sectors selectively. The industrial rationalization policies even involve crude state intrusion into the detailed operation of individual enterprises with measures intended to improve their operations (Johnson 1982). This state intervention tries to influence business activities to serve public goals. Because profitability signals that are used in private business decision making may not necessarily promote national economic interests, there was a belief that private decisions over consumption and savings, work and leisure, and sectorial distribution of investment funds might not conform to national development priorities.

Such a belief led to direct state intervention in big private business in Japan and South Korea, and a large public sector consisting of many state enterprises in Taiwan.19 In the latter case, the state was able to control directly production activities and the investment pattern. In the former case, the boundary between the private and the public sector was not rigid, as it is in Western capitalism. State and private businesses maintained a close, long-term, cooperative relationship, and the state participated in enterprise decision making almost like a business partner. C. Lee (1992) conceptualizes the close relations between the government and large firms in Korea as a "quasi-internal organization" along the lines of Williamson's (1975) transaction cost economics. Similar networks between the state and big firms existed in Japan. The so-called administrative guidance (gyosei shido), meaning non–legally binding guidance that is issued by ministries mostly in written form but on occasion orally, was based on a long-term, multifaceted, and intense relationship (Eads and Yamamura 1987).

Direct state intervention in Japan, South Korea, and Taiwan in business can be deemed successful in the sense that it significantly affected the rate of investment in certain economically strategic industries and led private businesses to do something other than what they would otherwise have done without the intervention, or it even created new actors to undertake initiatives (Amsden 1989; Johnson 1982; Wade 1990). These cases suggest that the state has a comparative advantage vis-à-vis markets as an implementation mechanism. Based on transaction costs economics, C. Lee (1992) argues that "internal implementation" by a quasi-internal organization could be more effective than "market implementation" in achieving necessary developmental goals. Nonmarket hierarchical allocation helps to resolve the problems of imperfect markets and policy implementation because such a network structure allows for the specialization of decision making, economizes on communication costs, and reduces uncertainty by coordinating the decisions of interdependent units in adapting to unforeseen contingencies.

A comparison of the Taiwanese and Korean experiences of import substitution of heavy and high-technology industries in the 1970s shows the difference between market implementation and internal implementation. In Taiwan, private entrepreneurs were unable and unwilling to make large capital investments with a long gestation period (Park 1990). As a result, government had to rely on state-owned enterprises to undertake the investment and the results were not totally successful. In contrast, South Korean *chaebols* (conglomerates), supported by ambitious government schemes, jumped in without caution, which resulted in excessive and duplicative investment. This example shows that internal implementation can be quick in achieving tangible, but not necessarily economically efficient, outcomes. Eads and Yamamura (1987, 447–48) also warned against the belief that the state's industrial policy has the unquestionable ability to create competitive advantage, by illustrating several cases of failure despite MITI's aggressive guidance and assistance. The point is that industrial policy cannot totally substitute for underlying economic conditions; rather, it acts within the framework of those conditions.

One question that remains is why direct state intrusion in business activities (especially state-owned enterprises in Taiwan) was effective on average in these three countries and did not result in bureaucratic rigidity and inefficiency. Other than the existence of a large number of small and medium-size private businesses that supported the basic vitality of the economy, the unique discipline mechanism in Japan, South Korea, and Taiwan should be noted.

The Dual Discipline: Markets and Networks

Although state intervention reflects some suspicion about markets and individual economic actors acting in their self-interest, state intervention in these three countries did not ignore the markets. State intervention was "market augmenting" in the sense that it reduced uncertainties and risks related to business, generated and disseminated information about opportunities, and inspired an attitude of expansion among the people. That is opposed to "market-suppressing" planning, where increasing fragmentation of the market or proliferation of rent-seeking opportunities occur (Y. Lim 1981, 4–8). The effort to increase competitiveness in markets provides evidence of the respect the three governments had for the disciplining function of markets and their willingness to accept market outcomes.

The principal function of a market organization is to relate responsible economic actors to an adequate level of payoff, namely, rewards and penalties. The socialist maximal states replaced the resource allocation function of the market with central planning at the cost of cutting the link between performance and payoff, which resulted in low incentives. The lesson to be learned from this experience is that, whatever the form, state intervention should not suspend the most important function of the market, that is, the disciplining of producers against the wasteful use of resources. State intervention in Japan, South Korea, and Taiwan either did not paralyze the disciplining function of the market or effectively supplemented it with an alternative discipline mechanism whenever the intervention weakened market discipline.

In Japan, although domestic producers were immune from competition with imported goods and were less dependent on the world market than were Korean and Taiwanese producers, Japanese producers expanded through severe discipline in a partly government-created oligopolistic competition in a relatively large domestic market (Hadley 1970). South Korea and Taiwan, with their smaller domestic markets, allowed more monopolistic production in some industries. Nevertheless, the South Korean government strongly encouraged infant industries to begin exporting very early (Westphal 1984) and thus exposed them directly to international competition. Taiwan relied more on the threat of allowing imports if the prices of domestic substitutes rose much higher than the international prices (Wade 1988).

These facts answer in part a theoretical question: why can outward orientation be an effective development strategy? Aside from the obvious benefits—such as obtaining essential inputs, technologies, capital, and markets to achieve economies of scale—what additional benefits does foreign trade offer? Naturally, participation in the world market means that the economy will be subject to external conditions; hence, a national government faces constraints on policy choice. However, these constraints are not necessarily costly relative to their benefits. Export orientation imposes market discipline, which the domestic market is not able to offer to protected producers, and thereby imposes a set of constraints on domestic economic policies that prevent the adoption of measures which are severely antithetical to growth (C. Lee 1992). World market prices, which are externally determined, force the export-oriented firms and the political leadership to be economically and politically efficient. In other words, the lack of both economic and political competition within a country is complemented by competition in world markets. This is why Korean chaebols and Taiwanese state-owned enterprises were able to maintain efficiency and competitiveness despite domestic protection. In contrast, an inward-oriented economy, which lacks this disciplining effect, is more prone to resource waste and rent-seeking activities (Srinivasan 1985). China's restriction on international trade, particularly after the Sino-Soviet dispute, was one reason for the slow productivity growth.

In addition to domestic or world market discipline, administrative interference supplemented the market in terms of a more immediate and constant discipline. The continual discipline function of the government was effective since an intimate network existed between the state agencies and the big firms. The government as a supplier of credit has a strong incentive to stay well informed about the conditions of the firms. Firms that do not show satisfactory performance or that borrow without due commercial caution cannot normally expect the continuation of loans. The combination of the goal-committed government and the unique government–business relationship made it possible for even protected producers to be under strong pressure and given incentives to become more efficient in the future (Jones and Sakong 1980; C. Lee 1992).

However, the efficacy of the network organization requires a growth-committed hard political leadership and market verification; the possibility of collusive and inefficient behavior by the bureaucrat–business collusion and unjustifiably prolonged protection should be checked.[20] These conditions are generally met in these three countries, but not in China, which also has a network connecting the state authorities and the enterprises. In China, the network resulted in collusion between local state authorities and enterprises in expropriating state assets for irregular private gains (Keun Lee 1991).

Conclusion

It is impossible to give a context-free answer to the question of whether the state can be relied on to do the "right" thing and avoid doing the "wrong" thing. The three East Asian countries of Japan, South Korea, and Taiwan represent a strong case for state activism. Their experiences suggest that a certain mechanism of state activism exists in the economy, which is effective for speeding up economic development, and that the effective mechanism varies in each country because of the different conditions. In these East Asian medium activist states, the mechanisms were different from those found in either maximal socialist states or minimal noninterventionist states.

Aside from the existence of a growth-committed hard political leadership and national consensus on the goals, our investigation has identified three important constituents of the mechanism. First, state activism in the Japan, South Korea, and Taiwan was based not only on purely political state authority but, more important, on their real economic power, which derived from state ownership of banks or loanable funds; the state's financial control over big business worked as a highly discretionary and qualitatively different control instrument that was not available in minimal states. Second, their businesses were subject to a double discipline mechanism—namely, market discipline, especially to exogenous world markets in the cases of the more outward-oriented Taiwan and Korea—and market-conforming network discipline based on the intimate long-term relationship between the well-informed state agencies and business. Third, state activism played a part, not in the small-business–oriented private sector, but only in targeted strategic sectors and big businesses, where the private-public boundary was ambiguous or did not exist (as in the case of Taiwanese state-owned businesses).

The above three elements can be a blueprint of a new economic system for any pro-growth political leadership in a capital-scarce economy. The ideal economic system would be based on market operation and private ownership of all businesses (except state ownership of banks, a few natural monopolies, or strategic industries) and would be run by a network of efficient bureaucrats and ambitious entrepreneurs with a strong outward orientation. Clearly, this system is neither a minimal state's free-market economy nor a maximal socialist state's planned economy; it is also different from the conventional picture of market socialism by Lange (1964). China, which is today a medium socialist state, may want to emulate this system, but this will require privatization of more state enterprises, more entrepreneurs, and a greater outward orientation than exists at present.

Of course, the performance of this system also depends on other factors, as shown by the past experiences of Japan, South Korea, and Taiwan. In the case of East Asia, despite the great diversity at concrete levels, one important and common initial condition was the historically inherited hard Confucian state. The authoritarian regimes of these three countries were hard enough to resist partisan pressures from social forces, to convince the population of the public-good nature of economic growth, and to conduct well-designed industrial policies; at the same time, the regimes could take advantage of the private initiatives, and their political stability lengthened time horizons for private entrepreneurs. Thus, their model can be defined as late, capitalistic nation building, given the tradition of Confucianism and nationalism, led by hard bureaucracy through well-informed industrial policy including selective protection and an outward orientation.

For simplicity, if we think of the degree of state activism as ranging from a minimal state, on the right, to a maximal state, on the left, the optimal developmental state must lie somewhere between the two. Given the initial conditions, the optimal balance was struck in Japan, South Korea, and Taiwan, while socialist China went too far to the left. The history of the Japanese state indicates how difficult it is to find the optimal degree of state activism.[21]

Korea and Taiwan had different experiences in their search for an optimum intervention mechanism. Right after independence in 1948 and during the post–Korean War period in the 1950s, the South Korean state under President Syngman Rhee was softer and smaller than the state since the 1960s under President Park Chung Hee, an ex-military modernizer. The Rhee regime was preoccupied with how to build its political support and was not capable of mobilizing human and physical resources for economic development (Lim 1985, 48–49). The soft nature of the state can also be seen in the compromising nature of the land reform. Unlike Korea in the 1950s, Taiwan possessed not only a strong political leadership but an economic policy apparatus that was staffed with reformist technocrats (Haggard 1990, 86). The nationalist regime in Taiwan was harder than the Rhee regime and conducted comprehensive land reform between 1949 and 1953. The government established the Economic Stabilization Board in 1951 and shifted toward a more centralized economic policy with its first four-year economic plan in 1953. The South Korean "waste" of the ten years in the 1950s can be related to the gap in the growth record between Korea and Taiwan.

In contrast to South Korea under the Rhee regime, North Korea under Kim Il Sung adopted a maximal hard state approach. The well-acknowledged superior performance during the 1950s of North Korea relative to South Korea is consistent with the view that the maximal hard state is a better choice for the task of initial mobilization and postwar reconstruction. The Chinese experience also confirms this view, and the maximal hard Chinese state thus seemed optimal until about 1957, when China claimed the establishment of a socialist base with the first five-year plan. Showa Japan also experienced something close to the maximal state between 1935 and 1955, which covered the Manchuria and Pacific War period, followed by postwar reconstruction. After this time, Japan shifted back toward the right to enter into a high-growth period.

In contrast, the Chinese maximal state has continued to persist until recently. This happened because the Soviet-type maximal state was chosen in China, not because it was "plan-rational," but because it was "plan-ideological," to use Johnson's terms. In socialist China, state ownership and central planning were not rational means to a developmental goal; they were fundamental values in themselves, not to be challenged by any economic criteria (Johnson 1982, 18). Partly freed from the "plan-ideological" stance, the reform-minded post-Mao leadership is trying to find a new optimal level of state activism somewhere to the right of the original position.

In terms of the prospects for state activism in East Asia, two theoretical points should be made. First, the initial conditions, such as the hard Confucian nature of the state, change. Second, with the changing internal and external conditions, both the actual and optimal degree of state activism also changes. Depending on the adaptability and other intrinsic ability of the state leadership and bureaucrats, a gap between the actual and optimal level of state activism may or may not emerge. The hard nature of the East Asian state seems to be changing, with authoritarianism being gradually replaced by more democratic rule. At the same time, the implementation capability of the state is being weakened. Some Confucian values that had acted positively in the past—such as collectivism and high work morale—as well as a sense of the national imperative toward the goal of economic development (namely, growth ideology) are losing their influence among the people.

Moreover, there are signs that the three essential features of East Asian state activism are also changing. First, privatization of banks and capital market liberalization would reduce the effectiveness of the most powerful control instrument, financial control, of the activist state. This would also mean a loss of control over the investment pattern. In a sense, capital market liberalization can be considered a critical turning point in terms of state ability to intervene. Second, the network discipline is losing its effectiveness as state autonomy is decreasing and the influence of the dominant class or big business is increasing.[22] For instance, Korean chaebols, which the state once helped to grow, now complain about unnecessary bureaucratic interference and want to be freed from state control or even want to gain over the state (E. Kim 1988; Lee and Lee 1992). In other words—and this leads into the third feature—the boundary between public and private business is becoming more rigid as the scale and complexity of the private sector increases. From the state's point of view, this in turn means less leverage over, and less information about, private business. Put together, these phenomena indicate a trend toward the minimal state, which is to be expected as one country graduates from the imperative goal of economic development.

If the autonomy of the state is no longer guaranteed, it might be better to have the minimal state, especially from the point of view of those who have no influence on state policy-making. In the cases of the soft medium or soft maximal state, the neoclassical economists' view that economic growth is best achieved when economic decisions are left to private, competing individuals or firms will become increasingly valid. However, if economic development remains an incompletely achieved goal for East Asia and if necessary structural shifts do not occur by market forces alone, the case for continuing state activism remains. As a sort of emulation of Japan, even the United States began to show some signs of a new developmental, industrial policy orientation. This is not to say that the NIEs and Japan should continue their current levels of state intervention. It is obvious that the East Asian model defined above can no longer sustain future economic growth in East Asia. The tendency toward liberalization and deregulation, however, does not necessarily mean that the mix of authority and exchanges in the future will soon become more like the pattern observed in the Western advanced economies. Given the current difficulties facing South Korea and Taiwan, a new appropriate development model has yet to be designed.

Notes

1. The terms *state* and *government* are used interchangeably in this chapter, although the former is generally more inclusive than the latter.

2. Other than providing public goods, the main reason for a minimal state to intervene is macroeconomic stabilization to manage unemployment and inflation rates.

3. Recognition of the possibility that the state is partially endogenous to vested interests of the society is the difference between the neoclassical political economy and the traditional neoclassical welfare economics (Colander 1984; Srinivasan 1985).

4. The opposite of the hard state as defined here is the soft state of South Asia (Myrdal 1968, 66–67). The term *hard state* was also used in Jones and Sakong (1980).

5. Johnson (1982, 19–20) distinguished the developmental state from the regulatory state. The regulatory or market-rational state concerns itself with forms and procedures and does not concern itself with substantive matters. In contrast, the development or plan-rational state has as its dominant feature the setting of substantive social and economic goals.

6. See H. Lee (1991) on the formation and transition of political elites in socialist China.

7. On the early history of Meiji Japan, see Livingston, Moores, and Oldfather (1973).

8. See Mardon (1990) on how the Korean nationalist state shaped the pattern of foreign capital integration to facilitate the expansion of domestic firms.

9. This paragraph relies on Tsou (1986).

10. Of course, some Confucian values are obviously antithetical to capitalist ethics. Indeed, some scholars believe that certain Confucian traits were the cause of East Asia's previous inability to develop economically.

11. Kornai's (1986) concept of the soft budget constraint refers to the relax-

ation of the strict relationship between earnings and expenditure, which occurs when firms expect that excess expenditure will be paid by some other institution, typically the state, in the form of "soft subsidies and soft credits." In this situation, firms are not sensitive to their performance, since their continuing operation is almost guaranteed by the state regardless of whether they make profits or losses.

12. The so-called growth ideology that was supported by political stability of harsh or soft authoritarianism contributed to lengthening time horizons and made manufacturing a much more feasible alternative to commerce as a field of entrepreneurial activities (Johnson 1987).

13. According to Zysman's (1983) definition, the three countries had a so-called credit-based financial system, as opposed to the capital-market–based financial system that prevailed in the United States and England. Firms in Taiwan and South Korea depended more heavily on bank credits than did most other developing countries (Wade 1988, 132).

14. Given the relatively high rate of private savings, Taiwan's private sectors were less dependent on state-owned banks for credit. Moreover, for political reasons, indigenous Taiwanese businessmen wanted to be less dependent on the mainland-origin government (Haggard 1990; Ho 1978).

15. In the 1950s, state-owned enterprises accounted for an average 50 percent of manufacturing value added in Taiwan (Park 1990).

16. For an explanation of the differences, see Wade (1988) and (Park 1990).

17. Of course, this is not the case for Taiwanese state-owned enterprises. Explanation about their performance will be provided later, with regard to the discipline mechanism.

18. Park (1990) mentioned risk taking in the form of excessive and duplicative investment in the heavy industry drive in South Korea in the late 1970s.

19. In the case of Taiwan, the Kuomintang government's effort to build the state sector was partly based on political rationale (see Haggard 1990; Ho 1978).

20. Regarding the uses of credit by Korean chaebols, the impression of the ordinary Korean is that credit diversion was substantial and that the chaebols earned substantial amounts of money by credit diversion. Thus, rather than trying to say that the diversion was small, we can say that it contributed to the chaebols' capital accumulation and hence, enabled them to invest in new risky lines of business.

21. Modern Japan between 1868 and the early 1880s went too far to the left with direct state operation of economic enterprises (Johnson 1982). Meiji Japan began to shift toward the right to correct the earlier failure. However, even during Showa Japan with the establishment of MITI in 1925, the history of the degree of state involvement is checkered.

22. This is related to the fact that effective state intervention makes it more clearly an arena of social conflict and makes the constituent parts more attractive targets for a takeover.

Chapter 3

Sustaining Economic Development in South Korea: Lessons from Japan

As a result of the rapid economic growth it has achieved in the past three decades, South Korea is now labeled a new giant in Asia and has become the object of envy and a model for other developing countries (Amsden 1989). There are now increasing doubts, however, about South Korea's ability to maintain sustained economic growth and eventually catch up with the industrialized countries. The partial political liberalization implemented with the birth of Roh Tae Woo's regime in 1987 has not been without cost to the economy. This so-called democratization cost has strained economic performance as every social stratum has demanded compensation for its past sacrifice. Workers have waged intense large-scale strikes for higher wages, better working conditions, and even direct participation in enterprise decision making. Although rapid wage rate increases have eroded the international competitiveness of Korean products, big business has done little to prevent this erosion through investing heavily in R & D. Instead, it has indulged in real estate and stock market speculation.

The performance of the Korean economy has suffered further because of changes in external conditions. Low oil prices, low interest rates, a strong Japanese yen, and a weak Korean won, which were all favorable to the rapid expansion of the Korean economy during the mid-1980s, ceased to prevail in the late 1980s. In fact, for the first time since 1974, South Korea suffered negative real growth in exports in 1989 and has yet to regain its past vigor in export growth. The balance of trade, which recorded enormous trade surpluses in the mid-1980s, turned into a deficit of U.S.$2 billion in 1990. For 1991, the deficit was as much as U.S.$7 billion.

Can South Korea sustain the high economic growth rate of the past three decades to the point that it can join the ranks of the industrialized countries? One now hears pessimistic forecasts about the future of the South Korean economy as its exports become less competitive in the world market and as it seems unable to catch up with Japan in technology. Although the government has not sat idle in the face of declining economic performance, its effort to boost that performance with traditional macroeconomic policies has not been successful. The problem that the South Korean economy now faces cannot be fixed with traditional macroeconomic policies; because its root lies in the basic structure of the economy, its solution requires structural reform. Japan's development strategies have served as a model for Korean policymakers, and Japan has succeeded in achieving sustainable economic growth, so a comparison of Japanese and Korean economies for the purpose should yield useful lessons for the latter.[1]

A basic premise underlying this chapter is that both the Japanese and South Korean economies have developed with active state intervention, especially in big business. Given this premise, the changing role of the state in the Korean economy should be examined and compared with that of Japan. We will then address the following three specific characteristics of the industrial system, focusing on large manufacturing enterprises: (1) the structure of firm ownership and owner–management relations, (2) time horizons of various economic agents, and (3) management–worker relations.

State–Enterprise Relations

Supremacy of the State Over Business

The state in both Japan and South Korea has been characterized as a developmental state, as opposed to the regulatory state of the West, because it has played an active, intervening role in economic development (Johnson 1982). The East Asian tradition of the "hard" state, nurtured through the influence of Confucianism and nationalism, has helped make the state a mobilizer of resources for national economic development. Their growth ideology, supported by the political stability of authoritarianism, has contributed to the lengthening of the time horizon of business undertakings and has made manufacturing a feasible alternative to commerce as a field of entrepreneurial activity (Johnson 1987).

One important necessary condition for successful state activism in the economy is its "hardness" (see Chapter 2 in this volume). At a minimum, the state must be autonomous from partisan interests of various interest groups, especially the dominant class. Such a state may even be able to place an obligation on all social strata, forcing them to trade current for uncertain future benefits (Myrdal 1968, p. 277). Given its growth ideology and unencumbered with distributional strife, the hard state can thus initiate the process of capital accumulation.

Although the relationship between the state and big business has been generally cooperative in both South Korea and Japan, they were not partners of equal standing, especially during the period of rapid economic growth (Wade 1988; Jones and Sakong, 1980). The state was the senior partner, providing big business with leadership. In fact, the state–business relationship in the two countries can be characterized as having a hierarchical, quasi-internal organization, in which administrative and other guidance by state authorities affects the decision making of large business enterprises (Chung Lee 1992).

The supremacy of the state over private business derives from a diverse set of interacting factors. First of all, the state controlled financial resources by nationalizing the banking sector (Korea) or by controlling the city banks and postal savings (Japan)(Eads and Yamamura 1987). As they were highly leveraged, private enterprises had to rely heavily on bank credit allocated by the state. Thus the acceptance of state supremacy was a necessary cost of the financial liquidity essential for the survival of an enterprise.

There were also several politico-economic events in postwar Korea and Japan that helped the state consolidate its dominance over the society, especially big business. There is, however, a certain difference in this process between the two countries, which accounts for the increasingly divergent pattern in their industrial system.

A series of reforms carried out immediately after World War II, such as the dissolution of zaibatsu, the purge of business executives responsible for the war, and a land reform, led to the emasculation of family owners' control over big business (Kiyonari and Nakamura

Table 3.1
Ownership and Control in South Korean and Japanese Firms

	South Korea		Japan	
	1983	1986	1936	1966
Managerial control (SDS less than 10%)	7.4%	1.8%	41.0%	60.0%
Minority-owner control (10% ≤ SDS ≤ 50%)	88.6%	82.8%	46.5%	38.0%
Majority-owner control (SDS larger than 50%)	5.0%	13.2%	12.5%	2.0%
Total	100%	100%	100%	100%
Number of firms	149	226	200	200

Source: South Korean data are from U. Lim (1988, 69). Japanese data are from Kiyonari and Nakamura (1980, 268).

Note: SDS stands for the share of the dominant shareholder including his/her relatives.

1980; Toshio 1989). Such reforms, which diminished the power of the society but left intact the power of state bureaucracy such as the MITI, strengthened the autonomy of the state and its dominance over the society in Japan.

One of the important consequences of these reforms was the weakening of the power of former zaibatsu families and the consequent separation of management from ownership. In fact, as can be seen in Table 3.1, many of the large enterprises in Japan are now controlled by professional managers, some of whom were formerly junior executives in the prewar zaibatsu period.[2] Between 1938 and 1966, the share of the firms under managerial control increased from 41 to 60 percent but the share of majority owner-controlled firms decreased from 12.5 to 2 percent.

The political leadership in Korea did not face anything like the zaibatsu in Japan. When the military under the leadership of General Park Chung Hee took over the government in 1961, there were a few *chaebol* groups (Korean, conglomerate). These groups, which had prospered by processing imported materials financed by U.S. aid, were, however, brought under control by the government, which charged them for accumulating wealth illicitly. At about the same time, the government nationalized the banks and took over the power of credit allocation.

The Park regime saw the chaebol as a useful and necessary instrument for its objective of economic growth (E. Kim 1988). This policy of relying on existing private firms instead of establishing new state enterprises, as the Kuomintang regime did in Taiwan, however, laid the foundation for the subsequent growth of the chaebols' power. Their power has now grown so much that it weakens the policy autonomy of the state. In other words, chaebols whose growth the state initiated and fostered have now become monsters that it can no longer control. This eventual outcome was inevitable because the government did not foresee the importance of keeping chaebols out of family ownership and thus away from control by a small number of tightly knit groups of people.

Since the mid-1970s, the Korean government has undertaken various measures to control the excessive concentration of economic power in chaebols. In 1974, special presidential directives were issued in order to open up privately held firms to public ownership and reduce reliance on debt financing. The same year, the government also introduced a new bank credit control system under which chaebols' major customer banks were to monitor their heavily indebted customer companies. Those chaebol groups with outstanding bank credit exceeding a specified amount and with a high debt-equity ratio were ordered to improve their financial structure.[3] They were prohibited from establishing or acquiring additional business, receiving loan guarantees, purchasing stocks of other companies, or acquiring nonbusiness-related real estate. With controls such as these, the government, at least during the tough Park regime, kept increasingly powerful chaebols under control.

Eroding State Supremacy

In the 1980s, the regime of President Chun Doo Hwan initiated an era of deregulation, privatization, and liberalization, and state–enterprise relations turned from discretionary governance to rule governance. The Korean state is now more like a regulatory state although it retains some discretionary power over the chaebol; it can still control credit allocation through remaining state-owned special banks or the privatized commercial banks that are nevertheless under de facto state control.

To control excessive concentration of economic power, in 1984 the Korean government introduced a system under which an upper limit is imposed on the total aggregate amount of credit for each chaebol group, including bank loans and loan guarantees, that each group can avail itself of. In part because of this measure, chaebols' share of bank loans has decreased since the early 1980s (Young Ki Lee 1990). However, freed from tight discretionary control by the state, they are now freer than before to allocate resources even into the activities that are regarded as socially undesirable and unproductive.

Korea's economic success in the 1960s and 1970s was due to two important accomplishments of the Park regime. First, it created manufacturing-oriented big business out of formerly mercantile business. Second, it directed those firms to produce for world, instead of domestic, markets. In recent years, however, the chaebol groups have been increasingly reverting to their former mercantile role. In the 1980s, they invested increasing amounts of resources in nonmanufacturing business, especially land and real estate speculation and financial profiteering. Furthermore, since the late 1980s, when the Korean won underwent rapid appreciation and when the competitiveness of exports began to decline, the market orientation of chaebols has turned increasingly inward. They even started importing items that they used to export.

From a business point of view, it was natural to invest in land or stocks rather than in manufacturing when the rate of increase in land and stock prices was several times higher than profitability in manufacturing. For instance, Table 3.2 shows that in 1988 capital profitability was only 9.2 percent, whereas the rates of increase in land and stock prices were 27.5 percent and 66 percent, respectively. It is estimated that the ratio of capital gains from holding land to gross national product (GNP) jumped from 14 percent in 1986 to 33 percent in 1987 and 54.9 percent in 1988.

Real estate prices, which rose more rapidly than nominal wages, aggravated workers' morale because they led workers to feel a sense of relative impoverishment. In a survey conducted in 1990, only 24 percent of employees owned their own home, and among the employees currently without their own home, more than 70 percent saw no possibility of purchasing a house or apartment within five years.[4]

In sum, the Korean government has failed to control undesirable activities by chaebols and to sustain growth in labor productivity. This failure can be traced to mainly two causes: the increasing power of chaebols and the decreasing autonomy of the state and resulting policy failure.

Under the pressure of public outcry over various undesirable eco-

Table 3.2

Profitability, Land and Apartment Prices, and Wage Rates in South Korea

	1985	1986	1987	1988	1989	1990
1) Where to invest?						
Manufacturing capital profitability [a]	8.4	9.1	9.4	9.2	4.9	–
Land price increase rate	7.0	7.3	14.7	27.5	32.0	20.6
Stock price increase rate	5.4	63.4	83.6	66.0	32.5	–
Capital gains from land price increase [b]	10,923	12,342	34,807	67,902	–	–
as% of GNP	14.0	13.6	33.0	54.9	–	–
2) Working hard for housing?						
Nominal wage increase rate	9.9	9.2	11.6	19.6	25.1	24.6
Apartment price increase rate [c]	–	–5.0	6.9	22.0	21.7	29.4

Source: Capital profitability and (2) are from Korea Development Bank, *Measures to Increase Productivity for Enhanced International Competitiveness* (Seoul: Korea Development Bank, 1991). Other variables in (1) are from Jae-Young Son, "Analysis of and Reform Proposal for 'The Land Problem' in Korea," paper presented at the Workshop on Korea's Political Economy. Honolulu, East-West Center, August 1990; the original source is the Ministry of Construction, *Land Price Statistics,* various issues, and National Bureau of Statistics of Korea, *Major Statistics of Korean Economy 1990.* Economic Planning Board, *Economic White Paper* 1989 (in Korean), also provides land price increase rate figures.

[a] Capital profitability (measured as a percentage) = current profit / total asset value; current profit is net of financial expenses such as interest payments, but includes corporate taxes.

[b] Capital gains are measured in billions of won.

[c] Apartment prices refer to the average prices of small apartments.

nomic activities carried out by chaebols and others, the government planned two reform measures. The first was to impose heavier restrictions on the use and ownership of land in order to control land and real estate speculation. The second was to require the use of real names in all bank accounts so as to keep track of true identities of depositors and their transactions. Despite a general consensus in favor of these reforms, the government did not implement them. It was dissuaded from doing so by big business, which argued that the reforms would plunge the economy into a recession. In fact, given their size and importance in the economy, chaebols were able to use the economy as a hostage in bargaining with the government.

Since the late 1980s, the Korean government has tried to rein in the power of chaebols with several measures. It has tried to induce them to sell the land they own, but are not using for active business (the so-called May 8 Decree of 1990); to designate a maximum of three companies for each chaebol group to specialize in product lines in which it has the strongest comparative advantage and growth potential; and to reduce ownership concentration by disposing of some of the shares held by owner families. The penalty for not following the first policy initiative is higher interest payment for bank debt and an eventual credit moratorium. The incentive for the other two policy initiatives is the lifting of upper limits on credit for the three companies each chaebol group is to specialize in and for whatever number of other companies in which the owner-family share is less than 10 percent of the outstanding stock.

In spite of the various financial and tax incentives offered to chaebols, the government has not yet been successful. Chaebols have not cooperated with the government, and in fact in certain cases they have resisted the implementation of the initiatives either by circumventing the restrictions or by using delaying tactics. For instance, one month after the deadline (the end of March 1991) set by the government, the chaebol groups disposed of only 60.1 percent of the nonbusiness-related land and have resisted selling the remainder.[5] Some of the chaebols said they were willing to pay the interest penalty since they figured that the appreciation in land value would more than offset the penalty.

The incentives for ownership decentralization could also be ineffective as chaebols can receive the same kind of credit benefits by designating any of their companies for a specialized product line and then change the designation after three years. Thus, the net effect of the incentives is, as argued by some, only to free chaebols from credit control with no effect on their ownership and specialization. The situation is worse than before!

Structure of Ownership and Owner–Management Relations

The structure of ownership of a firm is one of the most important determinants of its behavior and performance. Highly concentrated ownership often implies owner-picked management or management by owners. Such management saves the agency cost of hiring management but does not in general result in management capable of handling the complexities of running a modern enterprise. In contrast, open and dispersed ownership corresponds to professional management. Its superior capability comes, however, at the cost of an agency problem between shareholders and hired management.

The relationship between ownership and management also has implications for relations between management and workers. Professional management tends to be neutral between the interests of owners and those of workers, whereas owner–managers would be clearly biased in favor of owners' interests.

In Japanese firms, ownership is widely dispersed, and shareholders rarely have an effective voice in management (Aoki 1990). For most of the listed companies, financial institutions are the largest stockholders, and a city bank called the "main bank" is commonly the biggest of a company's shareholders. This bank has close ties with the firm in terms of cash management and loans, but the management is left alone so long as it maintains a certain minimum rate of profits (Komiya 1987). Because a large portion of the equity held by banks and other corporate entities is extremely stable, Japanese managers are insulated from takeover raids through open markets. This insulation, however, does not mean that stockholders' interests are neglected. While management is immune to the threat of a hostile takeover, the possibility of its collusion with workers against shareholders' interests is checked by various monitoring mechanisms. These include bank-oriented financial control and mutual monitoring by the managers themselves, especially when firms belong to an enterprise group.[6] In fact, there seems to be a close positive correlation between the degree of management freedom and the level of corporate profits (Aoki 1990).

When a Japanese company is in financial difficulty, its main bank intervenes, but usually before the problem reaches a crisis point (Aoki 1990). This early intervention is possible because the main bank can detect early signs of the problem through its management of commercial accounts and short-term credits and through its long-term personal contact with the top management and its business partners. Recognition of the problem leads to an internal overhaul of management and various rescue operations. Finally, a takeover may take place, but only when it cannot be avoided. In fact, one could argue that because of continual information flow between the troubled firm and its main bank and because of close ties, the firm's reorganization may occur sooner than under a market-oriented system, where the relationship between banks and firms is at arm's length (Berglof 1989, pp. 237–62). It is thus likely that the incidence of bankruptcy is lower in Japan than, say, in the United States.

As mentioned above, in Korea the founder-families are the dominant owners of large enterprises, and they are the ones who effectively control management. In the case of a chaebol group, the owner maintains his control through a combination of direct share-holding and cross-holding among affiliated firms. A study of 355 listed firms found that as of the end of 1986 the largest shareholder of one firm and persons related to him together held an average 35.62 percent of the company's total outstanding shares (Ungki Lim 1988). The same study also found that the founder–owner held far more shares than necessary for maintaining control. The proportion of the Korean firms under managerial control is extremely low—less than 2 percent at the end of 1986—in contrast to Japan, where the proportion was 60 percent in 1966 (Table 3.1).

Although the large Korean firms may save the agency cost associated with hired management, their ownership structure has several inherent weaknesses. First, as the firms rely heavily on the limited pool of owner-families for managerial services, there is little room for the development of professional management. Second, there is an agency problem between the dominant shareholder, on the one hand, and small shareholders and employees, on the other. This problem arises because there is no mechanism for checking the power of the dominant shareholder, and, consequently, important decisions, including the use of retained earnings, are solely at his discretion. In a situation like this, the dominant shareholder has an incentive to expropriate the firm's earnings, for instance, for his own use since the cost of using them is shared by others (Ungki Lim 1988). For the employees, however, the firm's earnings are best used for reinvestment, as it would lead to the growth of the firm and thus to a better chance for quicker promotion and larger compensation in the future. But, typically, they have no say in the use of the company's earnings.

The origin of the owner–manager system and the lack of a professional managerial class in Korea can be found in the conditions prevailing during the initial stage of Korea's industrialization (Moskowitz 1989). When capital was extremely scarce and their technological capability rudimentary, the firms had to rely on the state for credit and trade-quota allocation. In addition, the imported technology, which was simple and unsophisticated, did not require much professional management. What mattered most for the survival and growth of the firm then was the owner's ability to manage relations with state authorities.[7]

There is now increasing need for professional management in Korea, as it is no longer capital-poor, as private firms are freer to run their own businesses, and as their products are technologically more sophisticated. It is, however, unlikely that there will soon be an increasing number of professional managers unrelated to owners in chaebols, though there already are some. What is more likely is the professionalization of owner–managers of the second or later generation, with little change in the ownership–management structure. Thus, it is likely that all the problems related to the present ownership—management structure will remain for the foreseeable future.[8]

Time Horizon and Productivity

Shareholders, managers, and workers of a firm generally have different time horizons and different discount rates for future income streams. Consequently, they generally disagree on the size and type of investment and the use of profits the firm should carry out. Thus, how to manage the different time horizons for the successful performance of the firm is an important task in management.

It can be generally argued that the longer and the more similar the time horizon is among the various constituents of the firm, the better its long-term performance is. One might, however, suppose that for an economy at an early stage of development, there is an advantage in having the practice of short-term employment contracts, since the pace of diffusion of standardized skills and technologies would be high with the easy movement of workers from one firm to another. But, for a firm in an economy on its way to mature development, there are reasons for instituting long-term employment practices.

First, for a firm in such an economy, employees' firm-specific know-how is important, as quality competition and product differentiation are critical ingredients in its competitiveness in the world market.

The employees will invest more in firm-specific know-how if they expect to stay with the firm for a long time. Second, employees with a long time horizon would be more willing to trade current for bigger future wages if they expect the present sacrifice to lead to a higher rate of growth for the firm and better prospects for promotion.

A long time horizon for shareholders likewise has a favorable effect on the long-term performance of the firm, as shareholders would be more willing to refrain from excessive demand for cash dividends and to accommodate managerial initiatives for R & D investment.

In Japanese firms, shareholders, managers, and workers all have a long time horizon. First, institutional shareholders are mostly long-term shareholders. This is especially true of financial institutions that have developed long-term business relationships with the firms in which they hold a dominant position. Second, managers come from the ranks of employees who have worked for the same company for a long time and are guaranteed long-term tenure, owing to the low possibility of hostile takeover. Workers are also guaranteed "lifetime" employment.

The lifetime employment practice, however, is not without its own drawbacks. Employees may shirk if there is no threat of being fired, and, given the difficulty of screening prospective employees, the firm may find itself stuck with unqualified employees for their lifetime. These problems of moral hazard and adverse selection associated with lifetime employment can be adequately dealt with through some modification in the policy. According to Aoki, lifetime employment is not an absolute guarantee, and the seniority system is not rigid. There is always the possibility of a midcareer discharge, and there are differences in the speed of promotion among the employees as they climb up the corporate ladder (Aoki 1990). In other words, there is a rank hierarchy in the Japanese firm, which functions as a primary incentive device.

In a rank hierarchy, promotion criteria become stricter with the advancement of an employee through the hierarchy. If an employee does not exhibit continual progress, he may be separated from the firm by being posted in a less promising quasi-outside job at a minor sub-sidiary or other related firm. What is in fact practiced in Japan is not lifetime employment but long-term employment. The long term tends to become a lifetime for most employees, since the rank hierarchy system is effective as a monitoring device, and actual dismissal is seldom carried out as a disciplinary measure. Moreover, the potential loss of seniority and of retirement benefits linked to the length of employment discourages the midcareer exit of trained employees.[9]

In Korean firms, owner–managers naturally have a long-term interest in the firm because of concentrated ownership. Workers have not had a similar long-term interest in the firm, especially in the 1970s, when they had no job security. Table 3.3 clearly shows that the Korean industrial system maintains short-run–oriented employment relations. In 1981, only 16 percent of the labor force between ages 35 and 50 continued at one firm for longer than ten years, whereas in Japan 60 percent stayed on.

Furthermore, workers in Korea are not induced to stay on at a job for a long period as the disadvantages associated with quitting—such as the loss of seniority and retirement benefits—are not very large. According to one survey, about half the Korean workers who responded were considering transfer to another company because they were dissatisfied with promotion procedures and possibilities at their present company (Table 3.3).

The short time horizon of Korean workers must be attributed to Korean management, which views labor as a disposable resource and invests little in human capital. Given the short-term employment practices, the workers themselves have little incentive to acquire firm-specific skills. This situation is exactly the opposite of what one observes in Japanese firms.

The basic condition that led to this short-run–oriented view of labor in Korean firms was the abundance of labor when modern industrialization began. This condition has changed since the mid-1970s. Now, faced with an increasing scarcity of skilled labor, firms have begun investing more in employee training and in developing more stable internal labor markets.[10] The long-term employment rate increased from 16.1 percent in 1981 to 24.1 percent in 1986 (see Table 3.3).

Management–Labor Relations

Relations between management and workers have an impact on the performance of the firm. If the interests of both parties are harmonious and are generally identified through efficient bargaining with the good performance of the firm, they could be cooperative. However, if workers see management as representing only the shareholders' interests or regard their compensation as inadequate and unfair, relations could be noncooperative, if not confrontational. In such a case, even a routine

Table 3.3

Time Horizons of South Korean Workers

1. Long-term employment rates of employees age 35 to 50 (percents):

	1981	1986
South Korean workers	16.1	24.1
Japanese workers	59.4	65.3
American workers	32.6	32.6

2. Employment career and turnover:

	Total employment career		Employed at current place	
Average	6.2 years		4.1 years	
Years	%	persons	%	persons
0–2	30.9	672	49.5	1,076
3–7	39.6	861	35.9	781
2. 8 or more	28.4	618	18.3	298
No response	1.1	24	0.9	20

3. Attitude about attachment to current job:

	%	persons
Regard current company as a permanent place	29.1	633
Considering transfer to a different company	49.4	1,074
Wait and see	21.1	459
No response	0.4	9

4. Perception about promotion process:

	%	persons
Virtually excluded from promotion ladder	31.5	686
Automatic with seniority	19.1	415
With exam or training after required period	22.7	494
Only after transfer or promotion of immediate seniors	16.7	363
Other process or no response	10.0	217

5. Perception about promotion possibility:

	%
Satisfied	15.0
Unsatisfied	35.7
Strongly unsatisfied	49.3

Notes and Source: (1) is from Hyo-Soo Lee, "A Comparative Analysis of Labor Markets in Korea, the United States, and Japan," *No-dong kyung-Jae non-Jip* (in Korean) 11 (December 1988): 29–55. Here, long-term employment rates measure the proportion of workers who have worked more than 10 years at their respective companies to the total number of workers belonging to the same age-group. (2) to (5) are from Korea Labor Institute (1990). The survey was conducted in September 1989 for 2,200 workers in 119 workplaces hiring more than 30 workers. The proportion of blue-collar to white-collar workers is 2 to 1, and that of males to females is 6 to 4.

operation would require close monitoring and strict discipline with additional costs to the firm. Furthermore, good potential employees would shy away from a firm with confrontational relations, and even those who are hired would feel little inclined to invest in firm-specific training. Thus, such a firm is likely to lose its competitiveness in the long run.

Another possibility is that relations between management and workers could be collusive. This possibility increases when shareholders fail to implement a monitoring mechanism to ensure that the management represents their interests vis-à-vis workers'. By forming a coalition, management and workers could expropriate the firm's assets to their mutual benefit at the expense of the shareholders. Such collusion could further degenerate into short-run–oriented behavior on the part of management and workers who indulge in current consumption at the expense of the firm's long-run net worth.

In Japanese firms, the employees are recognized implicitly as well as explicitly as one of its constituents, and their interests are thus taken into account in the formation of managerial policy (Aoki 1987, p. 265). Thus, while pursuing the general interest of the firm, management acts as a mediator between shareholders and employees, balancing their respective interests. This characteristic of Japanese firms contrasts sharply with the standard neoclassical view of the firm, in which the employees are simply hired inputs, the shareholders control and take risks, and managers simply manage the firm on behalf of shareholders.

Aoki has shown that in the neoclassical firm management makes decisions about employment and investment unilaterally after wages are bargained over individually or collectively with a union, and that this system of unilateral decision making may not be efficient for a large firm with an internal labor market (Aoki 1984, part 2). More efficient, he argues, is the Japanese system in which management simultaneously coordinates wage determination and other managerial decisions in cooperation with the enterprise union. In such a system, management tends to hire more employees and to strive for higher sales growth than the maximization of the share price might warrant. The system induces employees to substitute expected utility for job security and better prospects for career advancement within the firm for the immediate satisfaction derived from bigger current wages. In other words, the bargaining system found in the Japanese firm allows the exploitation of a mutually beneficial trade-off between current wages and future benefits, and thus contributes to improving the long-term performance of the firm.[11]

In Korean firms, where management itself is the biggest shareholder, there is no possibility for collusion between management and workers against shareholders, and management is primarily interested

Table 3.4

Labor Disputes, Wage Rates, and Productivity

	1985	1986	1987	1988	1989
1) Labor disputes					
Number of incidents	265	276	3,749	1,873	1,616
demand for					
wage increase	84	75	2,629	946	742
Workers involved	28,700	46,941	1,262,285	293,455	409,134
Number of unionized					
workers	1,004,398	1,035,890	1,267,457	1,707,456	1,932,415
2) Wage rate and productivity in manufacturing					
Nominal wage rate					
index	100	109.2	121.9	145.8	182.3
growth rates	9.9	9.2	11.6	19.6	25.1
Labor productivity					
index	100	117.8	134.6	154.2	172.5
growth rates	7.1	17.8	14.3	14.6	11.6
Real wage index	100	106.2	115.1	128.5	152.1
growth rates	7.3	6.2	8.3	11.7	18.3

Source: (1) is from the National Bureau of Statistics, *Korea Statistical Yearbook 1990* (1990), 93–94. (2) is from the National Bureau of Statistics, *Major Statistics of Korean Economy 1990* (1990), 93–94.

in profit maximization for shareholders. During the early stage of industrialization, labor was in fact an easily replaced resource and did not have to be regarded as an object of human capital formation (Sookon Kim 1990). Productivity increases were maintained with intense monitoring and discipline of workers, and whatever union they had did not represent them adequately to the management. If relations between management and workers occasionally seemed cooperative, they were only apparently so as the workers were always under the threat of discharge. Fundamentally, relations within the Korean firm were those of latent confrontation.

Political democratization, which began in Korea in the late 1980s, has brought to the surface the latent confrontation between management and labor. The number of labor disputes suddenly increased from fewer than 300 per year in 1985 and 1986 to more than 3,500 in 1987 and more than 1,500 in 1988 and 1989, and between 1985 and 1989 the number of unionized workers almost doubled (Table 3.4).

The overall consequence of these disputes was a rapid increase in wage rates and a narrowing of the gap between the growth rates of labor productivity and real wages. As real wages continued to increase, the gap finally turned negative in 1989, when real wages were pushed up by 18.3 percent against a 12 percent increase in labor productivity. Such a divergence between wage-rate growth and productivity growth does not bode well for the competitiveness of Korean firms in world markets.

What is needed in South Korea now is the transformation of the present labor system, which is based on confrontational relations and weak labor unions, into a system based on cooperative management–worker relations and strong labor unions (Soonkon Kim 1990). This transformation may not be easy, as there needs to be a lengthening of workers' time horizon—this change, however, is unlikely to occur unless workers can trust management. To illustrate this point, suppose that the workers agree to the trading of wage increases now for job security or better opportunities for promotion associated with the firm's future growth. After such an agreement is made and wages are fixed accordingly, management has an incentive to manipulate managerial variables such that the agreement is violated (for instance, reducing the amount of profit to be reinvested). If this opportunistic behavior on the part of management is expected by the workers, they will not be willing to forego higher wages now for future benefits. In other words, cooperative bargaining is possible only if there is sufficient mutual trust between the bargaining parties (Aoki 1987). How to develop this trust, and trust among various segments of the society, is a challenge that Korea must surmount if its economy is to continue to develop.

Conclusion

South Korea has an industrial system with closed or concentrated ownership, an owner–manager structure, forced cooperation or confrontation between management and workers, and a conflicting time horizon between the long-term–oriented owner–manager and short-run–oriented workers. Nevertheless, South Korea was able to maintain rapid economic growth until recently because the state could control big business and labor to achieve its developmental objective. As the capacity and autonomy of the South Korean state has decreased, the old industrial system has become increasingly inappropriate to sustainable growth in a changing political and economic environment. What South Korea now needs is a change in its industrial system; it should become more like the Japanese system, which has open and dispersed ownership, professional management, and long-term–oriented, cooperative shareholder–management–labor relations.

Closed or concentrated ownership is harmful because it tends to result in unproductive interference with managerial initiatives, reduce the scope of managerial service markets, and lead to higher capital costs. Independent management is critical to a firm's performance and should be promoted, provided that there exists an effective disciplinary mechanism.[12] Only with independent management can cooperative relations among shareholders, managers, and workers be formed and can they be more efficient in terms of long-run performance than the kind of confrontational relations or noncooperative relations found in the United States.[13] So long as there are appropriate incentive schemes to deal with the moral hazard problem, long-term employment for managers and workers will improve performance, as it would lengthen their time horizon. Of course, this requires provision of material incentives for workers so that they will not change jobs frequently.

In the past, a coalition between the state and owner–managers helped firms to realize large profits and suppress workers' demands. With changes in the political climate in South Korea, this coalition is no longer viable, and management must find its partner in the employees. Both workers and management must learn Japanese-style cooperation so as to maximize their benefits by first improving long-term performance of the firm instead of maximizing their short-run benefits at the expense of the other, as in the past.

It is no longer necessary, and in fact less feasible, that the state directly intervene in individual private business.[14] But in certain nonbusiness areas, such as sociopolitical and structural issues, the state can still play a useful role. It should especially restrain chaebols from engaging in socially unproductive activities and separate management from owner-families. To this end, the state will have to form a coalition with workers and the general public and enforce compliance by chaebols, which are becoming increasingly powerful and noncooperative. In South Korea, the state is the only institution that can initiate this change.

The state should also act as a mediator between the owner–management and the workers so long as there are no independent managers who can mediate between the shareholders and workers and mutual distrust between the management and workers continues.[15] In 1987 and 1988, when labor strikes were most serious, the Korean government took a noninterventionist or neutral position that industrial conflict should be resolved between management and workers. In numerous cases, however, management and workers could not reach peaceful agreements, and the state had to step in to stop or prevent violent strikes, siding mostly with management. In the future, the state should take a more neutral position as a reliable and trusted mediator.

Notes

1. Articles by Korean and Japanese scholars in Chung Lee and Ippei Yamazawa (1990) deal with various aspects of the economies of Japan and Korea. Chapter 8 of Keun Lee (1991) compares firms in South Korea, China, and Japan.

2. As pointed out by Komiya in his argument against claims by Marxists such as Nagasu, postwar Japanese capitalism cannot be labeled "monopoly capital." The reasons are, besides the separation of management from ownership, facts such as the share of property income in GNP, which decreased substantially after the war. For details, see Ryutaro Komiya (1980) and Kiyonari and Nakamura (1980).

3. For details of various government measures to control chaebols, see Kyung Tae Lee (1991) and Young Ki Lee (1990).

4. Korea Labor Institute (KLI) (1990, 141). See also notes to Table 3.3 for more on the survey.

5. Report by the Bank Supervision Office of the Bank of Korea, which appeared in *Han-kuk il-bo*, April 25, 1991. Although since then the government achieved some success in forcing chaebols to sell land, the whole delayed process revealed the weakened power of the government over big business.

6. The lack of stock market discipline on managers may pose a potential problem, including collusion with workers. See Aoki (1987).

7. Chandler's analysis of the emergence of managerial capitalism in the United States focuses on two factors: (1) the relative importance of managerial capacity to the capital provider, given the relative abundance of capital;

and (2) the scale, capital intensity, and technical complexity of U.S. industry, which necessitated sophisticated coordination by professional managers. These clearly contrast with the initial conditions that prevailed in Korea. See Chandler (1977).

8. According to a survey by the Korean management association of 318 manufacturing firms in 1990, in 80 percent of the firms, ownership and the management are not separated. See *Han-kuk il-bo*, February 16, 1990.

9. The Japanese rank hierarchy contrasts with the American system, which is a relatively decentralized market approach, with clear employment contracts relating specific jobs and competitive wages written and workers' careers oriented more to a market than to an individual firm.

10. For more on personnel policies, including employee training in Korean chaebols, see chapter 7 of Steers, Shin, and Ungson (1989).

11. The Japanese enterprise union, covering all regular blue- and white-collar employees, does not negotiate a single wage rate for each job category. Instead, it negotiates the base pay for the bottom rank, pay differentials among ranks, and the speed of promotion. Within the negotiated agreement, however, the personnel department has discretion over the ranking and job assignments of employees. In the Japanese firm, the personnel department is an important institution. It has full control over recruitment, designs and runs the rank hierarchy (pay scale and promotion criteria), and rotates white-collar workers for the purpose of having them develop the systemic interests of the organization. See Aoki (1990).

12. However, American-style discipline of the management by stock markets and markets for corporate control might be only a second-best alternative since it tends to bring about short-run–oriented managerial behavior in management and collective bargaining with workers. In American firms, shareholders, management, and workers play a noncooperative game, pursuing separate self-interests. Their attachments to firms are defined by market transactions and contracts, which presuppose free, flexible, and higher short-term mobility. However, a noncooperative game incurs costs that might be saved in a cooperative environment, and a short-term orientation misses "externalities" of long-term attachment, such as voluntary investment in firm-specific human capital, possible long-range collective bargaining, and more reinvestment of retained profits.

13. Relations between management and workers in American firms, albeit noncooperative, rarely turn confrontational, since American managers are not dominant owners of the enterprises and they have incentives to pursue their own interests between the shareholders and workers. In contrast, Korean managers who are also dominant owners pursue their interest by suppressing worker demand with the help of state authorities.

14. If there remains one important area that still requires state–business cooperation, it would be R & D investment to fill the technology gap between Korea

and other advanced economies. Since 1991 the Korean government has vigorously moved into this area. In this effort, the Japanese experiences can still serve as a good example.

15. In a survey conducted in 1989, more than 70 percent of workers responded that active or selective state intervention is necessary in the case of extended labor strife. See notes to Table 3.3.

Chapter 4

China and the Former Soviet Union: Comparing the Reform Process

The sudden collapse of Mikhail Gorbachev's reformist regime and the Soviet Union itself may not have been as much a surprise to Soviet citizens as it was to outsiders. The Soviet economy before August 1991 was truly in crisis. For the first time in the postwar period, official Soviet sources reported a drop in net material product (NMP) and gross national product (GNP) of 4 percent and 2 percent, respectively, in 1990.[1] In contrast, China has not experienced negative growth since the beginning of reform; in fact, growth of real GNP averaged 9.6 percent annually during the reform period. In China, the problem was rather to cool down the overheated economy. While it was directly caused by economic corruption of state bureaucrats and emerging inequalities in economic opportunities and income distribution, the Tiananmen crisis of 1989 was, from an economic point of view, a call for economic adjustment. After partial and short-lived recentralization, the policy direction turned more liberal, and the economy recovered from a downturn (Central Intelligence Agency 1991). Thus, the Chinese reform leader, Deng Xiaoping, continued to reign, with reformists like Zhu Rongji rising to the top leadership in 1991.

Today, Chinese openly say that Russians should learn from the Chinese experience. China exported consumer goods to the former Soviet Union to help ease shortages. Given that the Chinese leadership used to be more conservative than Gorbachev's leadership, how can one explain the contrasting postreform economic performances of the former Soviet Union and China?

With the aim of solving the "puzzle" of the differences in performance, this chapter will argue that in several important aspects of the reform strategies, Chinese leaders were more shrewd and radical than were Soviet leaders, although the initial conditions for success of the reform were indeed more favorable for China. Despite failure in state-sector reform in both countries, China alone has succeeded in creating many new nonstate economic entities, which have served as the "engine" of growth and which have contributed to the emergence of a new, more market-oriented economic environment.

After a brief comparison of the growth records of these countries and some theoretical observations, the chapter presents a comparative analysis of the former Soviet Union and China in terms of the creation of nonstate economic entities in rural and urban areas, state-sector reform, and the construction of a new economic environment. The final section provides an overall picture of the reform process in a theoretical perspective.

Growth Comparisons and Some Theoretical Observations

In the Soviet Union and China, the reform-minded leadership's intention was to build a new mixed economic system consisting of both state and nonstate economic entities operating in a mixed environment of plans and markets. The reform strategy in both was to decentralize state property rights in mainly two dimensions. The first decentralization involved the transfer of state property rights to economic entities with a view to changing the behavior of existing entities or to creating new entities. The second decentralization was to create a new, more market-oriented macroeconomic environment in which new economic entities were to operate.

Comparison of the postreform growth records of the Soviet Union and China show the contrast between China's success and the Soviet Union's difficulties. As shown in Table 4.1, while the Chinese economy grew at an annual average rate of 8.3 percent in real NMP terms during the first six years of the reform (1978–1984), compared to 5.3 percent growth in the previous period, the Soviet economy recorded an annual real NMP growth rate of 2.7 percent during the first five years

Table 4.1

Reform and Economic Performance of the USSR and China
(average annual growth rates in comparable prices)

	USSR	China
1. Prereform performance (1981–85 for USSR; 1971–78 for China)		
Net material product	3.2	5.3
Industry	2.9	8.0
Agriculture	1.0	1.8
Construction	3.2	2.9
Transportation and communications	2.9	5.7
2. Postreform performance (1986–89 for USSR; 1978–84 for China)		
Net material product	2.7	8.3
Industry	3.3	8.5
Agriculture	2.4	7.4
Construction	6.6	10.7
Transportation and communications	0.8	7.7
1990 official estimated NMP growth	–4.0	–

3. A decade of reform in China

Annual growth in constant values	1971–78	1978–84	1984–88	1978–88
Gross national product	–	8.90	10.80	9.60
Net material product	5.33	8.31	10.60	9.22
Industry	8.01	8.50	14.85	10.99
Agriculture	1.83	7.37	3.13	5.65
Construction	2.94	10.72	15.55	12.63
Transportation and communications	5.71	7.69	13.47	9.96
Grain production	–	5.00	–0.80	2.60

Annual growth in current values		1978–85	1985–88	1978–88
Gross agricultural output		14.6	17.5	15.4
Gross industrial output		14.8	23.3	15.7
State enterprises		11.4	18.0	12.1
Collective enterprises		21.9	28.3	21.4
Urban collectives		–	19.0	–
Rural collectives		24.3	35.6	24.9
Urban cooperatives		–	19.0	–
Rural cooperatives		–	38.1	–
Individual enterprises		–	63.8	–
Urban		–	27.1	–
Rural		–	70.2	–

Sources: IMF et al. (1991, vol. 1, table II.2.1); State Statistical Bureau of China (1986, 1989).

Notes: USSR figures are from IMF et al. (1991, vol. 1, table II.2.1). The original source is Goskomstat of the USSR. These NMP growth rates are widely believed to be exaggerated. The figures for China are the author's calculations based on data reported in various issues of *Zhongguo Tongji Nianjian* (Statistical yearbook of China).

of reform from 1986 to 1989 and − 4 percent growth in 1990, compared with 3.2 percent growth in the prereform period. How can this differential impact of reform be explained?

A closer look at the Chinese reform path reveals that the success of the reform mainly derives from the creation of new economic entities. Efforts to change the behavior of old economic entities, such as urban state enterprises, were generally unsuccessful. The Chinese growth record during the reform decade indicates a shift in the source of the economy's dynamism.

From 1978 to 1984, the main source of growth arose from the initial shock from the decentralizing reforms, and, in particular, the successes in agriculture that occurred with the transformation to individual peasant farming. Agricultural net output recorded real growth of 7.4 percent per annum between 1978 and 1984, compared with the prereform average of 1.8 percent.[2] However, industrial net output maintained a growth rate that was almost the same as that of the prereform period, indicating no improvement in the performance of the state industrial sector.

During the latter half of the reform decade, the engine of growth seemed to switch to new economic entities in the nonstate industrial sector, especially private and rural collective enterprises. After a peak harvest in 1984, grain harvest consistently declined in physical terms.[3] In contrast, during this period, the average annual growth rate of industrial net output jumped from 8.5 percent to 15 percent. This increase was due not to the vitalization of the state sector but to the remarkable growth and increasing importance of the nonstate industrial sector. During this period, gross industrial output of state units increased less than 20 percent per year in current terms, while gross industrial production of collective units and individual businesses grew almost 30 percent and more than 60 percent, respectively (section 3 in Table 4.1). To explain the differences in postreform economic performance of the Soviet Union and China, my arguments are basically as follows. First, whereas China succeeded in creating new dynamic economic entities in rural areas by a "revolutionary" demolition of the people's commune to create individual family farming, the Soviet Union did not dare to demolish its state and collective farms, but kept the centrally controlled system with only limited modifications, such as allowing groups of families or individual families to lease land. Second, the demolition of the commune and distribution of communal assets to individual families in China provided the material basis for the emergence of nonstate industrial enterprises in rural towns and suburban areas; the Soviet Union did not see such an emergence of nonstate enterprises. Third, increasingly market-oriented interaction between rural and urban economies thanks to the increasing dynamism of nonstate economic entities helped to absorb some of the disruptive effects of the transition from a planning-based resource allocation system to a market-oriented one, while at the same time providing a material basis for the emergence of nonstate economic entities in urban areas. Fourth, some differences in the initial conditions of the Soviet Union and China are also partly responsible for the different courses of the reform in the two countries. For instance, China's rural economy was more market oriented even before the reform than was that of the Soviet Union, the Soviet people had lived much longer under the more taut central planning system than did the Chinese, and the Soviet Union was facing a labor shortage, whereas China had a notorious labor surplus. The main processes of the urban state sector reform were basically the same in both countries, with no apparent success.

Creating New Economic Entities in Rural Areas

One of the most important changes that economic reform brought to China's rural areas was the end of the people's commune. Farmland was distributed to individual families for free production and market-ing so long as the families met certain production quotas set by the state.[4] In addition, the demise of the commune signified the separation of government administration from economic management. The new township governments were not supposed to exercise direct control over economic matters, while newly established corporate entities managed collective enterprises that were previously operated by the communes and brigades. Those enterprises that were formerly run by the communes and the brigades were changed into township enterprises (*xiangban qiye*) and village enterprises (*cunban qiye*), respectively.

With decollectivization, many commune-owned nonagricultural as-sets were sold, often at low prices. These assets formed the basis of new forms of individual and cooperative businesses (Odgaard 1988; Zhou and Hu 1989). Some families and individuals have jointly set up their own enterprises, which can be called cooperative businesses (*lianhu* or *hezuo*). There are also individual businesses (*getihu*). While township and village enterprises are based on collective ownership and

Table 4.2

Size and Feature of State vs. Nonstate Sectors in the USSR and China

A. USSR after 5 Years
  of reform (1990)

	Number (1,000)	Employment (1,000)	Share of emploment (%)	Share of NMP (%)
Cooperatives	215	5,200	3.1%	–
State units	–	–	84.0%	87
Collective farms (1988)	–	–	8.2%	–

B. China after 6 Years
  of reform (1985)

	Number (1,000)	Employment (1,000)	Share of employment (%)	Share of GVIO[a]
State enterprises	93.7	89,990.0	18.0	64.9
Urban collective enterprises	150.7	33,240.0	6.7	15.9
Urban private businesses	330.1	4,500.0	0.9	0.3
Urban cooperatives	–	–	–	–
All rural labor	–	370,650.0	74.3	–
Peasant farming	–	300,859.7	60.3	–
Township and village enterprises	849.7	41,521.4	8.3	14.6
Rural cooperatives and private businesses	3,759.4	28,268.9	5.7	3.1
Rural cooperatives	741.7	–	–	1.6
Rural private businesses	3,017.7	–	–	1.5
Total urban and rural private businesses	3,347.8	–	–	1.8
Total employment		498,730.0		

Sources: IMF et al. (1991); State Statistical Bureau of China (1989).

[a] Shares in GVIO means shares in gross value of industrial output only in current value terms. Thus, they refer to those involved in industrial production.

management, cooperative and individual businesses should be regarded as "private" since they are initiated by single or several rural entrepreneurs and can hire wage laborers. Thus, the term *rural enterprise* embraces the two types of collective enterprises and the two types of private enterprises.[5]

Rural enterprises have contributed significantly to the increase in rural income levels and employment. The share of employment in rural enterprises has increased rapidly. The fastest growth in terms of employment shares was achieved by rural cooperative and individual businesses, whose growth has been even faster than that of urban individual businesses. As of 1985, all rural enterprises accounted for about 14 percent of China's total employment (Table 4.2). Growth of rural enterprises in China was also outstanding in terms of gross industrial output. The share of all types of rural economic entities in total industrial gross output increased from less than 10 percent in 1978, to 18 percent in 1985, and to about 20 percent in 1988 (Table 4.2; State Statistics Bureau of China [SSB] 1989). This contrasts sharply with the trend of the shares of state industrial enterprises, which decreased from 78 percent in 1978, to 65 percent in 1985, and to 57 percent in 1988 (Table 4.2; SSB of China 1989).

With respect to the farm sector, Gorbachev placed heavy emphasis on the leasing of land to families since 1987 (Hanson 1990a), and the 1989 Supreme Soviet decree provided the framework for leasing, which seemed mainly concerned with arrangements in the farm sector (Tedstrom and Hanson 1989). However, the Soviet Union never made such a revolutionary decision as dissolving the state and collective farms.

Soviet agricultural reform only instilled a greater element of private motivation in what was still a socialized production system by introducing an output-oriented system of labor organization and remuneration in subunits of public farms. Even in leasing arrangements, the public farms had de facto control over the lessee, since they were the landowner, employer, input supplier, and buyer of products (Atta 1990; Wadekin 1990).

Thus, despite a partial reform effort since the early 1980s, the organizational structure of Soviet farms changed little from that of the late 1960s; the sector continued to be characterized by large state and collective fields and herds, tiny private plots, rigid wages, poor labor discipline, weak financial discipline, and little farm autonomy (IMF et al. 1991, vol. 3, 156–57). Despite official endorsement in 1989, few farm workers leased land; farm managers did not in general encourage leasing, and marketing relations of traditional collectivized agriculture were not supportive of private small-scale farming.[6]

In sum, given the continuing collective nature of agriculture, the Soviet Union did not have the opportunity to use the agricultural sector as the engine of postreform growth, as did China. This was bad not only for agriculture but also for industry and the entire economy. In the Chinese case, accumulation of wealth by rural families led to the emergence of nonfarm industrial production and corresponding markets in rural and suburban towns and townships. Rural industrial enterprises have also become an important vehicle for China's export-led growth, with exports of items such as chemicals, machinery, and light manufactured goods such as textiles accounting for about one-fifth (US$6.5 billion) of total exports in 1988 (*Renmin ribao*, December 12, 1989).[7]

Creating New Economic Entities in Urban Areas

China's urban nonstate sector has grown slowly relative to the growth of rural enterprises, mainly because the scope of central planning and the state sector is much greater in urban than in rural areas (Lockett 1988). Urban collective enterprises in China used to be "collective" only in name or ownership classification; in reality, they were under as tight state control as were the state enterprises.[8] The emphasis of reform has been on making the urban collective enterprises into "real" collective enterprises based on independent management by worker collectives (Xiao 1986). Further, many of them have been transformed into joint-stock companies in an effort toward corporatization.

Compared to the somewhat slow-moving, old urban collective enterprises, the new economic entities such as cooperative businesses have been much more active in China's urban nonstate sector (*China News Analysis* 1989b). These businesses, are initiated with the help of state authorities, mostly by individuals who are young or who have failed to acquire jobs in the state sector. While the number of this type of firm was almost negligible in the early 1980s, it had grown to 37,200 by the end of 1988 (SSB of China 1989).

Urban private enterprises also grew in terms of both numbers and output. In the Chinese classification system, there are two types of private enterprises: (1) individual private businesses (*getihu*), which are mainly based on single-family labor and have fewer than eight hired employees, and (2) private businesses with more than eight hired employees (*siren qiye*) (Ma 1988). The latter group is regarded as capitalistic and exploitive in nature, and may be called "private capitalist business."[9] Although their numbers have increased recently, individual private businesses existed before the reform period, though with some fluctuation. However, private capitalist businesses have been revived after almost completely disappearing; their official recognition and registration began only in 1988.[10]

According to reports published in recent issues of *Renmin ribao* (People's daily, November 30, 1989), there were 66,525 private capitalist businesses registered across all sectors by mid-1989, and 14,527,000 individual private businesses by the end of 1988. The average number of employees in private capitalist businesses is 16.2 persons, while that of individual private businesses is 1.6 persons (see table 7.3 in Keun Lee 1991). About 80 percent of private capitalist businesses are in the industrial sector, and about 75 percent of individual businesses are in the service sector. When we consider only industrial enterprises, gross industrial output by private and individual businesses doubled, from 3.3 billion yuan in 1985 to 6.8 billion yuan in 1988, and their numbers grew from 330,100 in 1985 to 452,800 in 1988 (SSB of China 1989).

In sum, in China's urban nonstate sector, there are four types of enterprises: urban collective enterprises, cooperative businesses, private capitalist businesses, and individual private businesses.[11] The aggregate share of these enterprises in China's total gross industrial output was estimated at between 15 and 20 percent in 1985 (Table 4.2).

In comparison, in the Soviet urban nonstate sector, there were only two types of business entities: cooperatives and individual businesses. Individual businesses were encouraged by the Law on Individual Labor Activity, which was passed in November 1986.[12] The law permitted individuals to engage in several limited areas of business, such as production of handicrafts and consumer goods and the provision of services based only on family labor. Moreover, only pensioners, students, the disabled, housewives, and others not employed in the state economy were allowed to enter into individual business activity. Despite official efforts to encourage individual businesses, their legal status was still weak and ambiguous (they were not regarded as enterprises, only as labor activities), and it was difficult to run an individual business without breaking the law to acquire materials, premises, and so on. Many black-market entrepreneurs must have chosen not to register as individual businesses because of the many disadvantages (Hanson 1990a, 83). Once registered, they would be taxed, and would have to pay for licenses.

A more active and controversial form of business activity is the cooperative, which was authorized and defined by the 1988 Law on Cooperatives in the USSR.[13] Under this law, cooperatives could be formed by groups of three or more persons and could hire labor, lease or purchase business premises and equipment, and operate on as large a scale as desired. In other words, the law was much more generous to cooperatives than to individual businesses. Thus, by October 1988, there were already more people officially registered as engaged in cooperatives than in individual labor activities (770,000 versus 628,000) (Hanson 1990a, 84).

The rapid growth of cooperatives was remarkable. As shown in Table 4.2, by October 1990, there were approximately 215,000 cooperatives, which employed about 5.2 million people (including cooperative members and hired employees), and accounted for some 5–10 percent of GDP. Some 39 percent of cooperative enterprises in 1990 were in the manufacturing and construction sectors and accounted for about 49 percent of total cooperative output (IMF et al. 1991, vol. 2, 17).

According to Goskomstat, the great majority of these enterprises (some 170,000 cooperatives out of the total 215,000) were operating on the basis of leasing arrangements within the parent-state enterprises and were formed out of whole plants or work units in existing state enterprises (IMF et al. 1991, vol. 2). Such a heavy dependence of cooperatives on the state sector underscored the dominance of central planning in the economy and corresponding difficulties in running free enterprise in terms of acquiring inputs, bank credits, and even physical business premises.

China also has similar state-dependent collective enterprises, although their size in general appears to be greater than their counterparts were in the Soviet Union. In China, various state enterprises, with the help or implicit recognition of local authorities, have set up their own subsidiary collective enterprises, mainly to create jobs for their family members. These subsidiary collectives are more common in the Northeast, where heavy state industries are dominant, than in areas such as Shanghai, which are oriented toward light industries. Such collectives have provided parent enterprises with a way to manipulate many constraints of central planning.[14]

Greater degrees of management freedom and higher incentives have led to a marked increase in the physical efficiency and quality of production in these state-dependent cooperatives or collective enterprises. In the Chinese examples, profit, per capita profit, and employment grew much faster, in some cases twice as fast, in subsidiaries than in parents (see table 7.5 in Keun Lee 1991). However, some of the growth of these enterprises should be attributed to various kinds of regular and irregular assistance from parent units.

In China, the collective enterprises that are set up by parent-state units are supposed to be self-supporting and independent. However, in practice, the parent units often provide land, buildings, supplies, administrative support, investment subsidies, or a captive market for collective output (Byrd and Tidrick 1987, 72). In the Soviet case, too, many cooperatives started with state-owned capital, for which they have paid little and which they had no right to sell. As a consequence, the managers of cooperatives appeared to focus on short-term gain, with little attention given to enhancing long-term viability of the enterprises and the value of its assets (IMF et al. 1991, vol. 2, 21).

When compared with state enterprises, nonstate enterprises in China and the Soviet Union were in a disadvantageous position in several aspects; this situation forced them to adopt a peculiar behavioral pattern. First, the legal and political status of these private enterprises is still weak. For historical and ideological reasons, the general public still distrusts private businesses and cooperatives (Jones and Moskoff 1989; Tedstrom 1990). The fragile political and legal status implied an attenuation of property rights of private enterprises.[15]

The weak political status and attenuation of property rights of private enterprises have led to short-run–oriented behavior and prevented business from expanding on too large a scale (Jones and Moskoff 1989; Li et al. 1990; Ma 1988). For example, some private entrepreneurs who had profitable businesses did not dare to invest further, but instead placed the profits into social contributions in order to buy a good reputation in the community. Others made a quick profit and then quit the business. Some indulged in personal consumption to the neglect of investment; they can evade withdrawal restrictions by receiving high salaries as managers, rather than receiving profits as owners, or by purchasing personal goods through company accounts (Byrd 1990).

In sum, the state of newly created nonstate economic entities in urban areas of China and the Soviet Union was basically similar. Given the absolute dominance of the state sectors, the nonstate economic entities had remained marginal or dependent upon state sectors for their existence. The Chinese counterparts to Soviet cooperatives were private enterprises; in both the number of involved workers was between 15 and 25. However, of the two, China was ideologically more flexible in allowing private enterprises (owned by one proprietor) to emerge. Moreover, the Soviet Union did not have relatively large-scale urban collective enterprises that hire more than 200 workers per unit (Table 4.2). Although these collective enterprises used to be controlled by state authorities, they were being turned into joint-stock companies by distributing all shares to members. Thus the potential for success was much greater for these enterprises than for similar transformations of state enterprises into joint-stock companies, where the state intended to remain as the dominant shareholder.

Unsuccessful Reform of the State Sector

In China and the Soviet Union, reform of the state sector initially focused on enlarging the autonomy of state enterprises by transferring some property rights from the state bureaucracy to the enterprises (Ericson 1988; Hanson 1990b; Keun Lee 1991). State enterprises were allowed more rights in production, purchasing, and marketing decisions, and more important, they were given some income rights in the form of allowance for an increasing portion of profits to be retained and used for bonuses, collective welfare, and investment. Dual or multiple pricing systems allowed enterprises and peasants to sell products in excess of their plan quotas at prices above the plan prices. In other words, markets were supposed to function at the margin of the planned activities.

These actions were based on the belief that greater autonomy in these areas would lead to better incentives, higher profits, and hence increased state revenues. With more autonomy, enterprises were urged to be financially independent and responsible for their own profits and losses, so as to be under a hard budget constraint.[16] However, the separation of ownership and control was not as simple as central policymakers had expected, and state-sector reform encountered property rights and agency problems (Keun Lee 1991; Winiecki 1990).

First, increasing financial resources at the hands of the enterprise in the form of retained profits did not lead to corresponding increases in economic efficiency and productivity, but only to a reduction of state revenues and aggravated budget deficits. In China, ad hoc enforcement of the sharing scheme, which was subject to bargaining between enterprises and local state authorities, resulted in a failure to stimulate enterprise incentives (Bachman 1987; Lee and Mark 1989). In the Soviet Union, ministries continued to manipulate and redistribute profits of enterprises under their jurisdiction to maintain their control and keep their ministry-level autarky.

According to Gregory (1989, 1990), the rules of the game had not changed for Soviet ministries, and they continued to be judged on the basis of aggregate physical output in the same detail as before. In a world of uncertain supply and difficult interministerial relations, ministries could ensure plan fulfillment by being as independent as possible. For this purpose, each ministry had to have its enterprises produce diverse, unspecialized products, often at uneconomical costs. Profit redistribution was a way to keep loss-making enterprises with the help of more successful enterprises. For this reason, so-called full economic accounting, or hardening of the budget constraint, was not realized. For ministries, profit redistribution was also a means of keeping enough workers in loss-making enterprises under their jurisdiction. Without profit redistribution, loss-making enterprises would not have been able to pay bonuses to their workers and would have lost them to enterprises that could afford them.

While the persistence of paternalistic control by state organs over enterprises was the problem at one end, at the other end, the problem was collusive and opportunistic behavior by managers and workers. Since managerial authority over worker collectives was not strong and the workers exerted their influence in management decision making and sometimes even evaluation of managers through the workers' congress (China) or workers' council (USSR), the managers tended to be somewhat collusive with workers in allowing generous and egalitarian wages and bonus payments (IMF et al. 1991, vol. 2; Lee and Mark 1989). Thus, in the case of the Soviet Union, the Enterprises Law passed in 1990 repealed the provision in the 1987 Law on State Enterprises, whereby managers were nominated by workers' collectives, in an effort to reduce workers' power.

The figures in Table 4.3 are basically consistent with the above observations. In both China and the Soviet Union, increasing profit retention by state enterprises resulted in a decrease in enterprise profits remitted to the state budget despite the continuing real positive growth of profits and NMP or GNP. A large portion of retained enterprise funds were used to pay for generous bonus payments and workers' housing (especially in China) in the name of collective welfare.

However, no significant improvement in economic efficiency in terms of labor productivity, profit per capita, or output per capita was confirmed (Table 4.3). The combination of continuing fiscal subsidies to inefficient enterprises and the reduction of fiscal revenues resulted in enlarged and persistent fiscal deficits throughout the reform period, although China managed to check this tendency during the later period of reform. At the same time, the increasing accumulation of consumption funds in the hands of the population led to inflationary pressure or forced savings (monetary overhang) when they were not able to find ways to spend the money (as was also the case in the Soviet Union). In the Soviet Union, savings increased more than 30 percent per annum during the late 1980s (Table 4.3). Privatization of state enterprises through leasing arrangements or selling stocks to workers and the general public was finally tried, though on a limited scale, with a view to revitalizing inefficient enterprises (Feige 1990; Lee and Mark 1991).[17] It was also a means of reducing monetary overhang. Thus, the reform process of the state sector was similar in the Soviet Union and China—reforms in both have generally failed to revitalize the state sector.

Building a New Economic Environment

Table 4.4 on page 70 summarizes the reform process in terms of types of economic entities and identifies their plan or market orientation as their behavioral patterns. As section C in Table 4.4 shows, China has created many new economic entities that are market oriented rather than plan-oriented, unlike the Soviet Union.

Now, the Chinese economy consists of diverse economic entities, ranging from individual peasant farms, individual businesses, private enterprises, small-scale rural and urban cooperatives, and medium-scale rural and urban collective enterprises including joint-stock companies, to state enterprises including leasing arrangements with private groups and joint-stock companies. China's rural enterprises and urban collective enterprises together produced about 30 percent of China's total industrial gross output in 1985, and 35 percent in 1988 (SSB of China 1989). In contrast, the picture of the Soviet economy is much simpler. The Soviet economy consisted mainly of state enterprises, cooperatives, and individual businesses, and public farms in rural areas.[18] The NMP share of the state sector was very high in the Soviet Union, at 87 percent (Table 4.2).

What is the relationship between these new economic entities and the emerging economic environment in both countries? This question is important since both countries aimed to create a new, apparently more market-oriented, economic environment. The economic environment is more than just laws or decrees on paper, which abounded in the Soviet Union. Economic environment is to an important extent a

Table 4.3

State-Sector Reform and Economic Efficiency in China and the USSR

A. China

	1978	1980	1984	1985	1988	Avg. Annual Growth (%)		
						1978-84	1985-88	1978-88
GNP (billion yuan)	358.8	447.0	696.2	856.8	1,385.3	11.7	17.4	14.5
GNP (billion 1978 yuan)	358.8	416.6	597.8	673.8	900.6	8.9	10.2	9.6
GNP deflator (1978 = 100)	100.0	107.3	116.5	127.2	153.8	2.6	6.6	4.4
Central budget balance[a] (billion yuan)	1.01	-12.75	-4.45	2.16	8.05	-7.3	-1.2	-4.8
Collective profits (tax)[b] (billion yuan)	57.20	43.52	27.68	55.75	58.25	-11.4	1.5	0.2
Nonbudget enterprise funds[c] (billion yuan)	25.26	42.21	99.07	125.27	162.60	25.6	13.7	22.9
Bonuses and extra piece wage[d] (billion yuan)	1.13	6.09	14.39	15.47	35.30	52.8	31.7	41.1
Gross profit per asset (yuan)[e]	0.242	0.248	0.242	0.238	0.206	0.0	-4.7	-1.6
Gross profit per fixed asset (yuan)	0.248	0.243	0.223	0.224	0.202	-1.8	-3.4	-2.0
Gross output per fixed asset (yuan)	1.03	1.01	0.96	0.95	1.131	-1.2	6.0	0.9

B. USSR

	1985	1986	1987	1988	1989	Avg. Annual Growth (%)		
						1986	1988	1986-89
NMP (billion rubles)	578.5	587.4	599.6	630.8	673.7	1.5	5.2	4.7
Real growth rate (%)	-	2.3	1.6	4.4	2.5	-	-	-
NMP (billion 1985 rubles)	578.5	591.8	601.3	627.7	643.4	2.3	4.4	2.8
NMP deflator (1985 = 100)	100.0	99.3	99.7	100.5	104.7	-0.7	0.8	1.8
Central budget balance (billion rubles)	-18.3	-49.6	-72.8	-96.2	-89.5	-	-	-
Before-tax profits[f,g] (billion rubles)	186.9	215.6	223.7	260.1	290.1	15.4	16.3	10.4
Collected profits (tax)(billion rubles)	115.9	125.9	123.4	115.6	111.4	8.6	-6.3	-4.0
After-tax profits[g] (billion rubles)	68.5	87.1	97.4	141.7	174.6	27.2	45.5	26.1
Profit retention rates (%)	36.7	40.4	43.5	54.5	60.2	-	-	-
Wages (billion rubles)[h]	279.3	288.4	299.5	321.5	347.1	3.3	7.3	6.4
Premium paid out of profits[h] (billion rubles)	15.0	15.9	15.6	17.7	18.2	5.4	13.3	4.7
Savings of the population[h] (billion rubles)	24.4	28.0	32.0	41.9	61.8	14.8	30.9	30.2
Industrial NMP growth (%)	-	0.6	3.6	6.1	3.1	1981-85: 2.9		1986-89: 3.3

Labor productivity growth (%)	—	—	3.8	2.4	2.3	2.3	2.7	2.7
Real wage growth (%)	—	—	1.1	2.2	8.3	7.7	1.7	4.7
Retail price growth (%)	—	—	2.0	1.3	0.6	2.0	–	–

Sources: IMF et al. (1991); State Statistical Bureau of China (1986, 1989).

[a] The last three columns of the budget balance row represent the average budget balance during 1979–84,1985–88, and 1979–88, respectively.

[b] Due to the adoption of the tax-for-profit system, collected enterprise profits are called income taxes after 1985.

[c] Nonbudget enterprise funds are funds held by state enterprises and their supervisory organs. Because the 1988 figure is not available, a 1987 figure is reported. Accordingly, growth figures of nonbudget funds in the last two columns are over the period 1985–87 and 1978–87, respectively.

[d] Bonuses and piece-wage figures are for state enterprises only. Piece wages include only those paid for overfulfillment.

[e] Asset values are the sum of the net value of fixed assets and the average value of circulating funds. In figures of gross profit/fixed assets and gross outputs/fixed assets, assets and fixed assets are valued at their original values.

[f] Before-tax profits are operating surplus minus turnover tax plus price subsidies.

[g] Before- and after-tax profits refer to state enterprises.

[h] Wages, savings, and premium refer to populations reported in tables D.1 and D.2 of IMF et al. (1991).

Table 4.4

Diverse Economic Entities in the USSR and China

	China	USSR
A. Rural entities		
Individual peasant farms	New	Absent
State farms	Absent	Old
Collective farms	Abolished	Old
Leasing arrangements with collective or state farms	Absent	New
Township enterprises (formerly commune-run enterprises)	New	Absent
Village enterprises (formerly brigade-run enterprises)	New	Absent
Independent cooperatives	New	Absent
Private enterprises	New	Absent
Individual businesses	New	New
B. Urban entities		
State enterprises	Old	Old
State joint-stock companies	New	New
Leasing of state enterprises by individuals or cooperatives	New	New
Collective enterprises	Old	Absent
Collective joint-stock companies	New	Absent
Independent cooperatives	New	New
Private enterprises	New	Absent
Individual businesses	New	New
C. Plan vs. markets		
Plan-oriented entities:	3	5
	State enterprises	State enterprises
	State joint-stock companies	State joint-stock companies
	Urban collective enterprises	
		State farms
		Collective farms
		Leasing arrangements with state/collec. farms
Market-oriented entities:	8	3
	Individual peasant farms	
	Township enterprise	
	Village enterprise	
	Indep. cooperatives	Indep. cooperatives
	Private enterprise	
	Individual businesses	Individual businesses
	Leasing of state enterprises	Leasing of state firms
	Collective joint-stock company	

summation of economic entities, although the environment itself is more or less independent of the behavior of any individual entity. For instance, perfect competition prevails when no single economic actor can influence the market outcomes, and thus perfectly competitive markets are the summation of a large enough number of independent economic actors. Reform-related laws and decrees can help to create a new economic environment only when they are successful in changing the behavior of economic entities or in creating new ones.

China managed to build a market-oriented economic environment owing to emerging new economic entities, while in the Soviet Union, market-oriented entities remained marginal or even fragile. Of course, certain initial conditions exist that may facilitate or hamper the development of more market-oriented entities and environment. In this light, the conditions were more favorable in China than in the Soviet Union. The Chinese economy was more market-oriented, less centralized, and less concentrated during the prereform period than was the Soviet Union (Naughton 1986; Wong 1985).

In China's rural areas, dominant ownership was collective under more decentralized control by local authorities, whereas in Soviet rural areas, there appeared to be no practical difference between collective and state farms, since collective farms were controlled as tightly as state farms. In the urban industrial sector, there were also some differences. As shown in Table 4.5, while China centrally allocated about 210 commodities in 1978, the Soviet Union centrally allocated more than 10,000 commodities. In 1978, the first year of Chinese reform, state industrial enterprises accounted for less than 80 percent of total industrial output, while the proportion was more than 95 percent in the Soviet Union in the mid-1980s. In addition, the Soviet economy was highly concentrated in that some 30–40 percent of Soviet industrial output was composed of goods produced on single sites (IMF et al. 1991, vol. 1). The difference in the degree of industrial concentration is also reflected in the number of firms. Whereas China had about 83,700 state enterprises in 1978, and 70,000 in 1985, the Soviet Union had only about 47,000 enterprises in 1987 (Table 4.5).

The more centrally planned and more concentrated the economy was initially, the more difficult it was for new economic entities to find necessary input supplies and even physical premises, and the slower was the speed of marketization. Cooperatives and individual businesses did not grow as rapidly in China's urban areas as they did in

Table 4.5

Initial Conditions and Marketization in China and the USSR

A. USSR

1) Share of production by state order:

1988	1989	1990	
		Average	Range
90%	35% (planned)	75%	40100%

2) Share of locally controlled state enterprises in industrial
    output produced by state enterprises in 1990: 35%

Number of centrally balanced commodities: 15,000 in 1981.
Number of industrial enterprises: 45,840 in 1987.

B. China

1) Number of centrally allocated commodities:

1953	1957	1958	1964	1971	1978	1981	Late 1980
227	532	132	592	217	210	67	< 30

2) Proportions of key producer goods allocated by
    central government (in %):

	1965	1978	1980	1982
Finished steel	95	80	58	53
Cement	71	36	29	25
Coal	75	54	54	25

3) Proportion of planned economy by ownership in 1984
    (% of total output value):

	State firms	Urban Collective enterprises	Rural collective enterprises
Production decision	29.46	12.20	4.06
Marketing	71.05	4.40	1.67
Input supply	86.79	6.47	3.05

	1985
4) Number of state enterprises	70,342
Number locally controlled	66,517
Share of locally controlled state enterprises in gross industrial output produced by state enterprises	73.2%

Sources: Hewett (1988, 126); IMF et al. (1991); Naughton (1986 table 3); Reynolds (1987); State Statistical Bureau of China (1988, 6–7); and Wong (1985), 259).

rural areas. The majority of Soviet cooperatives in urban areas had to rely on assets, resources, and even marketing channels of the state entities and took the form of leasing arrangements with state entities. Although the 1987 Law on State Enterprises stipulated that enterprises could sell all production above the state order to whomever they wished and were expected to obtain inputs for that part of their output in similar fashion, it turned out that the state ministries did not release the allocation for free transaction but continued to monopolize the input supply (IMF et al., vol. 1, 39–40). Thus, enterprises found it virtually impossible to produce for the free market, and tried to receive the highest possible level of state order for which inputs were assured by the old system.

Thus, despite the plan to reduce the proportion of production accounted for by state orders to less than 35 percent in 1989, state orders accounted for an average 75 percent of production in the USSR in 1990. In contrast, China had moved faster than the Soviet Union. In Table 4.5, urban and rural collective enterprises in China are shown to have operated in a market-dominated environment as early as 1984. It is also shown that although state allocation agencies continued to supply the bulk of input requirements for state enterprises, the production decisions were left largely to enterprises in 1984. The table also indicates that the number and proportion of key producer goods had been rapidly reduced in the early 1980s. Such a difference in the speed of marketization is also related in the fact that the share of republic and locally controlled state enterprises accounted for only about 35 percent of total industrial output by state enterprises in the USSR in 1990, whereas in China, the share in 1985 was more than 70 percent in terms of gross industrial output.

These experiences suggest that markets are not easily created at the margin of planning by old state enterprises and that markets can be more easily created by new economic entities. In other words, new nonstate economic entities create their own markets, the expansion of which will gradually and eventually replace planned resource allocation in the economy unless they are artificially restricted by state authorities. As these new markets grow, state entities can also participate and learn market-oriented behavior. It is difficult to learn market-oriented behavior in markets that operate at the margin of plans.

The underdeveloped nature of the Soviet commodity distribution and circulation systems, together with the breakdown of the transport system, seemed to amplify the disruptive effect of the state-sector reform. Although some reform has occurred in the distribution system since 1985, the tendency has been growing disequilibrium, which was partially aggravated by a disruption of the traditional system of planning and supply without its replacement by a new smoothly functioning system. The situation was made worse since the Soviet rulers did not allow middlemen in commodity transactions even after the reform.

While many state enterprises tended to change their product variety and marketing channels as the incentive structure facing them changed, the existing market institutions were not able to support such new situations.[19] Thus, three presidential decrees adopted in late 1990 sought to deal with the growing disarray in the industrial supply system and halt the slide in production by ordering all state enterprises to keep all existing supply and marketing channels and contracts through 1991 and by declaring invalid all interenterprise and interregional arrangements that disrupted existing ties (Schroeder 1991; originally from *Pravda*, September 28, 1990, and *Izvestia*, October 5 and December 15, 1990).

Interaction of Diverse Economic Entities in a New Environment

It is true that nonstate economic actors are more efficient and dynamic than are state enterprises and hence should be promoted as the saviors of a stagnating socialist planned economy. However, the problem of state versus nonstate in socialist economies is much more complicated than that portrayed by a simple dichotomy. A simple dichotomous approach should be transcended by an analysis of interaction among the diverse forms of ownership.

In a transitional economy with mixed ownership, the alleged superior performance of private entities is partly due to their coexistence with state or collective entities, given the state-dominated dual economies of plans and markets, and the related ambiguity in property rights, as a consequence of the decentralization of state-monopolized property rights. In such an environment, state property tends to be expropriated for the benefit of nonstate actors, and collective property tends to be expropriated for the benefit of private actors (Grossman 1990; Keun Lee 1991). In other words, nonstate actors with strong private interests have incentives to utilize and divert, in unfair ways, common property for which no one has strong personal interests to protect in order to reap private gains.

The early socialist reformers' rationale for allowing growth of the private sector was that certain economic activities could be better performed by private actors, and the state should therefore not monopolize all economic activities. Their governments have never taken the more radical position that state enterprises are bound to be inefficient and hence should be replaced by nonstate enterprises. Thus relations between state and nonstate enterprises were envisioned as complementary rather than competitive and substitutive. State enterprises were supposed to be in charge of important urban industries, while nonstate enterprises were supposed to operate in urban secondary sectors, including services, and in rural areas utilizing locally available resources.

The nonstate sector in the Soviet Union can still be seen with such a traditional perspective about the role of the nonstate sector in the socialist economy. It is difficult to say that the Soviet nonstate sector had its own fully independent dynamism, as it was still marginal in the state-dominant economy. However, socialist reformers, especially in China, did not anticipate that when nonstate enterprises were allowed to grow without restriction, they would become competitive and even threatening to state entities. The Chinese reformers did not realize that they would soon have to make a fundamental decision on whether the private sector should be allowed to grow further and take a dominant position in the economy, or whether they should crack down on the private sector and end up with a stagnant, but still socialist, economy. This was the situation that actually occurred in China in the late 1980s, when the nonstate sector became much more dynamic, independent, and important in the national economy.

In China, nonstate enterprises took advantage of the general gap between the demand and the supply ability of state enterprises in a variety of items ranging from intermediate goods to consumer goods. The underdeveloped nature of China's distribution mechanism and infrastructure, including the transportation and communication systems, has also been taken advantage of by nonstate enterprises. Successful enterprises were more flexible and active in exploiting new markets, in seeking information about products, and in marketing beyond the boundary of their base localities.

As sales and purchasing activities expanded, rapid growth of the nonstate economy increased interaction between the urban and rural economies and across different regions of the country. Subsequently, a competition problem arose between nonstate and state enterprises, although China's nonstate enterprises grew under both restrictive and supportive state policies.[20] Since the late 1980s, the problem has been most prevalent in competition for raw materials and energy, as the rapidly growing national economy required more and more intermediate inputs, while more and more inputs were acquired in markets rather than allocated by plans. Only those enterprises that could afford to pay higher market prices were able to obtain necessary inputs, and state enterprises found it increasingly difficult to obtain an adequate amount of inputs.

In the late 1980s, at a time of serious inflation, financial decentralization and rapid growth of nonstate sectors were generally recognized as the main causes of inflation.[21] This situation led to hot debate on the competition issue as well as on the issue of how to judge the nature of growth of the nonstate sector. Especially since 1989, rural enterprises were increasingly criticized as economically inefficient, causing pollution and environmental destruction, engaging in tax evasion, and unjustifiably protected by local state bureaucrats pursuing local interests (Delfs 1989; Ignatius and Bennett 1989). The success of the rural enterprises was attributed mainly to strong private incentives, which, however, were not always consistent with the benefit of the whole economy. Such arguments provided an excuse for recentralization measures after the Tiananmen crisis in the spring of 1989.

The 1989 recentralization movement re-enlarged the scope of centralized allocation of key materials and re-emphasized the priority of large and medium-size state enterprises.[22] Many rural enterprises were closed or merged, and others were subject to strict taxation and controls. Nonstate enterprises were urged to rely solely on locally available resources. This situation signifies the dilemma facing the leadership between rapid modernization and socialist emphasis on state-owned industry. The recentralization and contractionary policies led the economy into an abrupt and serious downturn with the re-emergence of unemployment.

Concerned about the social implications of economic stagnation, the central leadership again had to promote the positive role of nonstate enterprises in creating jobs even before the end of 1989. The strategic decision on the role of the nonstate vs. the state sector remains one of the key issues for China's economy. We can expect that a similar set of issues will rise as a top policy agenda item in the former Soviet Union, if it takes more and more radical attitudes toward the nonstate sector, as evidenced by the Small Enterprise Law and the Privatization Law, in late 1990 and July 1991, respectively.[23]

Conclusion

Gorbachev's reform regime collapsed not simply because of worsening economic performance but, more importantly, because the reform did not generate any reliable pro-reform forces in the society that were fed by some tangible benefit from perestroika and more economically motivated. People cannot live on political freedom from glasnost alone. Everybody seemed to be losing and dissatisfied. Emerging cooperatives are not reliable and independent enough to be the engine of reform, and peasants have not received any apparent benefits from the reform. While urban workers have accumulated some money, they do not find enough commodities on which to spend their money, and the real value of their hoarded money is now being threatened by inflation. Gorbachev's reform was fragile, and the reform force was based on general dissatisfaction with the old system but without any material benefits from the new system.

In contrast, from the very beginning, Chinese reform identified peasants liberated from the communes as strong pro-reform forces, followed by a substantial number of nonstate economic actors and local state bureaucrats. Having already generated substantial vested interests, the reform has now become all but irreversible.

The experiences of China and countries in Eastern Europe indicate that privatization of state enterprises is not an easy process and involves a high degree of complexity and uncertainty. Transformation of public farms into individual farms would have much quicker and more certain results and could help the Russian government buy time for the more difficult reform of the state sector. The Chinese lesson is that the success of reform depends on the creation of a new nonstate sector large enough to become the new engine of growth. The nonstate entities are the only actors who are reliable enough to generate a new market-oriented economic environment more quickly and in an irreversible manner.

Still, both Chinese and Russian policymakers are more or less constrained in their policy choices, although they are showing increasing flexibility. Above all, a change in the perception about the role of the state sector relative to the nonstate sector is required. Corresponding to that change, a new economic mechanism that can make individual pursuit of self-interest compatible with the benefits of the national economy is essential. Market discipline and capital markets should be strengthened, and markets should be fair to everyone, both state and nonstate enterprises. Only with a new economic environment is it possible for the reform leadership to free itself from the trap imposed by the dilemma between growth and socialist priorities on economic equality and security. The trap may be superficial, the dilemma may be overcome, and tolerance for socioeconomic divergences may well increase if the popular perception is that any inequality is a result of a "fair" game.

Notes

1. Industrial production and agricultural production declined in 1990 by 1.2 percent and 2.3 percent, respectively (IMF et al. 1991; Schroeder 1991; originally from *Ekonomika i zhizn'*, no. 5, 1991).

2. Of course, there was a rapid increase in prices of agricultural products. However, there was also significant growth in physical terms, as seen by the average 5 percent growth of grain outputs.

3. Although one reason for this would be the possible exhaustion of the shock effects of the reform, a more important reason is that individual farming weakens investment in irrigation and fertility maintenance, which requires collectivist cooperation. State-initiated investment has also decreased since 1984. The 1984 record level of grain harvest was recovered only in 1989 as a result of massive investment since 1988.

4. For more details on the revival of the individual peasant farm in China, see Part 1, "Agriculture," in Perry and Wong (1985).

5. The Chinese equivalent for this term is *xiangzhen qiye*, which is used to mean only township- and village-run enterprises. Since 1984, the term includes cooperative and individual businesses in official statistical classifications (SSB of China 1986).

6. *Ekonomika i zhizn'* (no. 5, 1991, 5) reports that there were 40,600 individual peasant farms in operation by the end of 1990 (Schroeder 1991).

7. Even in the 1970s, compared to other socialist planned economies, China was very much export oriented and their trade in soft currency with the Soviet bloc was less than 10 percent of total trade volume (Lee and James 1991).

8. Traditionally, urban collective enterprises were classified into two groups, large enterprises and small enterprises. The large enterprises were under the jurisdiction of light industry ministries of city and town governments and were included in production and material supply planning by the state. They were not required to be self-responsible for profits and losses. Small collective enterprises were under the jurisdiction of district or neighborhood management bureaus of local governments. They were not included in central planning as much as the

large collectives, but were under various levels of control by local bureaus. Both large and small collective enterprises were given less favorable treatment by state authorities as compared to state enterprises in many respects, including material allocation, taxation, various administrative fees, recruiting of new workers, and wage rates (Lockett 1988).

9. Although the criterion of eight employees is arbitrary, the distinction the Chinese want to make is between private enterprises based mainly on self-labor versus hired labor.

10. Only in April 1988 did the constitutional amendment legally recognize such private businesses, with implementation regulations regarding taxation approved in July 1988.

11. If we add leasing of small state-owned enterprises by groups of individuals, there are five types altogether.

12. See Ioffe (1989) for more legal details of the law.

13. See Hanson (1988) for more on the law.

14. For example, parent enterprises often used subsidiary units to get around supply allocations, multiple prices, or tax differences (Byrd and Tidrick 1987, 72). Enterprises can also use the somewhat loose control by higher authorities over collectives to increase bonuses. Through such subsidiary collectives, they have been able to get around labor quotas from the Ministry of Labor. Thus, such subsidiaries are now discouraged by the central government.

15. For instance, in China the share of profits that owner–proprietors can withdraw for their own personal consumption is usually severely restricted (Byrd 1990); even without explicit restrictions, proprietors do not withdraw a substantial share of profits as a result of local community, social, and political pressures, and to evade severe personal income taxation.

16. Kornai (1986) argues that firms in the socialist economies tend to be under a soft budget constraint owing to arbitrary *ex post* fiscal intervention by state authorities in the form of soft taxation, soft credit, and soft subsidies.

17. There were reportedly 1,200 joint-stock companies in the USSR by the end of 1990 (Schroeder 1991; originally from *Ekonomika i zhizn'*, no. 5, 1991, 5).

18. Ioffe (1989) provides a somewhat legal analysis of each of the three different ownership-based sectors of the Soviet economy.

19. New alternative channels included interenterprise barter deals and various black markets where prices were much higher. Some of the products were kept by the producing enterprises, regions, and republics for their own use (IMF et al. 1991, vol. 3, 40).

20. On the diverse attitudes toward nonstate enterprises by state bureaucrats in China, see chapter 7 of Keun Lee (1991) and Byrd (1990).

21. The dual pricing system and price reform are also responsible for the shortage of intermediate inputs and inflation.

22. On more detailed aspects of the recentralization, see chapter 9 of Keun Lee (1991).

23. See IMF et al. (1991) for details of the Small Enterprise Law, and the *New York Times* (July 2, 1991) on the Soviet parliament's approval of a new law on denationalization.

Chapter 5

Industrial Systems and Reform in North Korea: A Comparison with China

The sweeping collapse of socialist regimes in the Soviet Union and Eastern Europe has raised the issue of transition from socialism to capitalism. In the meantime, China is still trying to solve its problems through ambitious systemic reform while maintaining its socialist identity. Somewhat in isolation, North Korea is showing no clear signs of radical political or economic change, although it has also attempted some economic reform since the mid-1980s in emulation of other socialist countries, particularly China.

Since the mid-1980s, North Korea initiated several reform measures (Kang 1989; H. Lee 1990; P. Lee 1987). They included a new emphasis on the financial accountability and relative autonomy of state enterprises, as well as on material incentives for labor, reduced scope for central planning with the adoption of the associated enterprise system, promotion of direct foreign investment and a nonstate sector in consumer goods and services. Some of these reform programs looked similar to those implemented in China and appeared to be influenced by the Chinese reform effort.

In terms of time, the "mid-1980s economic reform" was preceded by, or coincided with, numerous overseas visits during this time by North Korean officials, including Kim Il Sung himself (for the first time in twenty-three years), intellectuals, peasants, and workers, primarily to China and the East European socialist countries.[1] Reportedly, the North Korean leader Kim Il Sung and his successor and son, Jong Il, had a firsthand look at China's open-door policies and economic reform and were impressed enough to make a statement expressing their admiration (Kang and Lee 1990, 339). While recent North Korean reform efforts appear to be imitating China's, such imitation goes back to the so-called Chŏllima mass movement in the late 1950s, which was apparently inspired by the Great Leap Forward in China. Although North Korea first patterned its economic system on the Stalinist model, Chinese influence on North Korean economic policy has been increasingly important since the early 1960s.[2]

This chapter compares North Korea's economic reform program in the mid-1980s with the reform process and experiences in China. The analysis is based on descriptive elaboration of current North Korean industrial systems, using the Chinese economic system and its reform process as a reference point. Given the paucity of primary information about the North Korean economy, such an approach can be useful, but the limited and sometimes indirect nature of the empirical evidence will make my argument somewhat hypothetical. Because of the strong homogeneity among the socialist planned economies, which I confirmed as dominating other aspects of the North Korean economic system, I believe that my argument is valid.

In the next four sections, I discuss in sequence the following aspects of the North Korean industrial system: state–enterprise distributional relations, the enterprise decision-making structure, labor incentive provisions, and the emergence of the associated enterprises. Results of analysis in each of these four sections will be synthesized in the conclusion of this chapter.

State-Enterprise Relations and the Soft Budget Constraint

Under traditional state ownership, each state enterprise, as simply a part of the entire economic organ of the state, was not expected to be responsible for its own profits or losses. Profits were submitted to the state, and losses were covered by the state.[3] Remitted profits were reinvested at the state's discretion. The principal duty of enterprises was to fulfill plan targets. Profitability used to be only one of the many performance indicators, and fulfillment of output targets was emphasized as the primary goal. While the objective function of the socialist state enterprise can also be operationalized into the framework of constrained maximization, the profit constraint, if any, tended to be weak or soft. If sufficient state credits and subsidies were assured as a result of the "soft budget constraint," to use the term coined by Kornai, the manager of the state enterprise was less concerned about its profitability.[4] In other words, state assets would not be used in a financially efficient manner.

Rather than fully confiscating realized profits of state enterprises, various socialist economies in the Soviet Union and Eastern Europe allowed enterprises to keep a portion of profits. The retained profits were used for investment, collective welfare, and bonus funds. In return, enterprises were supposed to assume more responsibility for their own financial conditions. The idea was that decentralized investment and bonus payments would be more effective than central reallocation in stimulating enterprise and worker incentives. Of course, such decentralization also reflects high transaction costs and information problems associated with centralized reallocation.

Like East European socialist economies, which have implemented it since the first wave of reform in the late 1950s, North Korea has adopted the profit retention system by state enterprises. This differs from China, where the profit retention system began only in the late 1970s.

If we examine the fluctuation of profit retention rates in North Korea since the early 1950s, one noticeable fact is the decrease of the rate between the early 1960s and the mid-1970s and the sudden increase in the mid-1980s from the previous level.[5] Considering that the profit retention rate is one measure of decentralization, such a fluctuation corresponds to centralization or decentralization of the planning system in North Korea. After the early 1960s, North Korea experienced a further centralization, so-called unified and detailed planning. This process reduced the enterprises' autonomy and, hence, their profit retention rates. In contrast, the mid-1980s appeared to be a period of decentralization; State Council Decision No. 20 increased the portion of extra profits that the enterprise could retain from 20 percent to 50 percent (P. Lee 1987, 4).

In December 1984, the 10th session of the Sixth Central Committee of the North Korean Workers' Party revised the Provision on the Independent Accounting System (IAS) in state enterprises. The revision gave enterprises more autonomy (Kang 1989). Actually, three basic principles of the new provision hinted at some new elements in the North Korean industrial system.[6]

First, it stated the need for a correct combination of state planning and commodity–money relations through the introduction of economic levers such as costs, prices, and profit. Considering that the term *commodity–money relations* used to be an ideological substitute for *markets* in socialist economies including China, this principle can be regarded as indicating a combination of plans and markets. Second, enterprises are asked to cover their own expenses from their revenues and to fulfill their duty of contributing to state revenues. Third, it stated that enterprises should be allowed both political and material incentives, while their performance should be evaluated according to their plan fulfillment.

According to the new provisions, North Korean enterprises can retain part of their profits in two ways: enterprise funds (*gi-eop gi-geum*) and prize funds (*sang-geum gi-geum*). Enterprises can retain a portion of plan-quota profits and extra-quota profits as enterprise funds when they overfulfill profit plans and after first submitting a predetermined amount of state share of profits to the state and paying back to the state a portion of working capital that is supposed to be covered by enterprises themselves (the state still provides enterprises with the majority of working capital). Accumulated enterprise funds can be used for (1) production expansion and technology development (production development funds) and (2) worker welfare and cultural projects (welfare funds).[7]

The main emphasis in the new provisions was on financial accountability and independence of state enterprises, which also reflected serious fiscal deficits owing partly to heavy subsidies to enterprises. Merrill (1989, 10) stated that numerous articles have appeared in the North Korean media warning enterprise managers that they are now on their own and will get no sympathy (and, more important, will be held accountable) if they fail to meet production goals. Such efforts to disengage state enterprises financially from the state administrative budget are not new but, rather, are recurrent in socialist economies; such measures in North Korea would not seem to have much effect on hardening the budget constraints for state enterprises and hence on economic efficiency, as the Chinese experience suggests.

Although China introduced the profit retention system only in the late 1970s, it has long used the term *independent accounting* for state enterprises. However, as is well known, it has nothing to do with financial independence from the state. Emphasis on the financial independence of the enterprise rose only since the reform with the introduction of the profit retention system under the broader theme of the separation of ownership and management. It has developed into a contract between the state and the enterprises, through which enterprises acquire rights to manage themselves while fulfilling some duties, including submission of the contracted amount of profit.

There were two major problems: *ex ante* arbitrariness of the profit remission quota and the *ex post* weak enforceability of the contract. There was no objective basis for determining the appropriate level of the profit remission quota. This difficulty has resulted in soft *ex post* enforcement of profit remission quotas, as well as substantial *ex ante* bargaining between the state authorities regarding the determination of the profit quotas. Unexpectedly large profits often led to arbitrary requests from the state authorities to submit more than the contracted amount of profits, whereas too small profit or even losses elicited arbitrary generosity by state authorities, especially when accumulated enterprise funds were too small to cover losses (Lee and Mark 1989). Given such paternalistic and arbitrary state intervention and resulting soft budget constraint for enterprises, the intended incentive effects were limited.

The later, improved version of the profit contract system, the so-called contracted management system (*chengbaozhi*), sought to formalize the relationship between the state and the enterprise by introducing legal enforcement of contracts by the people's court and public notarization (K. Lee 1990). However, collusive behavior between local state organs and the enterprises in the determination and enforcement of the profit remission quota have persisted throughout the reform decade (Keun Lee 1991). The main consequences of the various versions of profit remission systems were a limited improvement of enterprise performance and the persistence of state fiscal deficits. The Chinese experience indicates the limited effectiveness of the socialist effort to separate ownership and control (management) formally without touching the real fundamental ownership issues.[8]

The renewed emphasis on the financial independence of state enterprises is an indication that North Korea, like other socialist planned economies, has also suffered from having a soft budget constraint for state enterprises. From the fact that no new innovative measures were suggested in the 1984 revision, and from the experience of other countries with similar measures, we can infer that there would be little improvement of the problem.

In fact, North Korean managers of firms not located in Pyongyang (the capital of North Korea) spend most of their time in the city dealing with state authorities to obtain stable supplies of intermediate materials needed and preferential tax or subsidy treatment.[9] As Kornai (1986) predicts, to the extent that such bargaining is successful in solving the financial problems of firms, enterprises will be less sensitive to real economic efficiency.

One symptom of the soft budget constraint problem is runaway demand for inputs. Such unconstrained demand for inputs happens since firms with a soft budget constraint are less sensitive to financial conditions. Although excessive input demand and hoarding aggravates material shortages, they are at the same time caused by the shortages. In other words, shortage and runaway demand form a vicious cycle in socialist economies. One article by a North Korean scholar (Hyun 1989) indirectly confirms the existence of a hoarding problem in North Korea. When discussing the efficient use of working capital and how to reduce its circulation period, Hyun argued that enterprises should always check whether they are holding an optimum level of circulating capital in the form of intermediate inputs and immediately turn over any excess inputs to the state material allocation agency (*ja-jae sang-sa*).

The simplest and most typical example of the soft budget constraint problem in socialist economies has been the nonexistence of bankruptcy in state enterprises. Since China experimentally introduced a bankruptcy law in 1986, more and more state enterprises have been subject to bankruptcy and related acquisition by and merger with other enterprises. Until now, we have not heard of similar legislation in North Korea. In North Korea, when enterprises incur losses, the state usually provides special loans for a year.[10] If losses persist over several years, the enterprises are reorganized.

Decision-Making Structure: Party Committee vs. Manager

The current model of the North Korean socialist enterprise, the so-called Dae-an Model (DM), originated when Kim Il Sung offered some on-the-spot guidance at the Dae-an Electric Factory in 1961. Incorporating some new elements since then, the Dae-an Model firmly established its constitutional status as "the" North Korean model for socialist enterprises.

The allegedly distinctive characteristic of DM is collective leadership by the factory (or enterprise) party committee in enterprise decision making, which signified the breakup from the earlier Soviet-inherited one-man (manager) responsibility system. The DM is supposed to ensure the priority of political guidance and worker participation over economic-technical guidance and top-down ordering in decision making. In the DM, every enterprise is run by a party committee, which consists of approximately twenty-five to thirty-five members elected from the ranks of workers, managers, and engineers (Kang 1989; Wickman 1981).11 A smaller "executive board" consisting of six to nine members, including the party committee secretary, top manager, and chief engineer, is in charge of day-to-day operations.

North Korean abolition of the Soviet-type manager responsibility system (MRS) happened several years after a similar move by China. In 1956, the Eighth Party Congress of the Chinese Communist Party decided to terminate the MRS so as to implement the "manager-responsibility system under the leadership of the party committee." This system would combine the collective leadership and the individual responsibility system with the party at its core (Zheng 1987).[12] While some political motivation to claim independence from Soviet-type communism underlay the abolition of the Soviet-type leadership system by China and North Korea, North Korea seemed to go to an extreme by adopting purely collective leadership by the party committee, compared to the Chinese compromise between individual and collective leadership as seen in the MRS under the leadership of the party committee. North Korean deviance from China has deepened since China entered the reform era beginning in 1978.

We do not have any strong theoretical method of proving absolute inferiority in terms of productive efficiency of collective leadership and worker participation. The current Western literature on this issue is controversial, and, more importantly, the actual impact of participatory collective decision making depends on the external economic environment. Given the environment of a centrally planned economy without horizontal competition, where individual performance and its payoff are only vaguely linked, collective responsibility could result in collective collusion, as one symptom of a negative behavioral pattern or situation in which no one is willing to take responsibility.[13] The difficulty of arriving at consensus in the collective could lead to inertial behavior, which prefers the status quo to innovation.

The above-mentioned symptoms exist in North Korea as much as in other formerly centrally planned economies, not simply because of collective responsibility but as an aggregate outcome of various elements present in planned economies. Collective and participatory decision making are not fully exercised in any of the socialist economies. Although we have little direct empirical evidence, the North Korean case does not differ much from the situation in China, where collective decision making was emphasized more than in other socialist countries.

In China, worker participation through worker assemblies did not have much input in management; it was concerned only with policies directly related to workers' rights and welfare. Most important managerial decisions were made between the enterprise leadership headed by the party secretary (under the old system before reform) and each enterprise's supervisory state authorities. The enterprise leadership itself was not collective in reality. It was, rather, a one-man dictatorship by the party secretary, which would definitely be worse than that by the manager, in terms of economic performance. The Chinese decision to revive the MRS in 1984 signifies an effort to separate the party from administration (*dangzheng fenkai*). The MRS introduced a division of labor between the party committee and management. The party committee's role was reduced to party organization and ideological work, while the manager assumed the unified authority over economic matters.

If theoretical justification is still weak, the main trend, including China, toward the manager responsibility system in socialist economies is strong empirical evidence of the inefficiency of collective leadership, especially by a party committee. There is a hint that North Korea may also be following this trend. A recent article by Kwang-Jeon Kim (1990) indicated some necessary division of labor among the party secretary, manager, and chief engineer, and the importance of tripartite leadership. Amid the same old slogans praising the collective leadership style of the DM, he stated that the party secretary should be responsible for party projects, the manager with administrative rights should conduct unified guidance, and the chief engineer, with his expertise over technical matters, should be responsible for production. Although it is not clear that such statements about division of labor among the three key positions indicates a new approach to leadership issues, such terms as "unified guidance by the manager" and "troika" leadership have seldom appeared in other North Korean literature.

If we understand such a statement as an indication of North Korean moves to separate the party from enterprise administration, the difference with the Chinese pattern in this regard is, first, that the division of roles is proceeding under the umbrella of the party committee. Thus, in this sense, we can say that North Korea is moving toward the model of the MRS under the leadership of the party committee, which China went through before adopting its current model of the MRS. Another North Korean peculiarity seems to be a broader and more active role played by the chief engineer. It is not the manager, as in China and other socialist economies, but the chief engineer who is in charge of overall production. Actually, the chief engineer is supposed to be the head of the factory advisory committee (*cham-mo-bu*), which is responsible for production planning and technical matters.

What, then, is the role of the manager? It seems that while the role of chief engineer is broader, with responsibility for overall production matters, the manager seems to be in charge of external relations, such as dealing with state planning and tax authorities. According to the DM, the manager is supposed to be in charge of administration (*haeng-jeong*). Such a view confirms the still traditional socialist perspective on enterprises, that they are seen as almost a part of the government and regarded as an object not of management but of administration. In the case of China, they have been trying to separate not only the party from administration but also administration (government) from enterprises (*zhengqi fenkai*) (Guisheng Zhang 1988). Their reform effort in this regard included requiring many double-status personnel to choose positions either in the government or in enterprises, as well as disengaging some government bureaus from business activities and entities.

However, in North Korea, the reform perception does not seem to have reached that level. A literal translation of the North Korean *ji-be-in* (*zhipairen* in Chinese), whose position is equivalent to the manager, would be "agent" rather than "manager." The word "agent" captures its subordinate status more than its other aspects including management activity. In other words, to a certain extent, such terminology seems to reflect their traditional view of the socialist managers executing handed-down orders rather than carrying out independent management activity as their duty. Thus, it appears that although North Korean firms might be trying some degree of separation of the party from the management, they are not ready for separation of the government from the enterprises.

The Chinese experience tells us that while more technical aspects of the reform program were relatively easily implemented, tasks such as newly defining the role of the Communist party in the enterprises and in the society were more sensitive. The reform of enterprise leadership was the only area in which China's leader, Deng Xiaoping, was personally involved, giving orders to start experimentation with the MRS in 1984.

In North Korea, the DM with its core of collective leadership by the party committee is allegedly created by its leader Kim Il Sung. While the need to reform such collective leadership in the enterprise increases, Kim's personal involvement will make any radical reform in this regard difficult. Any reform is likely to proceed under an ambiguous slogan that would claim the continuation of collective leadership at least in name.

Intra-enterprise Income Distribution and Incentives

In the North Korean industrial system, workers' income can be divided into three sources: basic living costs (*saeng-whal-bi*), bonuses (*jang-lyeo-geum*), and monetary prizes (*sang-geum*). Basic living costs are compensation for labor expended during the production process. Since this portion of worker income is for workers to contribute their labor power, it is paid regardless of plan fulfillment (Suh 1986). Bonuses are basically to reward labor performed beyond the average labor standard, which results in savings in production costs. The state sets maximum limits on total worker compensation, which is mainly the sum of living costs and bonuses paid to workers, in each enterprise. The relationship between the maximum amount of total worker compensation (WC) and the basic living costs (BLC) is defined as follows:[14]

> WC = (BLC) x (physical plan target fulfillment rates)
> + (adjustment according to fulfillment of cost plans)
> + (miscellaneous additional payment)

The BLCs are determined by the total number of workers in given enterprises and their composition in the grading system (a total of six grades for industrial workers). Then the difference between the WC and the BLC sets the upper limit of bonus funds available for workers.

Monetary prizes are paid from the prize funds that enterprises accumulate. Enterprises can retain a portion of profit as prize funds when they overfulfill both physical plan targets and profit plans. The amount of annual profits that can be retained in the prize funds is 20 percent of extra profits, and the amount cannot exceed 10 percent of the WC (*Economic Dictionary* 1985). These funds can be doled out as prizes for workshops and work teams to act as collective and individual incentives, and as supplementary prizes for the so-called socialist competition citation (Institute of Developing Economics [IDE], 1986).

One North Korean peculiarity is the distinction between bonuses and monetary prizes, which China did not differentiate in practical terms. The North Korean *Economic Dictionary* and Suh (1986) state that the financial source of bonuses is the cost savings from superior labor, and it is a part of the wage bill to be charged to production costs. In contrast, monetary prizes have their financial basis in extra profits. The distinction is that bonuses are counted as a part of variable capital, the V, in Marxian $C + V + S$ formula, and monetary prizes as a part of the surplus, the S in the formula ("C" stands for constant capital).

However, when we consider that cost savings from superior labor also lead to additional profits, the distinction seems only conceptual. Especially when it comes down to the individual worker level, whether superior performance should be rewarded by bonuses or prizes is a matter only of classification in accounting. Chinese firms use the same term, *bonuses* (*zhangjin*), even though a portion is charged to production costs and a rapidly increasing portion came from retained profits in the 1980s.

While the revival of bonus payments was initially good for workers' morale in China, given the twenty-year freeze of wage rates and upgrading, China failed to link bonus payments to performance. Chinese state authorities failed to control the tendency in firms to use more of their retained profits for bonuses and collective welfare expenses, at the sacrifice of productive investment. There was state regulation to set the guidelines on how to divide the retained profits into the three types of funds of productive investment, collective welfare, and bonuses; the state's function was to ensure that sufficient amounts of investment were guaranteed, while excessive bonus payments were checked.

However, state enforcement was lax, and firms had de facto discretion regarding the use of retained profits. As a consequence, bonus payments and housing construction from the collective welfare funds got out of control. Given loose monitoring devices and a weak power base, the managers tended to collude with workers in paying bonuses and using collective welfare funds for worker housing construction in an extraordinarily generous and still egalitarian manner.[15]

In light of the Chinese experience, the North Korean separation of enterprise funds and prize funds seems to be a better scheme. The separation would allow state authorities to control the size of prize funds more easily. Only after an enterprise first retained enterprise funds as some portion of quota profits and extra-quota profits could they retain prize funds out of remaining extra profits. However, in North Korean firms too, there is a relative distribution problem of enterprise funds between production development and collective welfare. The Chinese experience shows that when more enterprise autonomy is allowed and a more radical reform is pursued, collective welfare expenses absorb more and more enterprise funds. However, in consideration of the still highly centralized or limited reform nature of the North Korean economy, worry about the possible increase of consumption funds would be rather a "luxury." Their problem is in giving incentives rather than controlling consumption funds in the hand of workers.

If the prize funds in North Korean firms are too limited in size to motivate workers, incentive provisions for workers should come from bonuses charged as a part of wage costs. However, it is unclear how effective the North Korean bonus system is. As explained above, the size of bonus funds is basically determined by the difference between the maximum amount of total worker compensation (WC) and basic living costs (BLC), and hence by the rate of fulfillment of physical plan targets and cost plans. We can first say that the effectiveness of such a bonus system is limited because of the well-known ratchet effect. Workers and firms tend to hide their full capacity since the overfulfillment of plans can lead to upward adjustment of targets in succeeding plans. Thus, there is a trade-off between bonus scheme stability and dynamic incentive provision.

More important than the ratchet effect is the difficulty of implementing the bonus scheme effectively, as observed in many planned economies. Actual determination of the extent of plan fulfillment is always a matter of bargaining between state authorities and enterprises. Even after the size of bonus funds is determined, there remains the problem of distribution among workers within the enterprises.

Combined with the difficulty of measuring individual contributions to team production and the peculiar authority relations of socialist firms, increasing enterprise autonomy regarding the distribution of bonuses has often led to egalitarian bonuses in socialist economies. In China, since the revival of bonuses in 1978, there was an upsurge of contention among workers over bonus matters because of a lack of consensus over fair quotas and related evaluations and payments (Walder 1987). Managers sidestepped this problem by paying out bonuses equally. Furthermore, workers have resisted payment-by-results schemes because of their cultural and political orientation toward egalitarianism (Byrd and Tidrick 1987, 73–74). The egalitarian tendency also exists in North Korea, as indirectly evidenced by an article (Choi 1989, 10) arguing for the need to overcome the egalitarian tendency so as to keep the socialist principle of distribution according to labor.[16] Given the collective leadership style in North Korean firms and limited managerial authority, the manager is likely to take more opportunistic attitudes toward bonus payments. He cannot ignore the collective power of workers as represented in the Workers' Congress and the party committee. The opportunistic behavior by managers and workers was possible in North Korea since North Korean firms also had some autonomy regarding distribution of bonuses (Suh 1986, 47).[17] The consequence of opportunism and egalitarianism is a weakening link between bonus payment and plan performance, so bonuses have become a general wage supplement.

Changes in Planning Systems and the Associated Enterprises

Following the orders of Kim Il Sung in 1964, the North Korean economy implemented the so-called unified and detailed planning so as to centralize their material allocation system further. Despite acknowledged resistance from state planning bureaucrats, Kim was personally involved in setting up a tight and comprehensive planning system with up to 100,000 products physically balanced under the system (H. S. Lee 1990, 1862).

The aim was to control all economic activity for more coordinated development of the economy, avoiding a situation in which an emphasis on major important goods leads to disequilibrium in minor goods, which, in turn, jeopardizes the production of important goods (*Economic Dictionary* 1985, 334). However, seen from a long-term perspective, it is obvious that it was wrong to impose additional rigidities on the economy. Since the first seven-year economic planning period (1961–67), serious chronic shortages and bottlenecks have impeded economic development (Chung 1983, 177). Such a situation indicated that North Korean central planning was not able to cope with the increasing information and transaction cost problems, which increased complexities of the economy.

In recognition of the overcentralized nature of the economy, North Korea launched important decentralization measures in the mid-1980s. The number of ministries in the central government was reduced from thirty-four to twenty-four in November 1985. The power of local government was extended with the reorganization of the Committee for the Guidance of the Provincial Economy into a new Committee for the Guidance of Local Government and Economy (Kang and Lee 1990, 338). At the enterprise level, an important decision made in July 1985 was to implement on a wider scale the associated enterprises (*yeon-hap gi-eop*; *lianhe qiye* in Chinese), which implied an important expansion of enterprise autonomy and the reduction of the scope of planning.

By September 1986, there were reportedly 120 associated enterprises, 61 controlled by the central government and the remaining 59 under the management of provincial authorities (P. Lee 1987, 4). There are two types of associated enterprises. One is the vertical integration of a key enterprise with others that have backward or forward linkages in production or technical areas. The other is the horizontal integration of several enterprises belonging to the same product groups.

In the former central planning system, intermediate goods were first submitted to state material allocation authorities and then distributed to production enterprises. Vertical integration represented an effort to reduce uncertainty and transaction costs of detailed central planning by internalizing intermediate goods allocation within groups of enterprises closely related to one another.[18] This aimed at "normalization of production activities," which emerged as an important policy agenda because of frequent production stoppages caused by material and energy shortages (C. Kim 1986, 75). Horizontal integration seemed to be designed to overcome such departmentalism or localism, in which each enterprise or local authority pursues its own partisan or local interest at the expense of the whole interest (C. Kim 1986, 76; S. Lee 1986, 51).

Vertical or horizontal integration of enterprises was accompanied by an increase of enterprise autonomy at least at the association level, if not at the subordinate member enterprise level. The associated enterprises are now regarded as independent planning, production, and execution units, and are allowed to sign purchasing and marketing contracts with each other directly, without going through state material allocation agencies (C. Kim 1986, 71). Thus, the integration reduced the number of enterprises the state has to deal with, as well as the number of the middle links (middle-level state agencies).

Clearly, the move toward associated enterprises is a retreat from the former detailed central planning. Kim admitted the difficulty of detailed planning given the increasing complexities in production linkage among enterprises and factories (C. Kim 1986, 75). Now enterprises are supposed to solve their own input supply problems.

However, North Korean associated enterprises have encountered a coordination problem among the member enterprises because of their ambiguous property rights relations (both income and control rights). For instance, C. Kim (1986) says that while each member enterprise is subject to control and planning at the association level, each of them is also supposed to maintain independent accounting and relative autonomy. The coordination problem among member enterprises exists since the integration was not based on clearly defined property rights but conducted through administrative measures.

China had similar experiences in its efforts to implement the associated enterprises since the mid-1980s. Joining the enterprise group did not change the participating enterprise's relations with its supervisory state organs, and each affiliated enterprise was still owned by its supervisory organs and subject to various degrees of control. Thus, each enterprise gave priority to its responsibilities toward its supervisory state organs, as opposed to the interests of the enterprise group (Gangzhu Zhang 1988). Therefore, coordinated use of production capacities and resources was not possible, which hampered efficient resource allocation within the group. For instance, there was no group-level accumulation of funds for investment purposes since each supervisory state authority allocated funds only to its own subordinates (Liu and Hu 1988). Integration of the enterprise group was attempted by adopting a shareholding system, in an effort to clarify property rights relations among member enterprises and to reduce the role of state authorities from being owners and managers to being shareholders (Lee and Mark 1991).

However, North Korea is not yet showing signs of implementing such radical reform measures as transforming state enterprises into shareholding corporations, which is regarded as a stepping-stone to privatization. Moreover, their vertical or horizontal integration does not seem to represent marketization. Rather, the move still appears antimarket, just a transfer of authority from one tier to another in the overall planning hierarchy. Actually, every member enterprise that belongs to the association is supposed to be under the direct control of association-level planning (S. Lee 1986, 50). From the center's point of view, it would be easier to control directly a small number of big units than a large number of small enterprises.

In sum, the North Korean move to the associated enterprise strongly resembles the *Kombinaten* in the former East Germany, where vertical and horizontal integration was used to improve the planning system rather than for market reform (Andreff 1989). Thus, it is different from the Chinese experience in that the Chinese associated enterprises emerged with substantial marketization in the economy and more or less spontaneously, especially in late 1980s.[19] In our opinion, the North Korean associated enterprise should be understood as deriving from both recentralization and decentralization. North Korea emphasized that the associated enterprise system represents a correct model of combining central guidance and enterprise creativity (S. Lee 1986, 48).

Conclusion

This chapter has tried to describe the North Korean economic system and identify recent reform efforts, and then, by analogy with the Chinese reform experience, attempted to evaluate the effectiveness of North Korean reform measures.

Despite the alleged uniqueness credited to the creativity of Kim Il Sung, the North Korean economic system, especially the enterprise system, can be basically considered one variant of the centrally planned socialist economy with some incentive schemes such as profit retention and worker bonuses. Its recent reform effort since the mid-1980s was motivated by the increasing seriousness of problems typical of centrally planned socialist economies. Much direct and indirect evidence testifies to the existence in North Korea of such problems as the soft budget constraint, runaway input demand and hoarding, over-centralization and related disequilibrium (shortages), and ineffective worker incentive provisions, and related collusive and opportunistic behavior.

The mid-1980s reform program in North Korea included new emphasis on the financial independence of enterprises (to harden their budget constraint), on the role division among the enterprise party secretary, manager, and chief engineer, on material incentives and the payment-by-results principle, as well as vertical or horizontal integration and increased enterprise autonomy with the associated enterprise system. However, there is nothing innovative about these measures.

That there has been no significant improvement of performance in Chinese state enterprises, despite a decade of reforms through similar measures, suggests that the results of North Korean economic reform will not differ much from those of Chinese. The Chinese lesson was that without radical changes in property rights relations and the emergence of a harder and more competitive economic environment, any attempt to revitalize the state sector is likely to fail.

An additional handicap for North Korea is presented by the fact that its leader, Kim Il Sung, was personally involved in devising and implementing several important measures that have shaped the current economic system, such as the Dae-an Model of collective leadership and the so-called unified and detailed planning. This implies that reform programs, or at least reform slogans, will be more compromising or partially concealed under the veil of the same old phrases, so long as Kim is alive to exercise his absolute control over the society.

North Korea would feel more comfortable in allowing nonstate-sector and foreign joint ventures than in attempting radical reform of the state sector, and only in such areas will reform be successful, as evidenced by the Chinese experience. Already initiated with some vigor is the so-called August Third program, which encouraged the nonstate sector to rely on market mechanisms in 1984, the same year that North Korea promulgated a joint venture law (H. S. Lee 1990). However, the Chinese experience tells us that such a dualist approach will eventually create competition between the state and the nonstate sector and between plans and markets. This implies a possible divergence of interest among various groups and strata in the society, which could produce social instability.[20] Great uncertainty exists about the future of North Korea, probably greater than that facing China.

Notes

1. For more details on such overseas visits by North Koreans, see Kang and Lee (1990, 338–39).

2. See Brun and Hersh (1976) and Wickman (1981) on the North Korean economic system before the mid-1980s reform.

3. In the socialist state enterprise, enterprise profits remitted to the state constitute a combination of dividends and income taxes, since the state is the owner of enterprise assets. In contrast with capitalist corporations, where dividends are alienable residual claims of shareholders, remitted profits are not completely alienable to socialist enterprises because they are reallocated to enterprises for investment and operating expenses.

4. Kornai's concept of the soft budget constraint refers to the relaxation of the strict relationship between earnings and expenditure ability when firms expect that excess expenditure or losses will be paid by some other institution, typically the state, in the form of "soft subsidies" and "soft credits." See Kornai (1986) and chapter 2 of Keun Lee (1991).

5. According to table 1 in Kang (1987), retention rates from extra profits were 10 to 90 percent in 1960, 13 to 50 percent in 1962, and 0 to 20 percent in 1972. Then the rate rose to 50 percent in 1985.

6. See IDE (1986) for details of the new provision.

7. The provision also states that a portion of production development funds can be used for supplementary monetary prizes for several political prizes such as "socialist competition citation" and "innovator citation."

8. The later experiment to transform state enterprises into shareholding corporations by allowing nonstate shares was the first move by Chinese authorities to deal with the arbitrariness of distributional relations between the state and enterprises, and related incentive problems by addressing property rights issues (Lee and Mark 1991).

9. Information from an interview with North Korean scholars in Osaka, Japan, 1990.

10. Ibid.

11. In the case of Dae-an Electric Machinery Associated Enterprises (the new name of the Dae-an Electric Factory), which had about 5,000 workers as of 1976, the party committee consists of 35 members elected by enterprise members. See Brun and Hersh (1976).

12. In 1957, the Central Committee of the Chinese Communist Party emphasized mass supervision under the party committee leadership, and in this spirit the worker assembly was implemented. After the Great Leap Forward, during which the party secretary took command, virtually replacing the collective leadership, the Central Committee revived "the manager responsibility system under the leadership of the party committee" in 1961. Since then, this system was maintained except during the turmoil of the Cultural Revolution, when even the party committee was abolished and replaced by the revolutionary committee.

13. Here we use the term *collusion* only in a negative sense. For the positive meaning of collusion, we use the term *cooperation*. As Aoki (1987) argues, the Japanese firm is evidence of cooperation among owner, management, and work-

ers. See also chapter 8 of Keun Lee (1991) for a comparison of firms in China, Korea, and Japan in this regard.

14. See *Economic Dictionary* (1985, 189–90) for more details.

15. Walder (1987) observes that a tacit agreement emerged between managers and workers, with both parties seeking to retain as much as possible in the worker's bonus and welfare fund, while distributing it as equally as possible. Empirical analysis of the collusion is provided in Lee and Mark (1989).

16. Choi (1989) used the term *"pyong-gyun ju-eui."* This is equivalent to the Chinese term *"pingjun zhuyi,"* egalitarianism.

17. Suh (1986) argues that the peculiarity of bonuses, relative to monetary prizes, which are subject to stricter control by state authorities, is that the rules on distribution are basically determined by each enterprise in consideration of diverse firm-specific conditions. One of the reasons for the individualistic determination of the bonus rules is that the most important tasks differ from enterprise to enterprise, and bonus payments should be related to fulfillment of such tasks. Moreover, the different nature of production across enterprises requires different labor evaluation standards.

18. See Chandler (1962) and Williamson (1975) on the advantages of vertical integration and the so-called M-form structure as enterprise organization. Discussion of this issue regarding the case of Chinese firms can be found in chapter 8 of Keun Lee (1991).

19. In China, the associated enterprise or enterprise groups have also emerged since the mid-1980s: these are called *qiye jiduan* or general corporations (*zonggongsi*). The relations among group firms are also diverse, ranging from tight integration based on parent and subsidiary relations to a very loose integration that is based simply on intensive mutual transactions (Gu 1988). Komiya (1987) argued that most Chinese firms called *chang* (factory) cannot be considered firms in the modern sense. In their function and autonomy, they are more equivalent to factories belonging to corporations as in Japan. However, these new forms of enterprise in China, enterprise groups can be considered closer to modern corporations. See chapter 8 of Keun Lee (1991) for such an argument.

20. This problem is further dealt with in chapter 9 of Keun Lee (1991) in discussing China's 1989 recentralization.

Part II

International Division of Labor and Interdependence

Chapter 6

China's Open-Door Policy and the Asian-Pacific Economy

The year 1978 marks a momentous change in the economic policy of the People's Republic of China (henceforth China). That year China officially proclaimed an open-door policy. This opening up to international trade represents a sharp reversal of Maoist policy, which preached self-sufficiency and autarky. The Chinese policy changes, however, were gradual, first limiting and maintaining contact with world markets mainly through the four Special Economic Zones (SEZs) and then enlarging it to fourteen open coastal cities.

Since 1978, the importance of trade to the PRC economy has grown rapidly. Trade represented 28 percent of gross national product (GNP) in 1988, compared to 9.7 percent in 1978 (see Table 6.1). While GNP grew at an annual average of 9.6 percent in constant yuan terms from 1978 to 1988, exports increased 25 percent and imports 23 percent, in real terms. As a result, the Chinese share of world exports has more than doubled, increasing from 0.75 percent in 1978 to 1.67 percent in 1988, and China's export share rank increased from thirty-second in 1978 to seventeenth in 1987. Foreign investment in China also rapidly increased; its cumulative amount from 1979 to 1989 is estimated at U.S.$15.4 billion. In 1988, foreign investment amounted to 3.5 percent of China's total fixed investment.

Table 6.1

China's Open-Door Policy

	1978	1980	1985	1988	Average Annual Changes (%)		
					1985–88	1978–88	1980–88
(A) Values							
GNP, $100 million	2,135.7	2,980.0	2,914.3	3,723.9	8.5	5.7	2.8
real growth in constant yuan					10.2	9.6	10.1
Total trade, $100 million	206.4	381.4	696	1,027.9	13.9	17.4	13.2
Exports, $100 million	97.5	181.2	273.5	475.4	20.2	17.2	12.8
real growth					29.2	25.1	29.3
Imports, $100 million	108.9	200.2	422.5	552.5	9.4	17.6	13.5
real growth					9.6	23.0	28.6
Foreign investment, $100 million			16.61	31.93	24.3		
in SEZs			3.2	4.29	10.3		
in open cities			3.02	6.81	31.1		
(B) Ratios							
Trade/GNP	9.7%	12.8%	23.9%	27.6%	4.9	11.1	10.1
Foreign invest./tot. fix. invest			2.6%	3.5%	10.9		
China export/world exports	0.75%	0.91%	1.40%	1.67%	6.2	8.3	7.9
SEZ exp. procurement/tot. exp.			1.0%	1.9%	22.5		
Open cities exp. procurement/tot. exp.			23.6%	22.8%	-1.1		
Average exchange rate	1.68	1.5	2.94	3.72	8.2	8.3	12.0
Terms of trade	112.2	100.0	111.1	90.7	-6.5	-2.1	-1.2

Sources: Most calculations are based on data from MOFERT (various issues). Foreign trade figures are custom statistics.

China's Foreign Trade Pattern

Direction of Trade

China traded most intensively with other Asian-Pacific countries. By 1988, about 70 percent of two-way trade was with other Asian-Pacific countries, including the United States, Canada, Japan, Australia, New Zealand, and the NIEs (South Korea, Taiwan, Hong Kong, and Singapore) and ASEAN-4 countries (Table 6.2). The rise in trade intensity with Asian-Pacific countries has been most noticeable from 1978, when the share was slightly more than half, to the mid-1980s. Since then, the trend of increasing intensity slowed down slightly, while Western and Eastern Europe recovered some of their shares, replacing a portion of the U.S. and Japanese shares. During the late 1980s, trade with Hong Kong, Taiwan, and South Korea grew rapidly. Throughout the last decade, Hong Kong, Japan, and the United States remained China's largest trading partners, accounting for more than 60 percent of exports and more than 50 percent of imports.

Since Hong Kong represents about 60 percent of China's trade, information about China's re-export and re-import through Hong Kong is central to understanding the overall picture of China trade. For instance, according to Chinese statistics, which do not include China's exports to the United States via Hong Kong, the United States has consistently run a surplus with China. However, official U.S. figures including re-exports show a small U.S. surplus or even a deficit. Generally speaking, China has had trade deficits with the developed countries, mainly Japan, the United States, Australia, and Western and Eastern Europe (Table 6.3 on page 106). China has had a surplus with Hong Kong, Singapore, the Philippines, India, and all of Africa. In 1988, its trade surplus with Hong Kong alone more than offset the sum of official deficits with Japan and the United States.

Hong Kong has been the main entry port for China's indirect and unofficial trade with South Korea and Taiwan. China has had deficits in its trade with South Korea and Taiwan, and the size of deficits has been increasing since the mid-1980s. According to estimates by the Korean Trade Association, China's total trade with South Korea in 1988 was U.S.$3.2 billion, which was roughly equal to the size of China's trade with the ASEAN-4 (see Table 6.3 and Lee and Park 1989–90). Korea has surplus of $0.42 billion with exports worth $1.8

Table 6.2a

China Trade Statistics, 1978–1988 (U.S.$ millions)

Direction of Trade Statistics

Year	World	United States	Australia	Japan	Hong Kong	India	Indonesia	Malaysia	Pakistan	Phillippines	Singapore	Thailand	EC
Exports													
1978	9,745	271	118	1,719	2,533	–	–	163	89	86	248	71	1,195
1979	13,657	595	156	2,764	3,328	–	–	171	122	135	297	212	1,734
1980	18,139	983	224	4,032	4,353	–	21	184	140	258	421	312	2,363
1981	21,476	1,505	174	4,747	5,263	81	54	191	211	255	658	228	2,503
1982	21,865	1,765	224	4,806	5,181	101	46	181	203	236	648	168	2,169
1983	22,096	1,713	181	4,517	5,797	58	49	186	224	143	567	195	2,509
1984	24,824	2,313	218	5,155	6,586	37	70	196	261	233	1,209	251	2,234
1985	27,329	2,336	183	6,091	7,148	84	124	186	185	314	2,063	116	2,285
1986	31,367	2,633	209	5,079	9,776	89	143	203	207	157	1,217	159	4,016
1987	39,464	3,030	298	6,392	13,764	88	188	255	300	245	1,323	301	3,916
1988	47,663	3,399	362	8,046	18,239	149	236	309	330	268	1,494	512	4,746
Imports													
1978	10,915	721	715	3,105	75	–	–	111	43	57	46	74	2,021
1979	15,675	1,857	985	3,944	214	–	–	189	30	47	105	83	3,354
1980	19,505	3,830	1,063	5,169	570	–	14	240	176	70	190	140	2,814
1981	21,631	4,682	559	6,183	1,236	81	63	120	333	117	113	154	2,715
1982	18,920	4,305	914	3,902	1,314	75	151	156	143	137	103	347	2,180
1983	21,313	2,753	613	5,495	1,710	15	150	215	159	45	114	135	3,391
1984	25,953	3,837	897	8,057	2,830	25	214	193	47	82	141	188	3,325
1985	42,480	5,199	1,124	15,178	4,762	39	330	198	58	97	241	263	6,151
1986	43,247	4,718	1,403	12,463	5,572	39	324	180	25	136	553	287	7,759
1987	43,222	4,836	1,325	10,087	8,437	30	591	302	38	140	618	405	7,275
1988	55,352	6,633	1,113	11,062	12,005	98	681	570	55	135	1,018	633	8,176

Sources: International Monetary Fund, *Direction of Trade Statistics Yearbook,* and computer data tapes, 1988 and 1989.

Table 6.2b

Distribution of China Trade[a], 1978–1988

Direction of Trade Statistics

Year	World	United States	Australia	Japan	Hong Kong	India	Indonesia	Malaysia	Pakistan	Phillippines	Singapore	Thailand	EC
Exports													
1978	9,745	2.8	1.2	17.6	26.0	—	—	1.7	0.9	0.9	2.5	0.7	12.3
1979	13,657	4.4	1.1	20.2	24.4	—	—	1.3	0.9	1.0	2.2	1.6	12.7
1980	18,139	5.4	1.2	22.2	24.0	—	0.1	1.0	0.8	1.4	2.3	1.7	13.0
1981	21,476	7.0	0.8	22.1	24.5	0.4	0.3	0.9	1.0	1.2	3.1	1.1	11.7
1982	21,865	8.1	1.0	22.0	23.7	0.5	0.2	0.8	0.9	1.1	3.0	0.8	9.9
1983	22,096	7.8	0.8	20.4	26.2	0.3	0.2	0.8	1.0	0.6	2.6	0.9	11.4
1984	24,824	9.3	0.9	20.8	26.5	0.1	0.3	0.8	1.1	0.9	4.9	1.0	9.0
1985	27,329	8.5	0.7	22.3	26.2	0.3	0.5	0.7	0.7	1.1	7.5	0.4	8.4
1986	31,367	8.4	0.7	16.2	31.2	0.3	0.5	0.6	0.7	0.5	3.9	0.5	12.8
1987	39,464	7.7	0.8	16.2	34.9	0.2	0.5	0.6	0.8	0.6	3.4	0.8	9.9
1988	47,663	7.1	0.8	16.9	38.3	0.3	0.5	0.6	0.7	0.6	3.1	1.1	10.0
Imports													
1978	10,915	6.6	6.6	28.4	0.7	—	—	1.0	0.4	0.5	0.4	0.7	18.5
1979	15,675	11.8	6.3	25.2	1.4	—	—	1.2	0.2	0.3	0.7	0.5	21.4
1980	19,505	19.6	5.4	26.5	2.9	—	0.1	1.2	0.9	0.4	1.0	0.7	14.4
1981	21,631	21.6	2.6	28.6	5.7	0.4	0.3	0.6	1.5	0.5	0.5	0.7	12.6
1982	18,920	22.8	4.8	20.6	6.9	0.4	0.8	0.8	0.8	0.7	0.5	1.8	11.5
1983	21,313	12.9	2.9	25.8	8.0	0.1	0.7	1.0	0.7	0.2	0.5	0.6	15.9
1984	25,953	14.8	3.5	31.0	10.9	0.1	0.8	0.7	0.2	0.3	0.5	0.7	12.8
1985	42,480	12.2	2.6	35.7	11.2	0.1	0.8	0.5	0.1	0.2	0.6	0.6	14.5
1986	43,247	10.9	3.2	28.8	12.9	0.1	0.7	0.4	0.1	0.3	1.3	0.7	17.9
1987	43,222	11.2	3.1	23.3	19.5	0.1	1.4	0.7	0.1	0.3	1.4	0.9	16.8
1988	55,352	12.0	2.0	20.0	21.7	0.2	1.2	1.0	0.1	0.2	1.8	1.1	14.8

Source: Calculated from Table 6.2a.

[a] As a percentage of the Direction of Trade Statistics (IMF) World Total.

Table 6.3

Area Composition of China's Foreign Trade, 1988

	Shares (%)			Values, U.S.$ 10,000		
	Exports	Imports	Balance	Exports	Imports	Balance
Total	100.0	100.0	−100.0	4,754,034	5,525,073	−771,039
Asia total	68.6	50.1	64.0	3,260,843	2,767,612	493,231
H.K. & Macao	39.4	21.9	85.5	1,871,054	1,211,976	659,078
Hong Kong	38.4	21.7	81.6	1,826,858	1,197,326	629,532
Macao	0.9	0.3	3.8	44,196	14,650	29,546
Singapore	3.1	1.8	6.1	148,507	101,838	46,669
Taiwan	1.0	4.1	−22.9	47,900	224,100	−176,200
Japan	16.7	20.0	−40.7	792,208	1,105,709	−313,501
North Korea	0.7	0.4	1.4	34,535	23,367	11,168
South Korea	2.9	3.3	−5.5	138,700	180,900	−42,200
ASEAN–4	2.8	3.7	−9.0	132,396	201,792	−69,396
Indonesia	0.5	1.2	−5.8	23,644	68,152	−44,508
Malaysia	0.6	1.0	−3.4	30,820	56,888	−26,068
Philippines	0.6	0.2	1.7	26,950	13,506	13,444
Thailand	1.1	1.1	−1.6	50,982	63,246	−12,264
Burma	0.3	0.2	0.0	13,361	13,710	−349
India	0.3	0.2	0.7	14,862	9,771	5,091
Pakistan	0.7	0.1	3.6	32,995	5,522	27,473
U.S.	7.1	12.0	−42.2	338,003	663,109	−325,106
Canada	0.8	3.4	−19.0	38,988	185,583	−146,595
Oceania total	0.9	2.8	−14.4	42,579	153,840	−111,261
Australia	0.8	2.0	−9.7	36,154	110,779	−74,625
New Zealand	0.1	0.7	−4.8	3,915	40,735	−36,820
Latin America	0.8	4.0	−23.4	38,774	218,838	−180,064
Europe total	17.6	24.4	−66.7	834,871	1,348,988	−514,117
EC	9.9	14.7	−44.5	472,063	814,932	−342,869
West Germany	3.1	6.2	−25.3	148,451	343,355	−194,904
UK	1.4	1.6	−3.1	65,904	89,825	−23,921
France	1.1	1.8	−6.1	51,516	98,687	−47,171
Italy	1.6	2.8	−10.4	74,579	154,903	−80,324
EFTA	1.0	2.4	−10.7	48,691	131,272	−82,581
CPEs	6.5	7.0	−10.4	309,545	389,507	−79,962
USSR	3.1	3.2	−4.0	147,595	178,208	−30,613
Africa	4.0	0.5	20.7	188,384	28,897	159,487

Source: China Custom Statistics (1989), no. 1. Taiwan trade figures are esti-mations by the Ministry of Foreign Economic Relations and Trade of the PRC reported in *Renmin ribao*, March 20, 1990. South Korean trade figures are estimations by the Korea Trade Association. They include both indirect and direct trade.

billion in 1988. About 70 percent of the trade is estimated to be indirect trade via Hong Kong (Lee and Lee 1990b). According to official estimates by the Chinese Ministry of Foreign Economic Relations and Trade (MOFERT), China–Taiwan trade was U.S.$2.72 billion, of which Chinese exports were U.S.$0.48 billion and Chinese imports were U.S.$2.24 billion (*Renmin ribao*, hereafter *RMRB*, March 20, 1990). Thus, China has a deficit of U.S.$2.5 billion. Such a one-sided trade imbalance was maintained throughout the last decade (Y. Zhang 1988).

China's trade with Singapore has also increased rapidly, with China enjoying a steady surplus. This is because Singapore, like Hong Kong, is an entry port. The rapid rise in China's exports to Singapore increased almost fourfold between 1978 and 1985, mainly because of shipments of petroleum to Singapore's refineries. Whether Singapore can be China's gateway to the members of ASEAN remains to be seen. China's exports decreased after 1985, whereas imports continued to grow. China's trade has not expanded as rapidly with the ASEAN–4 countries as it has with the NIEs. Indonesia is an exception; China's trade relations with a highly suspicious Indonesia have recently been formally restored.

Complementarity and Competition

The future growth of China's trade will be concentrated within the Asian-Pacific region, but probably will be unevenly distributed. There is substantially less complementarity between China and the ASEAN–4 than between China and the four NIEs in economic structure and resource endowment; China is more similar to ASEAN members (and India) than to the NIEs (Ebashi and Hishida 1986).

The NIEs are likely to benefit more from rapid growth in China than other groups of developing countries in Asia. The NIEs can produce the type of consumer goods desired by the Chinese more cheaply and with better quality than the others. Exports of industrial inputs, machinery, and equipment from the NIEs will increasingly compete with those from Japan and the United States. The NIEs in turn can procure labor-intensive goods they need from China. Industries that the NIEs phase out can be relocated in China as well as in ASEAN and South Asian countries. China is accelerating its human resource development and is seeking to balance its economic structure by improving services, infrastructure, and the regulatory environment. The prospects for com-

petition between China and the NIEs in the U.S. and Japanese markets
depend on how rapidly the NIEs can move toward more skill- and
technology-intensive exports. It is unlikely that China will pose a serious competitive threat to the NIEs in more skill-intensive areas until
well into the 1990s.

China's labor-intensive manufactured exports may present stiff
competition to the ASEAN countries, as well as to South Asian countries in third-country markets. However, to date Chinese exports have
not crowded out those of other Asian less developed countries (LDCs).
Protectionist quotas in more developed countries are a far greater problem for Asian producers of textiles, footwear, and garments than is
competition from China.

China's trade links with the ASEAN–4 could be expanded because
of certain complementarities in overall resource endowments. ASEAN
producers of forest products, crude materials, and intermediate industrial goods (e.g., cement, plywood, iron and steel, fertilizer, and chemicals) may find a niche in China's markets, although competition will
come from other countries such as the United States, Australia, and
Canada. The ASEAN countries appear to have expanded exports of
such manufactured goods to China rapidly since 1983. China competes
to a certain degree with Malaysia, and even more with Indonesia, for
Japan's crude petroleum market. Through the 1990s, however, petroleum exports to Japan are unlikely to be sustained by these countries,
and competition will shift increasingly to labor-intensive manufactured
goods.

China's Rural Enterprises and Their Outward Orientation

Rural enterprises have come to be regarded as the most dynamic economic entities in China.[1] Two original forms of these enterprises were
the commune-run enterprises and brigade-run enterprises. Economic
decentralization since the late 1970s has generated new forms of rural
enterprises (Odgaard 1988; Zhou and Hu 1989). First, some families
and individuals have jointly set up their own enterprises that can be
called cooperatives (*lianhu* or *hezuo*). Second, there are individual private businesses (*getihu*). The growth of rural enterprises was remarkable in terms of both job creation and output. The fastest growth in
terms of employment shares was achieved by rural cooperative and
individual business, whose growth was even faster than that of urban

individual business. As of 1988, all rural enterprises together accounted for about 18 percent of China's total employment (Keun Lee 1991). All rural industrial enterprises, including private industrial enterprises, produced 26 percent of total gross industrial output in China, compared to 18 percent in 1985 (Keun Lee 1991).

However, especially after 1989, rural enterprises were increasingly criticized as economically inefficient and engaged in tax evasion, while aggravating shortages of energy and raw materials that were urgently needed in more important state-owned industry (Delfs 1989; Ignatius and Bennett 1989). Their success was attributed mainly to strong incentives and a competitive environment, which, however, have not always benefited the whole economy. In 1990, some rural enterprises were closed or merged, and others were subject to strict taxation and controls. Chinese policymakers cannot afford to abolish rural enterprises because they create jobs. Their emerging policy direction appears to be to induce rural enterprises to develop to the benefit of the national economy yet without competing with state enterprises (*RMRB*, December 1, 1989). Particular emphasis has been placed on making rural enterprises export oriented.

From the Chinese point of view, outward orientation seemed a satisfactory solution to the problem of competition against state enterprises for key materials and credits. Rural enterprises are thus encouraged to rely more on foreign inputs and capital and international markets. Already in 1988, total exports by all rural enterprises reached U.S.$6.5 billion, about a fifth of total national exports (*RMRB*, December 12, 1989). It is reported that before 1980 there were fewer than 1,500 rural enterprises in 13 coastal provinces of China that export (*RMRB*, November 6, 1989). As of mid-1989, there were more than 300,000 rural enterprises, exporting the wares of the chemical, machinery, consumer food, and textile industries. About 4,700 rural enterprises are reported to have contractual agreements with foreign and overseas Chinese businessmen (*RMRB*, November 6, 1989).

Direct Foreign Investment and Foreign Borrowing

Since the promulgation of the Chinese-Foreign Joint Venture Law on July 1, 1979, direct foreign investment has increased rapidly. The increase has been supported by legislation to provide greater incentives for foreign investors (United Nations Center on Transnational Corporations [UNCTC] 1988). During the initial years, however, foreign investment was concentrated in service industries, such as hotels and foreign trade companies. Since 1986, production-oriented, technology-oriented, and export-oriented ventures have invested more, thus altering the sectoral composition of direct foreign investment. According to the United Nations Center on Transnational Corporations (UNCTC) (1988, 62), between 1979 and 1985, only 45 percent of direct foreign investment was for production-oriented industry; the remainder went for hotels, tourist projects, taxi companies, and other service industries. But, in 1986, 76 percent of the total direct foreign investment was approved for such sectors as manufacturing, agriculture, transport, and telecommunications.

In terms of the country composition of foreign investment, the recent trend is a relative decline in the share of American and Japanese capital and a rising share from East Asian neighbors such as Taiwan, Hong Kong, Macao, and South Korea. The Chinese intend to form an export-processing zone comprising the mainland, Hong Kong, and Taiwan, in which plastic and petrochemical industries rely mainly on Taiwan capital, and electronics, light industry, and textiles rely on capital from Hong Kong.

The share held by Hong Kong and Macao increased from about 50 percent in 1984 to 65 percent in 1988, while the U.S. share decreased from 18 percent to 7 percent over the same period (Table 6.4). Although the amount of Japanese investment more than doubled after 1984, its share remained almost constant. The Tiananmen crisis in June 1989 and the subsequent economic sanctions imposed by the West caused an abrupt decline and even withdrawal of new direct foreign investment in China. The prompt negative responses by the Western economic powers contrasted with ever-expanding DFI from Taiwan and South Korea. While the initial shock of the Tiananmen incident wore off slowly for many foreign investors, those in Taiwan and South Korea soon resumed, and indeed increased their respective DFI in China.

The rapid growth of Taiwanese DFI was remarkable, especially after 1989. While the cumulative amount of Taiwanese capital invested in China was only about U.S.$100 million by the end of 1987, it reached U.S.$1 billion by the end of 1989 and doubled by the end of 1990. Taiwan has surpassed the United States and Japan to become the second largest investor in China, exceeded only by Hong Kong.

Compared to Taiwanese investment, South Korean investment

Table 6.4

Area Composition of China's Foreign Borrowing and Investment, 1984–1988

| | Shares (%) | | | | Value in U.S.$10,000 (utilized amount) | | | |
| | Borrowing | | Investment | | Borrowing | | Investment | |
	1988	1984	1988	1984	1988	1984	1988	1984
Total	100.0	100.0	100.0	100.0	648,673	128,567	319,368	141,885
World Bank	17.0	13.8	–	–	110,517	17,767	–	–
Asian Dev. Bank	0.0	–	–	–	260	–	–	–
UN Funds for Agri.	0.2	0.4	–	–	1,518	531	–	–
H.K. & Macao	10.5	0.5	65.6	52.7	68,139	628	209,520	74,753
Hong Kong	8.9	–	64.7		57,965		206,760	
Macao	1.6		0.9		10,174		2,760	
Singapore	1.5	0.0	0.9	0.1	10,000	0	2,782	120
Japan	42.5	65.9	16.1	15.8	275,611	84,741	51,453	22,458
ASEAN-4	0.0	0.0	0.4	0.5	0	0	1,135	731
Indonesia	0.0	0.0	0.0	0.0	0	0	32	0
Malaysia	0.0	0.0	0.0	0.0	0	0	130	57
Philippines	0.0	0.0	0.1	0.2	0	0	363	229
Thailand	0.0	0.0	0.2	0.3	0	0	610	445
U.S.	0.5	2.3	7.4	18.1	3,507	3,009	23,596	25,625
Canada	0.9	0.5	0.2	0.0	6,080	607	602	0
Australia	0.0	0.2	0.1	0.0	184	218	416	40
New Zealand	0.0	0.0	0.0	0.0	0	0	13	35
West Germany	2.4	1.5	0.5	0.5	15,356	1,925	1,490	756
UK	8.3	2.6	1.1	6.9	54,100	3,371	3,416	9,797
France	7.1	3.0	0.7	1.4	45,923	3,916	2,267	2,016
Italy	1.7	2.8	1.0	1.3	10,983	3,615	3,054	1,800

Sources: SSB of China, *Zhongguo tongji nianjian* (China statistical yearbook), 1989; MOFERT, *Almanac of China's Foreign Economic Relations and Trade*, 1985, 1989.

started late and its cumulative amount is still small; however, it has grown rapidly. As of September 1990, South Korean DFI in China reached U.S.$140 million disbursed over 71 projects, and South Korean investments have been in relatively bigger projects. Out of 26 ventures already in operation, 11 were projects exceeding a million U.S. dollars in invested capital.

With continued emphasis on direct foreign investment, the Chinese are seeking to attract a cumulative total of U.S.$40 billion by the end of this century, which means about U.S.$25 billion to be invested during the 1990s (RMRB, April 2, 1990). Competition will be fierce between China and the larger ASEAN countries wishing to attract foreign capital in the future. The NIEs have superior infrastructure, more efficient government bureaucracy, better regulatory and legal environments, and highly skilled and diligent labor forces. Thus, they will be more able to attract investment in skill- and technology-intensive industries than the ASEAN–4, China, or India. Out of this group, those that succeed in improving infrastructure and removing other deficiencies, such as corruption, will attract more DFI in labor-intensive areas.

International Implications of China's Foreign Borrowing

China needs to borrow from abroad to finance its modernization. However, the Chinese leaders appear much too cautious about foreign indebtedness, even though they are anxious to attract direct foreign investment. The Chinese want to avoid the burden of heavy payments of interest and debts, out of concern that debt repayment will constrain future growth. Thus they prefer not take out commercial loans at market interest rates, seeking instead preferential terms and loans from international organizations.

During the decade from 1979 to 1988, total Chinese borrowing already committed is estimated to be U.S.$33 billion (SSB of China, 1989). In terms of composition, the World Bank provided 17 percent of China's foreign borrowing in 1988, compared to 14 percent in 1984; Japan continued to be the biggest lender, accounting for more than 40 percent, which is, however, reduced from 66 percent in 1984 (Table 6.4). The shares contributed by Hong Kong and Macao increased from 0.5 percent in 1984 to more than 10 percent in 1988.

At the end of 1987, China's total gross debt was estimated at U.S.$36.5 billion, about two-thirds of which was long term (Table 6.5). Finance

Table 6.5

Chinese External Debt and Debt Service, 1980–1987
(U.S.$ 100 million)

	1980	1981	1982	1983	1984	1985	1986	1987	Growth rate 1982–87
Gross debt excluding IMF credit	–	–	80.60	100.58	128.91	205.22	258.61	365.04	35.3%
Long-term debt, total	41.98	35.09	57.47	60.87	67.44	106.17	171.31	245.11	33.7%
Long-term debt, unconcessional	0.11	0.32	7.64	12.53	16.94	28.55	42.25	62.20	52.1%
Debt service excluding IMF credit	14.56	23.33	20.46	19.66	14.20	23.17	31.12	45.35	17.3%
Amortization, long-term	–	–	13.13	11.38	5.56	12.68	18.75	28.50	16.8%
Interest, long-term	–	–	5.78	5.14	3.33	3.90	6.03	9.69	10.9%
Interest, short-term	–	–	1.55	3.14	5.31	6.58	6.34	7.15	35.8%
GNP	2,980.0	2,807.6	2,747.6	2,933.8	3,000.9	2,914.3	2,819.1	3,051.3	2.1%
Exports	181.2	220.1	223.2	222.3	261.4	273.5	309.4	394.4	12.1%
Debts/GNP	–	–	2.9%	3.4%	4.3%	7.0%	9.2%	12.0%	32.5%
Debt service/exports	8.0%	10.6%	9.2%	8.8%	5.4%	8.5%	10.1%	11.5%	4.6%

Source: Organization for Economic Co-operation and Development (OECD), *Financing and External Debt of Developing Countries, 1989;* China's GNP and exports are from SSB of China, 1989.

Note: China's GNP in yuan are turned into U.S. dollar values at official average exchange rates.

from international commercial banks and bond markets amounted to U.S.$12.3 billion, about half of which was long term, compared to less than a fifth in 1984. Although gross debt rapidly increased at an annual average of 35.3 percent from 1982 to 1987, China's indebtedness has been low by international standards. The ratio of debt to GNP quadrupled between 1982 and 1987, yet it was only 12 percent in 1987. The debt–service ratio hovered around 10 percent during the 1980s. The debt–service ratio has increased more slowly than that of debt itself, seemingly because China still relies principally on concessional loans from official sources rather than commercial sources.

Thus far, China has not been an important factor in reduced International Development Association (IDA, the World Bank's soft loan window) funding to Asian LDCs, though the World Bank's desire to increase lending to Africa has had such an impact. China has yet to borrow from the Asian Development Bank (ADB), but China's access to IDA and ADB funding has long-term implications for India and other Asian borrowers. Bilateral assistance from Japan is substantial, but that is not the case with other OECD members. The U.S. share as a source of China's borrowing decreased from 2.3 percent in 1984 to 0.5 percent in 1988 (Table 6.4). Since the United States has no aid program for China, the major source of credit was U.S. Export–Import Bank credit facilities and the Overseas Private Investment Corporation (OPIC). The amount of official U.S. bilateral funding to China has remained minuscule compared to that from Japan.

China's cumulative borrowing in international bond markets and cumulative commercial bank credits was estimated at U.S.$4.4 billion and U.S.$8 billion, respectively, at the end of 1987 (OECD 1989). The overwhelming majority of the bonds have been issued in Japan, and Japanese banks have also been the principal source of commercial credits to China. Under present circumstances and policies, China's presence in international financial markets is unlikely to raise the cost of borrowing by other Asian countries, so long as China preserves its strong credit rating and conservative borrowing policies wherein the "maximum permissible" debt–service ratio is 15 percent.

For the purposes of Chinese economic development, the Chinese have good reason to take a more active attitude toward foreign borrowing and to revise their perceptions about the optimum level of indebtedness. China's indebtedness is far below the levels of other heavily indebted developing countries, and China's export ability is much better than that of other European socialist countries that now carry heavy debts. Foreign borrowing is not simply debt accumulation but, more important, capital formation. The important matter is how to use borrowed funds efficiently so as to support accelerated growth. The heavy indebtedness of some developing countries derives from leakages of borrowed money to nonproductive, sometimes corrupt, purposes. Foreign borrowing and direct foreign investment both have costs and benefits. Policymakers believe that foreign borrowing might be a better choice than direct foreign investment because they do not have to worry about how to control the joint ventures. The example of South Korea, which relied primarily on foreign borrowing until the end of the 1970s, when more liberal policies were taken toward direct foreign investment, may be instructive in this connection.

China and GATT

In July 1986 the Chinese government submitted a formal request to join the General Agreement on Tariffs and Trade (GATT) as a full member; China was granted observer status in 1982. By citing the membership of six socialist countries—Cuba, Czechoslovakia, Hungary, Poland, Romania, and Yugoslavia—and its intention to abide fully by GATT regulations, China has sought to defuse some countries' opposition to its membership. Although some developing countries express concern that China may overwhelm them in the competition to export labor-intensive manufactured goods, most LDCs support China's application. Japan and most European countries have also been promoting China's GATT membership. The United States has some reservations about China's admission to GATT, but it is not likely that the United States will try to block China from attaining full membership in the organization. Hence, it is expected that within the next few years China will become a full-fledged member.

As of 1990, GATT had 92 members, which together account for 85 percent of world trade. The initial effect of China's membership would not be significant since China's trade volume is small despite its huge population. The long-run effects of China's participation in GATT, however, could be much greater.

China has requested that it be admitted to GATT as an LDC, which would allow it to invoke exceptions to GATT regulations that bind developed nations. However, China still maintains some features of a centrally planned economy (CPE), even though reforms have added elements of market mechanisms. Other CPEs admitted to GATT provide some precedent for the type of changes needed. Most often cited are the experiences of Hungary and Yugoslavia, which joined GATT as CPEs. Both adopted tariff concessions and committed themselves to ongoing reform. China's approach to membership will have to combine elements of LDC and CPE experience. Tariff and trade policy reforms to open China's domestic market and avoidance of improper export practices, for example, dumping (unrealistically low prices of exports), will be necessary elements. China's numerous bilateral trade agreements will also be superseded by GATT rules, which are based on the principal of multilateralism.

The United States has expressed concern that China's accession to full GATT membership, particularly during sensitive negotiations, may strengthen the position of LDCs that favor a "free rider" approach; that is, developed countries must continue to liberalize and open their markets, but LDCs are not obligated to follow suit. In the past, India has been a leading advocate of this position. In addition, some believe that granting China LDC status within GATT will actually slow the process of Chinese trade policy reform. In considering China's status, it is important to note that during the 1950s and early 1960s only a third of China's external trade was with non-CPEs. By the 1980s, however, almost 90 percent of China's external trade was with the market economies, most of them in the Asian-Pacific region.

China's open-door policy has also forced changes in its trade policy. The most difficult issue China and its trade partners will have to grapple with is that of equitable access to one another's markets. The Chinese cannot expect to be given full access to the markets of GATT members without granting these countries the right to sell in China's own domestic markets. The reform of tariffs and import quotas alone are not sufficient to open a centrally planned economy. Other trade and purchasing practices, particularly in the state-owned industrial sector, will be necessary.

Trade deficits and the partial recentralization drive in the late 1980s, however, have pushed China's policy back somewhat to a more closed system. In particular, the government has adopted a licensing system to control imports and exports. It adopted even more stringent control measures on imports in 1985 and in 1989 as the trade deficit worsened; for instance, most road vehicle imports are now banned. The system of tariffs in China is similar to that of many other LDCs. After 1985, nominal tariff rates varied from 3 to 150 percent for trade with countries that have concluded trade agreements with China; for other countries the range is even wider. This represents some improvement from previous rates, which ranged from 7.5 to 250 percent. China also has export duties covering twenty-nine basic staple items. These duties aim at ensuring adequate domestic supplies at prices that may diverge significantly from international prices.

The expansion of China's international trade will continue and thus so will China's prominence in multilateral trade negotiations. The Chinese have not yet developed firm positions on the issues to be addressed by the new GATT round, and their general stance has been more open minded than the strident LDC view characterizing India or Brazil. For example, China appears to have no objection to including services and intellectual property rights issues on the GATT agenda. China's primary objective is to become a full member of GATT, and it is currently studying the issues raised as they relate to its trade and development prospects. China has a particular concern regarding barriers to technology exports from the developed countries. China's position reflects its desire to give its exports the best possible access to external markets and to pursue its interests in improving access to the types of technology imports it views as indispensable to its defense and development objectives.

Prospects

At its first meeting after the Tiananmen crisis, the 13th Central Committee of the Chinese Communist Party (the fifth session, held on November 9, 1989) determined that China's austerity program would last three years or longer, including 1989, so as to alleviate the inflationary gap between aggregate demand and supply, to put the national economy on the track of sustained and coordinated growth, and to lay a good foundation for the strategic goal of quadrupling GNP by the end of this century.[2] The highest priority was placed on controlling excessive demand by reducing the money supply and restraining excessive growth by nonstate sectors, and some recentralization measures were emphasized, including some relating to foreign trade. For instance, the Central Committee document bans private entities from business dealings with the major means of production, from long-distance wholesale business, and from foreign trade; it also seeks to intensify supervision and control of incomes of workers in certain enterprises, people with two jobs, and owners of private and independent businesses. All foreign trade except that by authorized companies is also banned, and production enterprises authorized to engaged in direct import and export may neither export products of other enterprises nor sell their imported goods to others for profit.

Whatever their rationale, the opportunity costs of these measures will be greater than the short-run benefits if they are continued too long. There is widespread concern among China observers who agree with the rationale for short-run stabilization that if authorities overreact with a tightening of macropolicies and recentralization, not just the future of reform but also the pace of growth could be at stake. The tight macroeconomic policies have affected every aspect of the economy. First, normal production activities of even state enterprises and joint ventures were affected, and, second, unemployment problems re-emerged as nonstate sectors reduced their activities. Policy authorities responded by loosening credit for large and medium-size state enterprises and foreign joint ventures in 1990, indicating that foreign ventures are given priority as high as large and medium-size state enterprises. They also began to re-emphasize the positive role of collective and private enterprises in creating jobs.

Other than some recentralization measures toward domestic economy and some foreign trading practices, the Chinese authorities have been showing clear signs, both in rhetoric and in concrete measures, that they plan to stick with open-door policies. First, Chinese authorities devalued the renminbi against foreign currencies on December 16, 1989.[3] They were reportedly weighing the potential benefits devaluation could provide in boosting exports and dampening imports against the risk that it would hamper their effort to reduce the high rate of inflation. Since China finally took the step without waiting for inflation to be brought under control, most foreign analysts view the move as a sign that the current leadership places importance on maintaining an open economy.

Second, with a view to reboosting foreign investment, in April 1990, the Seventh National People's Congress revised the 1979 Chinese-Foreign Joint Venture Law, mainly to make foreign partners eligible for the position of chairman of the board and to relieve foreign investors of concern over the possibility of nationalization or takeover by the state (*RMRB*, April 6, 1990). The amendment also abolished the limits to the length of possible tax exemption for foreign ventures, as well as the former requirement of specifying the contract periods.

While China continues its open-door policy in the 1990s, its main partners are expected to be Hong Kong, Taiwan, Singapore, South Korea, and Japan. It has been increasingly apparent since June 1989 that China is giving the highest priority to economic cooperation with Taiwan, and Taiwan has responded strongly to signals from the mainland. South Korean–Chinese economic relations also seemed to be little affected by recent political events. While Japan was quick to resume economic transactions with China, changes for more active interaction with Western developed countries including the United States had arrived slowly because of political factors.

Notes

1. The Chinese for rural enterprise is *xiangzhen qiye*, which used to mean only township- and village-run enterprises; since 1984 it includes cooperative and individual businesses in official statistical classification (SSB of China, 1986)

2. For details of the plan for 1990, see chapter 9 of Keun Lee (1991).

3. The renminbi (or yuan) was devalued by 21.2 percent against the U.S. dollar, resulting in a new exchange rate of RMB4.71 to US$1.00. Before December 16, 1989, the last major devaluation was in July 1986, when the renminbi was devalued by 15.7 percent against the U.S. dollar. Since then, the official rate of RMB3.7 to the dollar was maintained until December 1989.

Chapter 7

Problems and Profitability of Direct Foreign Investment in China

Since China's open-door policy was initiated in 1978, direct foreign investment (DFI) flows into China have increased dramatically, aided by the promulgation of the Chinese-Foreign Joint Venture Law on July 1, 1979. While the total amount of actual investment between 1989 and 1983 was U.S.$1.8 billion, actual investment in 1988 alone reached more than U.S.$3 billion (Table 7.1). The cumulative amount of actual investment was estimated at U.S.$15.4 billion at the end of 1989. (DFI accounted for 3.5 percent of China's total fixed investment in 1988.)

Over the decade, Chinese policies toward DFI have shown increasing flexibility. However, while DFI in the Chinese economy is growing in importance, a decade of experience with China has revealed many problems and issues, especially the Chinese regulations regarding domestic markets and foreign exchange control.[1] This chapter investigates some of these areas, using actual survey data of DFI firms, and draws some policy implications for China's policymakers.

Direct Foreign Investment in China

The rapid increase of DFI in China has been induced in part by legislation providing incentives to foreign investors (UNCTC 1988). However, as the definition of DFI employed in their legislation is broader than the conventionally accepted one, we need to specify clearly what is included in DFI in China. In statistical reporting on DFI, the Chinese authorities distinguish the following four types: (1) equity joint ventures; (2) contractual joint ventures; (3) wholly foreign-owned ventures; (4) joint exploration of resources (mainly offshore oil).

The first three types are the so-called three foreign-invested enterprises (*sanzi qiye*), which have been given greater emphasis in Chinese policy. There were about 20,000 foreign enterprises categorized as such by the end of 1989 (Table 7.1).

An equity joint venture is a limited-liability company jointly managed by investors in proportion to their respective shares of investment. Profits are also distributed in a corresponding manner. Equity joint ventures are now the predominant vehicle for DFI in China, with more than half of the "three foreign-invested enterprises" being of this type by the end of 1989.

Contractual joint venture refers in Chinese usage to an array of arrangements that are not designated as equity joint ventures but nonetheless have as their common thread long-run cooperation. In such joint projects, Chinese and foreign parties write up a contract that sets forth their respective rights and responsibilities. Usually no new entity is created, and the parties involved simply contribute specified resources and perform the tasks prescribed in the contract, often under a management team composed of their respective representatives. Like compensation trade and processing and assembly arrangements, contractual joint venture is not, however, included in the conventional definition of DFI.

By the end of 1989, there were 6,250 contractual joint-venture enterprises, about half the number of equity joint-venture enterprises. Until the mid-1980s, contractual joint ventures as an investment vehicle were more popular than equity joint ventures because of their flexibility in allowing the parties involved to negotiate freely the manner and proportion of profit or output distribution (UNCTC 1988) However, since the mid-1980s equity joint ventures have accounted for an increasing portion of DFI in China (Table 7.1). This change reflects the Chinese preference for transferring technology and management skills, which the Chinese authorities believe can be better achieved through equity joint ventures without diluting their control over the enterprise. This preference has been adequately expressed in various measures, including tax incentives established in the 1980s.

Recently there has been a remarkable increase in wholly foreign-owned enterprises. Although there were only 1,410 wholly foreign-

Table 7.1

Direct Foreign Investment in China

(A) Utilized Amount Decomposed into Types (U.S.$ million)	1979–83	% of column	1983	1987	1988	% of column	1989	1979–89
Direct foreign investment	1,802.83	100.0	635.21	2,313.50	3,193.60	100.0	3,296	15,400
Equity joint venture	173.18	9.6	73.57	1,485.80	1,975.40	61.9		
Contractual joint venture	758.45	42.1	227.38	619.96	779.93	24.4		
Foreign-owned venture	83.07	4.6	42.76	24.55	226.16	7.1		
Joint exploitation	788.13	43.7	291.50	183.20	212.19	6.6		

Aggregates in years (U.S.$ million)	1979–83	1984	1985	1986	1987	1988	1989	1979–89
Total amount	1,803	1,258	1,661	1,874	2,314	3,194	3,296	15,400
Annual growth rates			32.0%	12.8%	23.5%	38.0%	3.2%	

(B–1)

(B) Number of firms

	Registered by end of 1989	Growth from 1988	Approved by end of 1989	Approved by end of 1986
Total	20,000	37.4%	22,000	7,815
Equity joint venture	11,449	42.4%	12,000	3,233
Contractual joint venture	6,250	17.8%	8,000	4,403
Foreign-owned venture	1,410	150.9%	1,500	138
Joint exploitation			58	41

(B–2)　　(B–3)

(C) Exports by "three ventures" (U.S.$ million)	1985	1989
	320	3,590

Sources: (A) are from various issues of *Zhonguo duiwai jingji maoyi nianjian* (Almanac of China's Foreign Trade and Economic Relations), except 1989 figures, which are from *Renmin ribao (RMRB)*, March 23, 1990. (B–1) is from *RMRB*, February 27, 1990. (B–2) is from *RMRB*, March 23, 1990, and (B–3) is from UNCTC (1988). (C) is from *RMRB*, April 2, 1990.

owned enterprises in 1989, their numerical growth was the highest among the three forms of joint venture for that year and for the period 1986 to 1989. Between 1987 and 1988, the amount of actual investment in wholly foreign-owned joint ventures increased almost tenfold, probably as a result of a change in policy in 1986. The change led to the replacement of preferential treatment for equity joint ventures with various beneficial incentives for either "export-oriented" or "technology-oriented" enterprises. These incentives were not discriminatory between equity or contractual joint-venture enterprises, but they were prohibited from service-sector enterprises such as hotels.

As part of the effort to attract foreign investment, China established four special economic zones (SEZs) in southern China in 1979 and 1980. These zones—Shenzhen, Shantou, and Zhuhai in Guangdong province and Xiamen in Fujian province—are testing grounds for economic liberalization and serve as models for economic development. They are in effect meant to be channels for Western technology, capital, and management skills to be introduced into China. In 1984 China also designated fourteen coastal cities as open economic development zones, or open cities. The rights and the extent of authority in the open cities are not clear and seem to depend on local conditions. Generally, however, the open cities, like the SEZs, receive preferential tax and duty treatment and have expanded autonomy in their dealings with foreigners, though not to the same extent as the SEZs.

Growth in both the SEZs and the open cities has been rapid. Between 1985 and 1988, gross industrial output grew at almost 40 percent in constant terms per year in the SEZs and at 13.2 percent in the open cities. Clearly, these growth rates compare favorably with a 10 percent growth rate of GNP for all of China during the same period (Table 7.2). In addition, the export performance of the SEZs and open cities were much better than the national average. Between the SEZs and open cities, the former performed better than the latter in terms of output growth and export procurement. Together the SEZs and open cities accounted for about a quarter of China's total export procurement and about 40 percent of total foreign investment.

The SEZs are "special" because of special economic and management policies permitted in the zones. In this respect they differ from free trade zones and export processing zones, although the SEZs perform these functions as well. Economic development in the SEZs depends on the absorption of foreign capital and on the use of that capital

Table 7.2

Special Economic Zones and Open Cities in China

	1980	1985	1988	Annual change 1985–88 (%)
China GNP, billion Yuan	447	856.8	1,385.3	17.4
GNP index	116.1	187.8	251	10.2
Gross industrial production (1980 prices, 100 million Yuan)				
4 SEZs		96.96	259.73	38.9
14 Open cities		2,015.85	2,924.87	13.2
China foreign investment, $100 million		16.61	31.93	24.3
4 SEZs		3.2	4.29	10.3
14 Open cities		3.02	6.81	31.1
Exports, 100 million yuan	271.2	808.9	1,767.6	29.8
Export procurement, 100 million yuan				
4 SEZs		8.48	34.1	59.0
14 Open cities		190.73	402.77	28.3
SEZ export procurement/China export.		1.0%	1.9%	22.5
Open cities export procurment/ China export.		23.6%	22.8%	–1.1
SEZ DFI/total DFI		19.3%	13.4%	–11.3
Open cities DFI/total DFI		18.2%	21.3%	5.5

Sources: SSB of China, Zhongguo tongi nianjian (Statistical Yearbook of China), various years.
Note: Foreign trade figures are custom statistics.

to produce export goods. The SEZs represent a mix of enterprises since the SEZ economy is based on joint ventures, joint operations, and wholly owned foreign operations. Foreign enterprises in the SEZs receive preferential treatment in taxes as well as in entry into and exit from the country. A key aspect of the SEZs is that economic activities and decisions there are supposed to reflect market forces more fully; the economies of the SEZs are more market oriented than economies anywhere else in China. Thus, a different management system and much greater autonomy are permitted in the SEZs than in the interior.

Although overall they have been successful in bringing about higher rates of economic growth and exports, the SEZs have been criticized by certain factions within the Chinese leadership. They have accused SEZs of fostering corruption, profiteering, and inflation, and they have questioned the correctness of the policy of letting the coastal regions lead the hinterland in development. The Chinese reformists, however, counsel patience and have argued that more time is needed before declaring such efforts a failure.

As a model for an export-led development scheme, the SEZs are under heavy pressure to produce substantial export earnings. Although the central government wants the SEZs to concentrate on foreign-currency–earning industries, they also want the SEZs to absorb foreign capital and technology to improve China's industrial capability. But to achieve the short-run objective of fulfilling export earnings quotas, enterprises in the SEZs carry out projects that rely on the available cheap labor and land and seldom undertake high-tech projects. The long-run objective is further hampered by the lack of good infrastructure. As a result, some 80 percent of the cooperative projects in Shenzhen are low-tech.

The SEZs also exist to allow experimental practices. The SEZs are already much more reliant on free markets than are most of the interior hinterlands. The SEZs also serve as testing grounds for the development of a competitive banking system. In March 1986 the first joint venture bank, the Xiamen International Bank, was established, breaking the monopoly of the Bank of China in Xiamen. The Xiamen International Bank is a joint venture between three state-run concerns and a Hong Kong bank. Xiamen also has thirteen other banks, trusts, investment companies, and other institutions providing financial services. Twenty international banks have opened branches or representative offices in Shenzhen to compete with local banks. Shenzhen enterprises are allowed to choose between local and foreign banks when seeking financing, and the state-run banks are allowed to do business with anyone they choose.

Profitability of Direct Foreign Investment

The preceding section discussed various measures undertaken by China to attract DFI. Its success in attracting DFI depends on whether or not joint-venture enterprises are profitable. Furthermore, by discovering the determinants of profitability we can propose measures for improving the policy on DFI. For this investigation we will rely on survey data of Sino-foreign joint venture enterprises in the Tianjin area.[2]

Direct foreign investment involves direct interaction between in-

Table 7.3

Problems and Benefits of DFI in China: A Survey of Forty-two Joint Ventures in the Tianjin Area

	Number of incidents	Intensity
Problems		
Shortage of energy, material, and working capital	37	1.30
Imbalance in foreign exchange	22	1.86
Problems associated with government intervention	10	2.40
Lack of marketing skill and channels	5	2.00
Conflict between partners	3	1.66
Other problems (economic sanctions, heavy taxation)	2	1.50
Benefits		
Imported technology, management, equipment, and information	27	1.52
Benefit from Chinese perspective (jobs, incomes)	22	2.09
Enhanced work force and product quality	17	1.82
Foreign exchange earnings by exports	11	2.09
Preferential treatment by Chinese government	6	1.67

Notes: Number of incidents counts how many firms answered that they had experienced such problems or benefits. Intensity measures the relative importance of specific problems or benefits; it ranges from 1 for the highest importance to 6 for the lowest.

vestment partners; consequently, how this interaction is managed affects the operation and ultimately the profitability of a joint-venture enterprise. In this regard we test the effect on its profitability of the share of capital contributed by respective partners and the composition of the board overseeing the enterprise. We also examine the performance of joint-venture enterprises that have experienced conflict between partners. In terms of intensity, conflict between partners is the second most important problem in DFI in China even though only three such cases have been observed so far (Table 7.3).

Joint-venture profitability can also depend on whether the Chinese partner is a state or nonstate enterprise. Out of forty-two enterprises in our sample, ten answered that they had problems dealing with related government agencies, which often interfered with management.

Other economic factors constrain the operation of joint-venture enterprises. First, the extent to which the production process is required to rely on domestic or imported inputs and, second, the composition of the labor force both affect the profitability of an enterprise. Studies on productivity of Chinese firms indicate that the proportion of permanent, full-time workers vis-à-vis temporary workers is negatively correlated with productivity (Keun Lee 1990). In the case of state enterprises, one reason for the negative correlation is that because of extremely rigid labor policies the larger the number of temporary workers in employment, the greater the flexibility in employment decision making and possibly the greater disciplinary control over the labor force. Although joint-venture enterprises now have the power to fire workers, the basic environment regarding labor policies is not, we suspect, flexible enough to allow them to fire workers freely. Third, the capital–labor ratio is one of the most important determinants of labor productivity and, hence, per capita revenue. This variable also to a certain extent represents the availability of working capital, which has been identified as a limiting factor in the operation of an enterprise in China regardless of its national origin.

Government policies toward joint venture enterprises also affect profitability. To analyze their effect, we compare the performance of joint venture enterprises located in the Tianjin Economic and Technological Development Zone (ETD Zone) with those located elsewhere. We also compare those that are designated as export-promotion or hi-tech enterprises with those that are not. Finally, we compare the performance of equity joint venture with that of contractual joint-venture enterprises.

There are 42 joint-venture enterprises in our data set, of which 32 are equity joint-venture enterprises and the rest, contractual joint-venture enterprises. In 29 cases out of 42, Chinese partners are state-owned enterprises and the remainder are collectively owned. Fifteen enterprises in the sample are located in the Tianjin ETD Zone, and 27 are classified by the Chinese government as export-promotion or high-technology enterprises.

The composition of the enterprise board reflects the relative capital contribution by Chinese and foreign partners. On average, the proportion of Chinese members was 61.7 percent, but it ranged from a minimum of 50 percent to a maximum of 92.3 percent.

Our data indicate that in procuring material inputs used in the production process, joint-venture enterprises relied on local suppliers for an average of 35.8 percent of their inputs, and their share ranged from a minimum of 0 percent to a maximum of 96.0 percent.

The standard definition of profitability is the ratio of profit to invested capital. We, however, cannot use this definition as our data set does not contain a profit variable.[3] We are thus forced to use per capita sales revenue as a proxy for profitability on the following grounds. Given the limited flexibility in labor and material input policies in China, revenues from sales of products would dominate costs as a determinant of profits. By dividing sales revenues with the size of employment, we can then adequately take into account the wage cost factor given the small variation in wage rates (or average wage) across enterprises. In fact, preliminary regression analysis shows that per capita sales revenue is the single dominant determinant of profitability, measured as profits divided by capital value, and most of the other variables are not significant.

Table 7.4 presents the results of log linear regressions of per capita sales revenue as a function of the capital–labor ratio, the proportion of Chinese board members, the proportion of full-time workers, the proportion of Chinese-made material inputs, and several dummy variables for the type of joint venture (equity or contractual), the type of ownership of the Chinese partner, location in the ETD Zone, high-tech or export-promotion enterprises, and incidence of conflict between partners. We derive our interpretation from the results based on Model 1 as they show highest R^2 values and F statistics values. We have tested three different models: Model 1 allows two separate dummies, each for export-promotion and high-tech firms, respectively; Model 2 combines export-promotion and high-tech firms into one dummy; and Model 3 has only one dummy for high-tech firms. Important results are basically consistent across models. In consideration of the fact that sample firms belong to all kinds of different industrial subsectors and no sectoral dummies are used in the regression, we can say that the results based on Model 1 fit well, as evidenced by the adjusted R^2 value of around 0.70 and the overall significance of the model at 1 percent.

The capital–labor ratio shows the most significant explanatory power: a 1 percent increase in the ratio results in a 0.66 percent increase of per capita sales revenue. As noted above, we interpret this ratio not simply as a technical variable but, more important, as a variable representing the availability of working capital, the shortage of which is most critical in Chinese firms. According to our survey of 42 enterprises, the most serious problem confronting their operation was the shortage of energy, material inputs, and working capital (Table

Table 7.4

Determinants of Profitability of Joint Ventures in China

Dependent variable: Log of per capita revenue

	Estimated coefficients of independent variables		
	Model 1	Model 2	Model 3
INTCPT	2.49 (3.63)**	2.12 (2.88)*	1.50 (2.21)*
K/L	0.66 (3.47)**	0.79 (4.0)**	0.80 (3.59)**
CBOARD	2.17 (1.70)	1.88 (1.33)	1.36 (0.90)
FULTIME	−2.00 (−2.75)*	−1.63 (−2.07)+	−0.88 (−1.27)
CINPUT	0.13 (0.41)	0.30 (0.92)	0.03 (0.08)
EJV	−1.34 (−3.05)**	−1.18 (−2.45)*	−1.02 (−2.00)+
STATE	0.42 (1.03)	0.44 (0.96)	0.31 (0.63)
ZONE	0.94 (2.29)*	0.89 (1.93)+	0.61 (1.28)
HITECH	−0.40 (−0.92)		0.24 (0.60)
EXPORT	−1.15 (−2.46)*		
EXPTECH		−0.69 (−1.53)	
CONFLIC	−3.11 (−3.19)**	−2.57 (−2.45)*	−3.28 (−2.74)*
Adj. R^2	0.72	0.64	0.58
F-value	5.82 (0.01)**	4.81 (0.01)**	3.86 (0.02)*

Notes: t-stat in parentheses; **, *, and + marks mean significant at 1%, 5%, and 10%, respectively.

Variables:
INTCPT: intercept term in regressions;
K/L: log of capital–labor ratio;
CBOARD: log of proportion of Chinese board members;
CINPUT: log of proportion of Chinese material inputs;
FULTIME: log of proportion of full-time workers;
EJV: dummy for equity joint venture;
STATE: dummy for state enterprise as Chinese partner;
ZONE: dummy for location in the Tianjin ETD Zone;
EXPTECH: dummy for firms classified as export-promotion or high-tech;
HITECH: dummy for firms classified as high-tech firms;
EXPORT: dummy for firms classified as export-promotion firms;
CONFLI: dummy for incidence of conflict between partners.

7.3).[4] As pointed out by Professor Kornai, this problem is typical of a planned economy and shows the symptoms of a "shortage economy." The shortage problem was most important in terms of both the number of incidents and the degree of intensity.

Relatedly, we may hypothesize that per capita sales revenue is negatively related to the proportion of Chinese-made material inputs used in the production process. The results do not, however, confirm this hypothesis. The variable of Chinese-made input is not statistically significant, but when we omit this variable in regression the R^2 ratio and overall fitness level of the model decrease substantially.

Regression results support the hypothesis that the higher the proportion of full-time workers vis-à-vis temporary workers the lower per capita sales revenue.

The proportion of Chinese board members is shown to be "not so significant" or only marginally significant at 12.5 percent. We may interpret this variable as indicating that more Chinese board members can mean a better relationship with state authorities who are in charge of material and labor allocations. They can facilitate obtaining a better and more stable supply of energy and other intermediate inputs and credit and receiving a favorable tax treatment.

The coefficient of the dummy for state-owned enterprise as the Chinese partner is not significantly different from 0, although its sign is positive. This might be because in our sample nonstate enterprise, the Chinese partners are all collectively owned enterprises; as is well known, there is no significant difference between urban state enterprises and collective enterprises in terms of their relation to state authorities and operational behavior. A positive sign of this dummy might, however, capture the size effect in that state enterprises tend to be bigger than collective enterprises. Moreover, proportionately more joint venture enterprises with a state enterprise partner are located in the Tianjin ETD Zone than are joint venture enterprises with a collective enterprise partner. Although it was not found to be significantly different from 0, the overall fitness of the model decreased substantially when the state dummy was omitted. In other words, we cannot safely ignore the importance of being owned by the state in a state-dominated economy like China's.

As expected, the results show that joint-venture enterprises located in the Tianjin ETD Zone tend to have better per capita sales revenue. This might be due to some preferential treatment. But as those designated by government as high-tech or export-promoting are not shown to be superior, we may conclude that they receive no additional preferential treatment. In the results based on Model 1, the coefficient of the export-promotion venture is shown to be negative, against our expectations. This is because several joint-venture enterprises have had extraordinarily outstanding performance, but are not designated as export-promotion firms.

Quite interesting and important are significantly negative coefficents of two dummies, one for equity joint ventures and the other for conflict between partners. Although it is not certain to what extent inferior performance is directly caused by conflict between partners, the conflict dummy is consistently negative when we control for all other important factors included in the regression.

The negative results of the dummy for equity joint ventures support the hypothesis that contractual joint ventures are superior to equity joint ventures—reinforcing our earlier observation that the former was a more popular investment vehicle than the latter because of its flexibility in freely negotiating the manner and proportions of profit or output distribution among partners. Such flexibility might be partly responsible for the superiority of contractual joint ventures. The numerical majority of equity joint ventures in our sample (32 vs. 10) might, however, indicate that they regained popularity thanks to recent preferential treatment in tax treatment; nevertheless, our findings suggest that their renewed popularity might not owe to their intrinsic strength in performance and before-tax profitability.

Policy Implications

Our survey results and regression analysis support the view that there are systemic contraints on the profitability of DFI in China. Shortages (of inputs and foreign exchange), typical of a centrally planned economy, as well as rigid labor policies, have a clear negative impact on profitability. The importance of cooperation between partners and relations with state authorities is also confirmed by our results. It has been also demonstrated that although more superior joint venture enterprises are located in the ETD Zone, whether the government labels them export-promotion or high-tech enterprises has little effect on their profitability.

The empirical results presented in this chapter—the importance of working capital, flexibility in hiring and firing workers, and flexibility in negotiation between partners as determinants of profitability of a joint venture enterprise—all point to one important conclusion. That is, an enterprise cannot be profitable if it suffers from a shortage of inputs, is not free in making operational decisions, and is constricted in its operation with unnecessary regulations. And it should be clear to everyone that foreign capital comes to China to make a profit, not for any other reason. If China is thus to benefit from the inflow of DFI, it must allow joint-venture enterprises to make profits without undue restrictions on their operations. Obviously, the issue is not whether or not China has the right to control the inflow of DFI, but whether the present policy regime serves China's welfare.

The shortage of working capital faced by joint-venture enterprises is a symptom of what is commonly called financial repression. The state controls the allocation of credit and the access to credit may depend on political or personal connections. In such a situation, it is common to find rent-seeking activities or corruption. What therefore needs to be discussed as a fundamental policy issue is whether there is inherent contradiction between the economic system currently in existence in China and its policy of relying on DFI for its economic development. To promote DFI, China may need to liberalize its financial systems, but then with liberalized financial systems the central government will lose its control over the allocation of financial resources. China may not have to go this far to promote the inflow of DFI, but it certainly should not introduce further distortion in other parts of the economy in order to compensate for the effects of distortion in the financial market.

Broadly speaking, there are two different reasons for a foreign enterprise to invest in China. The first is to produce output for China's domestic market; the second is to utilize China's abundant supply of inexpensive labor to produce exports for the world market. China does not face as much competition from other labor-abundant developing countries for the first type of DFI as it does for the second type. For that reason, China may be able to impose various conditions on the first type of DFI without significantly affecting the volume of its inflow. But China may not be as interested in inducing this type of DFI as the other since it has fewer direct effects on foreign exchange earnings. In other words, if China is interested in encouraging the inflow of DFI to increase the export of labor-intensive manufactured products, it faces severe competition from many other developing countries for

DFI. Whether it succeeds in this competition or not will depend on the profitability of joint venture enterprises in China and thus on the various factors discussed in this paper as the determinants of profitability. It will be up to China's policymakers to decide whether the conditions imposed on DFI benefit China.

Notes

1. Shen (1990) provides an excellent review of a decade of DFI in China.

2. The survey was designed and conducted jointly by the Chinese (Tianjin Municipal Government and the State Science and Technology Commission) and the East-West Center during the fall of 1989. In this survey, distributed questionnaires were answered by Chinese officials.

3. It is a pity that such fundamental variables as profit and gross and net output values are not asked for in the survey and thus are missing in the data set.

4. A similar survey on problems facing South Korean firms in Southeast Asia and China can be found in Hong (1990).

Chapter 8

South Korea–China Trade: An Asian-Pacific Perspective

In the late 1970s the People's Republic of China (PRC) instituted various economic reforms, including the adoption of an open-door policy. It even began indirect trade with the Republic of Korea (henceforth, South Korea), a country with which it had not had any relations for a long time. The trade between the two has been increasing ever since, and according to one estimate the value of trade (exports plus imports) reached HK$9.2 billion in 1987 (Y. Zhang 1988). PRC exports to South Korea are commodities such as textile fibers and yarn, metal ores and nonferrous metals, various animal and vegetable products, corn, and coal. In return, South Korea exports manufactured products such as synthetic fabric, paper products, steel, organic chemicals, television sets, and various machinery and equipment.[1] There has also developed a vertical division of labor between the two, with South Korea supplying synthetic fibers and yarns to Chinese weaving mills. Direct, albeit unofficial, trade between South Korea and the PRC was estimated to account for about 34 percent of total trade between the two in 1987 (Yun 1989).

According to the PRC's coastal development strategy, each coastal region is to be matched with a particular foreign economy or region in its trade and investment relations (Zou and Ma 1989). For instance, the Fujian delta is to be linked with Taiwan, the Zhujiang delta with Hong Kong and Macao, the Changjiang delta with Japan, Hainan Island with the ASEAN countries, and finally the Liaoning-Shandong Peninsula with South Korea. The purpose of this chapter is to investigate the economic effects of one such arrangement—the link between South Korean and the Bohai (Bal-Hae in Korean) region of China (this region includes the three provinces of Hebei, Liaoning, and Shandong and the two municipalities of Tianjin and Beijing)—and the current state and future prospects for trade between Bohai and South Korea.

There are several reasons why trade between Bohai and South Korea will expand rapidly. First, Bohai and South Korea are close to each other geographically; thus trade between the two can save on transportation costs. Second, Bohai may find imports from South Korea—consumer as well as capital goods—more appropriate, as they are technologically more advanced than their own but not as advanced as those from the West or Japan. Third, Korea may find Bohai a good source of raw materials and inexpensive consumer goods.

The following section provides basic economic profiles of South Korea and Bohai, including their trade patterns. The section beginning on page 139 explores trade prospects between the two with the aid of indexes of export similarity and of trade complementarity. The next section then examines the trade creation and diversion effects between 1981 and 1988, and the final section presents two alternative projections for the expansion of trade between Bohai and South Korea.

Economic Profiles of South Korea, China, and the Bohai Region

Table 8.1 presents some basic economic data for South Korea and Bohai. In 1986 South Korea's gross national product (GNP) and per capita income were $95.1 billion* and $2,287.80, respectively, while Bohai's GNP and per capita income were $63.1 billion and $333.60, respectively. Thus, while South Korea's GNP was only 1.5 times larger than Bohai's, Bohai's per capita income was only one-seventh of that of South Korea, because its population is five times bigger. Bohai is, however, a relatively advanced region in the PRC; its per capita GNP is about 25 percent higher than the average for the country as a whole.

In 1986 Bohai exported $82.5 million, only 13 percent of its GNP, whereas the same year South Korea exported 36.5 percent of its GNP. Bohai is certainly less export oriented than is South Korea, but

---

*Unless specified otherwise, all figures are in U.S. dollars.

Table 8.1

Basic Economic Data of South Korea, China, and Bohai China, 1986

	South Korea (A)	Bohai (B)	Total for China (C)	Ratios		Cities and provinces in Bohai China				
				A/B	B/C	Beijing	Tianjin	Hebei	Liaoning	Shandong
1. Basic comparison										
Population (10,000)	4,157	18,913	105,721	0.2	17.9%	975	819	5,617	3,726	7,776
GNP (current U.S. $ bill.)	95.1	63.1	281.4	1.5	22.4%	8.3	5.7	12.9	16.3	19.9
Per capita GNP (U.S. $)	2,287.8	333.6	266.1	6.9	125.3%	855.8	696.8	229.1	436.4	256.0
Exports (U.S. $100 mill.)	347.1	82.5	309.4	4.2	26.7%	7.2	12.6	10.5	30.8	21.4
Exports/GNP ratio	36.5%	13.1%	11.0%	2.8	119.0%	8.7%	22.1%	8.2%	18.9%	10.7%
2. Bohai's economy (100 mill. yuan)										
Net material product earned		1,664.3	7,790.0		21.4%	194.5	150.9	340.9	425.7	552.3
Net material product used		1,552.6	8,312.0		18.7%	212.2	139.9	328.3	370.5	501.7
Net outflow		111.7	−522.0			−17.7	11.0	12.6	55.2	50.6
Gross agri. product		732.7	4,013.0		18.3%	28.1	26.9	174.4	142.0	361.2
Gross heavy ind. product		1,654.6	5,863.9		28.2%	212.0	170.3	290.6	598.0	383.7
Gross light ind. product		1,228.8	5,330.4		23.1%	159.7	180.8	215.6	274.5	398.2

Sources: Korean data from *Korea Statistical Yearbook*, 1987. Chinese data from SSB of China, various years. Bohai region's total exports figure provided by the China Asia Pacific Institute.

Note: Exchange rates: U.S. $1 = 3.453 yuan, U.S. $1 = 861.4 Korean won.

nonetheless more export oriented than China, which exported only 11 percent of its GNP that year. Given the currently low export orientation and the enormous population with low per capita income, Bohai trade will expand rapidly if its economy continues to grow and modernize.

Although there are good reasons why the two economies would gain by establishing a direct trade relationship, Bohai would gain more by carrying out economic reforms that will lead to greater interprovincial trade. In other words, thorough economic integration of Bohai with the rest of China may benefit the country more than internationalization in the presence of existing barriers to interprovincial trade. Internationalization alone may bring about an enclave economy in Bohai, and the limited benefits of such an economy have been amply demonstrated in the history of many developing countries.

The importance of Bohai in China's economy can be seen in the proportion of its total output accounted for by Bohai. While it comprises 18 percent of the PRC's population, Bohai accounts for about 22 percent of the country's GNP. In terms of sectoral output, in 1986 Bohai accounted for 18.3 percent of PRC gross agricultural products, 28.2 percent of gross heavy industrial products, and 23.1 percent of light industrial products. It is thus clear that Bohai is a relatively industrialized region, with greater industrialization in heavy than light manufacturing.

It is also clear that Bohai is relatively more production oriented, or less consumption oriented. This observation follows from an examination of the pattern of resource flows between Bohai and the rest of China. Table 8.1 shows that in 1986 the PRC was a net resource importer, whereas Bohai was a net resource exporter to China and the world. Bohai's net resource outflows depended heavily on the industrial economies of Liaoning and Shandong, while Beijing was, as expected, a consumption city with a net resource inflow. In other words, China is dependent on Bohai for its economy and current living standard and is a net debtor to Bohai.

In order to find the trade pattern that may possibly emerge with internal economic integration, we have calculated the revealed comparative advantage of Bohai vis-à-vis the rest of China (Table 8.2). Our calculations show that Bohai has a comparative advantage in native products and animal by-products; light industrial products; chemicals, petroleum, and gas; and machinery and equipment. The rest of China has a comparative advantage in cereals, oils, foodstuffs, and beverages;

Table 8.2

Revealed Comparative Advantage of Bohai vis-à-vis the Rest of China

1. Exports from Bohai, the rest of China, and all China, 1988
Commodity composition (U.S.$1 million)

	Bohai Region		Rest of China		Totals for China	
	Value	Share	Value	Share	Value	Share
Total (all SITC categories)	110.46	100.0%	364.94	100.0%	475.40	100.0%
Cereals, oils, foodstuffs, and beverages (0, 1, 21, 22, 29, 41, 42)	13.51	12.2%	64.31	17.6%	77.82	16.4%
Textiles, silks, and garments (26, 65, 84)	24.15	21.9%	105.86	29.0%	130.01	27.3%
Native products and animal by-products (23, 24, 25, 27, 28, 29, 43, 61, 62, 63, 64)	8.29	7.5%	15.15	4.2%	23.45	4.9%
Light industrial products (8–84)	11.35	10.3%	22.61	6.2%	33.96	7.1%
Metal and mineral products, coal (32, 66, 67, 68, 69)	6.17	5.6%	33.86	9.3%	40.03	8.4%
Chemical, petroleum, and gas (33, 34, 35, 5)	35.09	31.8%	27.65	7.6%	62.75	13.2%
Machinery and equipment (7)	7.63	6.9%	20.05	5.5%	27.69	5.8%
Other products (9)	4.23	3.8%	82.62	22.6%	86.85	18.3%

2. Index of revealed comparative advantage

	Bohai	Rest of China	Difference
Cereals, oils, foodstuffs, and beverages (0, 1, 21, 22, 29, 41, 42)	74.7	107.6	–32.9
Textiles, silks, and garments (26, 65, 84)	80.0	106.1	–26.1
Native products and animal by-products (23, 24, 25, 27, 28, 29, 43, 61, 62, 63, 64)	152.3	84.2	68.1
Light industrial products (8–84)	143.9	86.7	57.2
Metal and mineral products, coal (32, 66, 67, 68, 69)	66.4	110.2	–43.8
Chemical, petroleum, and gas (33, 34, 35, 5)	240.7	57.4	183.3
Machinery and equipment (7)	118.7	94.3	24.4
Other products (9)	21.0	123.9	–103.0

Sources: Bohai's trade data provided by the China Asia Pacific Institute; China's total exports data are from China's customs statistics; Rest of China exports are the difference between total and Bohai exports.

textiles, silk, and garments; metal and mineral products; coal; and other products. Clearly, these are some of the potential exports from Bohai to South Korea and the rest of the world.

Table 8.3 presents the commodity and country composition of Bohai's foreign trade. Bohai's major trading partner is Asia, which accounted for 62 percent of its total export value and 66 percent of its total import value in 1988. Within Asia, Japan is by far the most important trade partner, followed by Hong Kong and Macao combined, and then Singapore. The United States, which has been the major trade partner for the Asian NIEs, accounted for only 10.4 percent of Bohai's total exports and 8.8 percent of its total imports in 1988. Thus, unlike the NIEs and Japan, the United States has not been a major source of trade expansion for Bohai. It is possible that Japan and the NIEs may play for China the role that the United States has played for the trade and economic expansion of these countries. Bohai and China generally are now in the fortunate position of being able to export to Japan and the Asian NIEs as well as the United States (Table 8.3).

Some of Bohai's exports to Japan, Hong Kong, and Macao were indirect exports to South Korea and were converted to direct trade after a formal trade relationship was established between the PRC and South Korea in 1992. Data on indirect trade between South Korea and the PRC carried through Hong Kong from 1981 through 1987 underestimate total indirect trade between the two countries. However, they would overestimate indirect trade between South Korea and Bohai, as the figures are for all of China. Even with this caveat, the figures indicate a rising trend in trade between Bohai and South Korea and the extent of trade diversion that would result from a formal trade relationship between the two countries (see Table 8.4 on page 141).

Effects of the Trade Opening between South Korea and China

As noted above, establishing a direct trade relationship between Bohai and South Korea will to some extent replace already existing indirect trade. Furthermore, as both Bohai and South Korea trade with the rest of the world, opening direct trade between the two is conceptually similar to forming a customs union and consequently will have similar economic effects. Specifically, the following three possible effects may result: (1) replacement of indirect trade with direct trade, (2) trade

Table 8.3

Foreign Trade of China's Bohai Region (U.S.$ 100 million)

	Exports		Imports	
	Value	Share	Value	Share
Commodity composition, 1988				
Total	110.46	100.0%	26.78	100.0%
Cereals, oils, foodstuffs, and beverages	13.51	12.2%	0.36	1.4%
Textiles, silks, and garments	24.15	21.9%	2.89	10.8%
Arts and crafts	4.68	4.2%	1.21	4.6%
Native products and animal by-products	8.29	7.5%	0.29	1.1%
Light industrial products	6.67	6.0%	2.13	8.0%
Metal and mineral products, coal	6.17	5.6%	2.41	9.0%
Chemical, petroleum products	35.09	31.8%	3.00	11.2%
Machinery and equipment	7.63	6.9%	3.46	13.0%
Other products	4.23	3.8%	10.98	41.0%
Country composition of Bohai regional trade, 1988				
Total	110.44	100.0%	22.98	100.0%
Asia	62.46	56.6%	15.16	66.0%
Hong Kong, Macao	17.05	15.4%	6.36	27.7%
Japan	37.81	34.2%	7.50	32.7%
Singapore	6.43	5.8%	0.36	1.6%
Africa	1.15	1.0%		
Europe	22.11	20.0%	4.89	21.3%
USSR, Eastern Europe	7.24	6.6%		
Latin America	0.85	0.8%	0.37	1.6%
North America	12.27	11.1%	2.23	9.7%
USA	11.53	10.4%	2.03	8.8%
Oceania and Pacific Islands	0.75	0.7%	1.19	5.2%
Australia	0.68	0.6%	0.51	2.2%
Others	10.82	9.8%	3.22	14.0%

Source: Data provided by the China Asia Pacific Institute.
Note: Import data include only transactions administered by local-level trading companies.

diversion from the rest of the world, and (3) trade creation. If direct trade simply replaces indirect trade, the gains from direct trade are limited to savings in transaction costs relating to indirect trade—the cost of third-party intermediation and possibly additional transportation costs. If direct trade leads to trade diversion from the rest of the world, both parties will gain, provided that there is no preferential treatment on direct trade between the two. They will gain as each gets lower-cost imports and as transportation costs decrease thanks to geographic proximity. Thus, unlike in a standard customs union, countries

Table 8.4

Trades Trends in South Korea, China, and Bohai China

	1981	1982	1983	1984	1985	1986	1987
Bohai's foreign trade (U.S.$ million)							
Current value							
Exports	91.69	88.01	85.6	99.04	107.81	82.52	105.93
Imports	4.15	4.22	4.97	6.83	15.48	17.31	19.91
In 1980 prices							
Exports	88.9	90.8	99.1	112.2	131.2	115.1	139.2
% change		2.1%	9.1%	13.2%	16.9%	-12.2%	20.9%
Imports	4.0	4.6	6.4	8.7	20.9	23.6	27.6
% change		15.5%	39.2%	34.6%	141.0%	12.6%	17.1%
South Korea's indirect trade with China through Hong Kong (HK$ million)							
Exports	811.0	338.2	327.3	1,254.1	2,786.6	2,154.7	4,196.3
Imports	413.2	569.0	839.2	1,444.7	1,942.9	2,939.3	5,065.5
Balance	397.8	-230.8	-511.9	-190.6	843.7	-784.6	-869.2

Sources: Bohai data is from the China Asia Pacific Institute; In deriving constant values of trade, price indices of China's total trade are used, which are from MOFERT (1988), *Almanac of China's Foreign Trade* (Chinese version); Korea's indirect trade data are from Hong Kong government statistics; I took these data from Yinfeng Zhang (1989).

Note: Bohai's import figures include only those administered by local-level trading companies. Thus, their values are significantly smaller than export values.

establishing a direct trade relationship will gain unambiguously from the trade-diversion effect of direct trade. (For example, with the establishment of direct trade Bohai will be able to import automobiles from South Korea instead of Japan. A savings will then be realized because South Korean automobiles are less expensive and will cost less to transport from Inchon than they would from, say, Osaka.)

The trade-creation effect of direct trade results from a more efficient internal resource allocation within Bohai and within South Korea. Imports will now substitute domestic production, and trade will be created between the two economies. This trade is in addition to the trade diverted from the rest of the world, and there will thus be gains in producer and consumer surpluses.

The replacement effect, the trade-diversion effect, and the trade-creation effect are all static effects in the sense that they are brought about as a result of establishing an official trade relationship. The trade pattern will not, however, remain unchanged over time as both Bohai and South Korea become further industrialized.

The trade-creation effect has two components: "pure" effects and "substitution" effects. The substitution trade-creation effect simply replaces domestic production with imports, resulting in a more efficient internal resource allocation. Pure trade creation leads to additional trade without involving substitution for domestic products. This effect may take place because of "getting to know each other" and because of reduced uncertainties and increased information flows. The initial trade opening between the PRC and South Korea must have involved some pure trade creation.

Here we calculate the index of export similarity and the index of trade complementarity as a measure of possible trade diversion. We will compare the trade patterns of Japan, the rest of China, and the ASEAN–4 (the Philippines, Indonesia, Malaysia, and Thailand) with Bohai and South Korea.

In order to find out how the opening of PRC–South Korea trade would affect the trade between Bohai and South Korea, we focus on the following two cases: (1) Bohai replacing the ASEAN–4 in South Korea's imports and (2) South Korea replacing Japan in Bohai's imports. The magnitude of the trade-diversion effect depends on the degree of similarity between the ASEAN–4 and Bohai exports to South Korea and that between Japanese and South Korean exports to Bohai. The greater the degree of similarity, the larger will be the potential trade-diversion effect. The extent of actual trade diversion will, however, depend on the price competitiveness of Bohai exports vis-à-vis ASEAN–4 exports and South Korean exports vis-à-vis Japanese exports.

The index of export similarity is defined as

$$S(ab,c) = 100 \times \left[\sum_{i} \text{Min} \left\{ X_i(ac), X_i(bc) \right\} \right]$$

It measures the similarity of the export patterns of countries a and b to country c. $X_i(ac)$ is the share of commodity i in country a's exports to country c. If the commodity distribution of country a's and country b's exports are identical, the index equals 100. If it is totally dissimilar, the index equals 0. If a measure of the index for Bohai and ASEAN–4 exports to South Korea is close to 100, the opening of a formal trade relationship between the PRC and South Korea will have a large trade-diversion effect, Bohai's exports replacing ASEAN–4 exports to South Korea. If it is close to 0, the opening will have a small effect.[2]

The index of trade complementarity between country a's exports and country b's imports can be measured by the following index:

$$C_{ab} = \frac{X_a'M_b}{\| X_a \| \cdot \| M_b \|}$$

where $X_a'M_b$ is the inner sum of country a's export and country b's import composition vectors, and $\|X_a\|$ and $\|M_b\|$ are the square root of the inner sum of vectors, X_a and M_b respectively. The value of the index approaching 1 indicates high complementarity.[3]

Bohai's Exports to South Korea

Results of our calculation of the two indices basically support our hypotheses that the opening of a direct trade relationship between the PRC and South Korea will expand Bohai's exports to South Korea at the expense of the ASEAN–4 (Table 8.5). The export structure similarity between Bohai and the ASEAN–4 is high, 0.67, whereas that between Bohai and South Korea is relatively low, 0.54. Exports from Bohai and the ASEAN–4 are thus competitive in the sense that they export similar items to the rest of the world. This fact reflects the fact that the exports of both Bohai and the ASEAN–4 are based heavily on primary resources.

Export similarity between Bohai and Japan is the lowest, 0.32, as expected. Japan is thus the remotest competitor for Bohai's exports. In terms of export structure, South Korea is between Japan, on the one hand, and Bohai and the ASEAN–4, on the other. If South Korea is to follow the typical structural change in trade pattern as its economy develops further, it will have to move ahead in the direction of the Japanese pattern before Bohai and the ASEAN–4 emerge as more serious competitors.

Trade complementarity between Bohai's exports and South Korea's imports is 0.70, almost as high as that between the ASEAN–4's exports and South Korea's imports. This again confirms our hypothesis that Bohai and the ASEAN–4 would be potentially tough competitors in South Korean markets. Many other factors will determine the actual outcome of the competition. While the ASEAN–4 may have greater experiences in trade and marketing, Bohai has an advantage in transportation costs, political relations, and the newcomer effect.

Our calculation also shows that complementarity in Bohai–South Korea trade is much higher than that between South Korean imports and exports from the rest of China, which is only 0.45. Thus, we can say that South Korea–PRC trade expansion will be concentrated in Bohai, not evenly spread throughout the PRC.

South Korean Exports to Bohai

Figures in Table 8.5 support our hypotheses that South Korea's potential competitor in Bohai is Japan and that there is strong complementarity between South Korea's exports and Bohai's imports. The index of export similarity between South Korea and Japan is high, 0.69, whereas that between Bohai and South Korea is lower, 0.54. Exports from South Korea and Japan are thus competitive, as they are exporting similar products. In fact, exports of advanced manufactured goods account for a large share of exports from both South Korea and Japan. It is also shown that export similarity between South Korea and China is generally high, but slightly lower than that between South Korea and Japan.

Complementarity between South Korea's exports and Bohai's imports is 0.91, almost as high as that between Japan's exports and Bohai's imports, 0.92. This again shows that Japan and South Korea would be

Table 8.5

Competition and Complementarity in Asian–Pacific Trade

Export competition

	Index of export similarity
1. Bohai's export competitors	
Bohai and the ASEAN–4	0.67
Bohai and South Korea	0.54
Bohai and Japan	0.32
2. South Korea's export competitors	
South Korea and Japan	0.69
South Korea and the rest of China	0.66
South Korea and Bohai	0.54

Trade complementarity

	Index of Import–export complementarity
1. South Korea's import market	
South Korea's imports from Bohai	0.70
South Korea's imports from the ASEAN–4	0.72
South Korea's imports from the rest of China	0.45
2. Bohai's import market	
Bohai's imports from South Korea	0.91
Bohai's imports from Japan	0.92

Note: On the methodologies, see text.

in potentially tough competition in Bohai. It is possible, however, that both Japan and South Korea could find their own respective niches in Bohai markets. While Japan has a comparative advantage in high-tech products and machinery, South Korea has a comparative advantage in middle-level technology and cheap consumer electronics. South Korea may also have an absolute advantage in transportation costs, political relations, and the newcomer effect in Bohai markets.

Our calculations also show that the commodity composition of exports from South Korea and all of China is similar. This implies that South Korean exports to Bohai will face potential competition from domestic products from other regions of the PRC. The seriousness of this competition will, however, depend on the quality and cost of their products.

Trade Creation and Trade Diversion, 1981–1988

This section estimates and compares *ex post* income elasticities of import demand in Bohai–South Korea (intra-area) trade and of extra-area trade between 1981 and 1988. The *ex post* income elasticity of imports is defined as the ratio of the average annual growth rate of imports to that of GNP (in constant prices). It can be used to abstract from the effects of economic growth on trade flows and thus to achieve comparability between estimates of trade creation and trade diversion. The income elasticity approach was first used by Balassa (1974) in his estimation of the trade-creation and trade-diversion effects of the European Common Market. When it is applied to PRC–South Korea trade with some necessary modification, it can be interpreted as follows.

First, trade-creation effects of opening South Korea–Bohai trade, defined as a shift from domestic to partner-country sources, is captured by an increase in the income elasticity of South Korea's (Bohai's) import demand from all sources together.[4] Second, trade diversion—a shift from the rest of the world to Bohai (South Korean) producers—would be indicated by a decline in the "after-opening" income elasticity of South Korean (Bohai) demand for imports from the rest of the world except Bohai (South Korea). Third, total trade expansion effects of the opening of South Korea–Bohai trade defined as an increase in South Korean imports from Bohai (Bohai imports from South Korea), regardless of whether the increase comes from substitution for domestic products (trade creation) or products from the rest of the world (trade diversion), are indicated by an increase in the income elasticity of South Korean (Bohai) import demand for Bohai (South Korean) products after trade opening.

The income elasticity approach assumes that the income elasticity of import demand remained unchanged in the absence of trade opening. This is a strong assumption, as it follows that nothing else will affect elasticity. Thus, the effects of price changes other than those brought about by the Bohai–South Korea trade opening are disregarded, as are the effects of exchange rate changes. To the extent that reliable price data are available, the income elasticity approach should be supplemented by estimation of the price elasticity of import demand taking into account import liberalization and exchange rate appreciation.[5] In interpreting the results obtained with the income elasticity approach, we should thus take into account various uncontrolled factors. Further caution is needed in interpreting our results as the absence of reliable data on trade between South Korea and Bohai forces us to use South Korea–PRC trade data for our estimation.

Table 8.6

Income Elasticity in PRC–South Korea Trade

	1981–88	1981–83	1983–85	1985–88
Income elasticity of South Korean demand for imports from:				
1. the world	1.05	0.95	1.31	1.13
2. PRC	5.0	0.06	20.54	2.98
3. Other than PRC	1.01	0.95	1.23	1.10
South Korea real GNP growth	10.5%	8.5%	8.1%	12.6%
Income elasticity of PRC demand for imports from:				
1. the world	1.50	1.50	3.20	0.20
2. South Korea	3.30	–2.20	20.00	2.30
3. Other than South Korea	1.40	1.50	3.10	0.10
China real GNP growth	11.0%	7.8%	13.6%	10.2%

Source: China–South Korea trade data are from the Ministry of Commerce and Industry of the Republic of Korea, which include both direct and indirect trade.

Note: Income elasticity of import demand is calculated as the ratio of real import growth as a percentage of real GNP growth

South Korean Imports from the PRC

In Table 8.6, it is shown that the income elasticity of South Korean demand for PRC products is 5.00, compared with 1.01 for non-PRC products. In other words, while South Korean real GNP grew annually at 10 percent between 1981 and 1988, its imports from the PRC grew at average 50 percent per year. This confirms the active trade expansion between South Korea and the PRC during this period.

Dividing the eight-year period in three we find that the first subperiod, 1981–83, was a period of a "cautious experiment": the income elasticity of South Korean demand for PRC products was even lower than that for non-PRC products. However, the second subperiod, 1983–85, shows an explosion of PRC–South Korea trade. We identify this period as the "actual opening" of PRC–South Korea trade. However, it is difficult to decompose this trade expansion accurately between trade creation and trade diversion. Although there must have been some trade diversion, shifting imports from other countries to China, at least for this initial opening period, most of the expansion likely resulted from pure trade creation associated with the newcomer effect of new markets.

The income elasticity of South Korean import demand for non-PRC products increased from the first subperiod to the second subperiod. Thus there must have been other reasons for the overall expansion of South Korean imports that far offset any trade-diversion effect of the opening of South Korea–PRC trade. There were in fact two exogenous events in the 1980s that may have affected overall South Korean trade as well as South Korean trade with the PRC. The first was trade liberalization, and the second was rapid currency appreciation. As both would tend to increase South Korea's imports, the elasticity approach would overestimate the trade-expansion effect of PRC–South Korea trade.

During the third subperiod, 1985–1988, the income elasticity of South Korean demand for PRC products was remarkably low—2.98—compared to 20.54 for the preceding period. This may be an indication that the initial newcomer effect was exhausted by 1985 such that the trade-creation effect was probably negative. However, that does not necessarily mean zero or negative trade-diversion effects. Rather, the reduction of income elasticity of South Korean import demand for non-PRC products during this period indicates that there may have been some positive trade-diversion effects as South Korean importers had had enough time to compare imported products from China with those from elsewhere and to switch their business partners.[6]

PRC Imports from South Korea

Table 8.6 shows that the income elasticity of PRC demand for South Korean products is 3.3, indicating that when China's real GNP grew annually at 11 percent over the 1981–88 period, its imports from South Korea grew on average more than 35 percent. This is, however, lower than South Korea's income elasticity of demand for PRC products, which is 5.0. The higher figure for South Korea may reflect a more active Korean attitude toward trade with China than the reverse. But since the income elasticity of Chinese demand of 3.3 for South Korean products is much higher than 1.4 for non–South Korean products, it may be inferred that there was relatively strong Chinese interest in trade with South Korea.

Estimates of income elasticity for the three subperiods reveal some interesting information. The income elasticity of PRC import demand for South Korean products was –2.2 during the first subperiod, whereas that for products from other countries was 1.5. Thus, even during this subperiod the Chinese attitude toward trade with South Korea appears to have been ambivalent or passive. However, the second subperiod of 1983–85 shows an explosion of PRC imports from South Korea. Since the same pattern is seen in South Korean imports from the PRC, these findings support our judgment that the 1983–85 period should be identified as the actual opening of PRC–South Korea trade.

Again, it is difficult to divide accurately such trade expansion into trade creation and trade diversion. But, as noted above in the case of South Korean imports from the PRC, it is likely that most of the trade expansion during the second subperiod resulted purely from trade creation. The income elasticity of PRC import demand from non–South Korean sources increased between the first and the second subperiods, indicating that other factors must have been responsible for the expansion of overall PRC imports.

The subperiod was the beginning of the second phase of economic reform in China. The reform was extended to include urban areas after its success in rural areas, and more active and confident attitudes toward economic reform were observed. In contrast, the subperiod of 1981–83 was the first adjustment or partial recentralization period to ameliorate some unexpected side effects of the initial reform undertaken in 1978. Thus, in interpreting the results obtained with the income elasticity approach we need to take these factors into account. As they would tend to increase PRC imports during the second subperiod, the elasticity approach would overestimate the trade expansion effect of the opening of PRC–South Korea trade.

The income elasticity of PRC demand for South Korean products for the third subperiod, 1985–88, was only 2.3, a significant decline from 20.0 of the preceding period. The same decline was also observed in the case of South Korean imports from China, and again this may be an indication that the initial newcomer effect had been exhausted by the second subperiod. It is, however, difficult to know how much of the decrease derived from this, because at the same time the income elasticity of PRC demand for non–South Korean products decreased significantly.

Prospects for Korea, China, and Bohai Trade toward 2000

This section offers some prognosis for trade between Bohai and South Korea in the 1990s, based on the results of our historical analysis of such trade between 1981 and 1988 as well as alternative economic scenarios for China and South Korea.[7]

Specifically, we assume that South Korean imports from the PRC are determined solely by South Korean GNP growth and the income elasticity of South Korean demand for Chinese products.[8] Since Bohai –South Korea trade data are not available, we first estimate South Korean imports from the PRC in the 1990s and then assume that 25 percent of PRC exports to South Korea come from Bohai. Bohai's share of China's total exports decreased from about 40 percent in the early 1980s to 23 percent in 1988, while its share in China's total GNP remained around 25 percent. Thus, the 25 percent assumption seems to be a reasonable, if not slightly optimistic, estimate for the future.

A similar procedure is also applied to our estimate of Bohai imports from South Korea in the 1990s. That is, we assume that PRC imports from South Korea are determined solely by the PRC's GNP growth and the income elasticity of PRC import demand for South Korean products. Then we assume that Bohai imports from South Korea are 20 percent of total PRC imports from South Korea. This figure is based on Bohai's share of total PRC "national income used," which was 18.5 percent in 1986.

South Korean Imports from the PRC and Bohai

Table 8.7 presents two projections for South Korean imports from the PRC and Bohai in the 1990s. The optimistic scenario assumes (1) that the South Korean economy will maintain the same 10 percent average annual growth rate in the next decade as it did in the past, (2) that the income elasticity of South Korean import demand for goods from China for the 1991–96 period will be the same as that for the 1985–88 period, 2.98, and (3) that this will decrease to 2.00 for the 1995–2000 period, which is an arithmetic average of 2.98 and 1.01 (the income elasticity of South Korean import demand for non-PRC products for the 1981–88 period).

The pessimistic scenario assumes (1) that the South Korean economy will grow 7 percent, (2) that the income elasticity of South Korean import demand for goods from the PRC during the 1991–96 period will be 2.00, which is an arithmetic average of 2.98 and 1.01 (the income elasticity of South Korean demand for non-PRC products

Table 8.7

Projections of South Korean Imports from the PRC and Bohai

	Scenario 1 (pessimistic)	Scenario 2 (optimistic)
Trends of the South Korean economy		
Annual GNP growth rates 1981–88	10.5%	10.5%
Annual import price change 1981–88	–0.7%	–0.7%ii
Scenarios		
Annual GNP growth rates 1991–2000	7.0%	10.0%
Income elasticity of imports from PRC, 1991–95	2.00	2.98
Income elasticity of imports from PRC, 1996–2000	1.01%	2.00
Bohai's share of PRC exports	25.00%	25.00%
Projections for South Korean imports from the PRC (current U.S.$ millions)		
1989	1,705.0	1,705.0
1995	3,588.0	7,817.5
2000	4,874.5	18,781.1
1989	426.3	426.3
1995	897.0	1,954.4
2000	1,218.6	4,695.3

during the 1981–88 period), and (3) that for the 1995–2000 period this elasticity will be the same as the South Korean income elasticity of demand for non-PRC imports of 1.01.

In other words, an important difference between the two scenarios is that the pessimistic one assumes a quicker regression of the income elasticity of import demand for PRC products than for those from other countries. The difference in income elasticity takes into account different scenarios about future Sino–South Korean economic relations. The most optimistic scenario corresponds to the establishment of a Sino–South Korean trade agreement allowing a direct trade relationship and tariff reductions. Without these, it would be difficult to maintain even the 1985–88 level of income elasticity. Accordingly, the pessimistic scenario assumes no such changes. The past trend will continue but there will be a gradual decrease in the income elasticity of import demand.

For both scenarios, we assume that import prices will decline 0.7 percent per year from 1991 to 2000, continuing the trend from 1981–88. Then the pessimistic scenario predicts South Korean imports from China of $3.6 billion for 1995 and $4.9 billion for 2000. South Korean imports from Bohai are then $0.9 billion and $1.2 billion for the respective years. The optimistic scenario predicts $7.8 billion for 1995 and $18.8 billion for 2000. South Korean imports from Bohai are then $2.0 billion and $4.7 billion for the respective years.

PRC and Bohai Imports from South Korea

Part A in Table 8.8 presents Chinese GNP growth projections. They are based on the growth trend of the Chinese economy in the 1980s and economic performance since the 1989 political crisis. China's economy recorded an annual average growth rate of 9.3 from 1979 to 1989. In 1989 economic performance was determined mainly by the recentralization drive undertaken after the Tiananmen crisis and the macroeconomic austerity measures adopted by the Third Chinese Communist Party Central Committee Plenum in September 1988. These are contained in the three-year adjustment program, "improving the economic environment and rectifying the economic order." It consists largely of curtailment of investment, especially in resource-intensive processing industries, postponement of price reform, and tightening of the money supply and credit lending with the aim of reducing extrabudgetary investment by state units and investment by collective and joint-venture enterprises. According to official releases by the State Statistical Bureau (*Renmin ribao*, hereafter RMRB, January 25, 1990, and February 22, 1990), the PRC's economic growth in 1989 fell to 3.9 percent, less than half that for 1988 and for the decade of 1979 to 1988.

China's economic plans and goals for the next few years are revealed in various documents including the communiqué of the Fifth Plenary Session of the Thirteenth Central Committee of the Chinese Communist Party held on November 9, 1989.[9] The party Central Committee determined that their austerity program would last three years or longer, including 1989, so as to alleviate the inflationary gap between aggregate demand and supply, to put the national economy on the track of sustained and coordinated growth, and to lay a solid foundation for the strategic goal of "quadrupling GNP" by the end of this century. According to quantitative targets for 1990 revealed in various documents, real GNP is planned to grow at 5 percent, which is 1 percent higher than the level achieved in 1989, but much lower than the 9.6 percent average annual growth rate for the past ten years.

The economic policies implemented and decreed in the past two years make clear that the highest priority was placed on control of

Table 8.8

PRC and Bohai GNP and Trade Projections

	Scenario 1 (pessimistic)	Scenario 2 (optimistic)
Chinese economic trends		
Annual GNP growth rates 1979–89	9.3%	9.3%
Annual population growth 1979–89	1.3%	1.3%
Annual per capita GNP growth 1979–89	7.8%	7.8%
Changes in GNP deflator 1979–89	4.9%	4.9%
Per capita GNP in 1989 in U.S. dollars	300	300
Annual change of import price index, 1981–88	−1.7%	−1.7%
A. Projections of PRC GNP:		
Scenarios:		
Annual growth 1989–91	5.0%	5.0%
Annual growth 1991–97	5.0%	9.0%
Annual growth 1997–2000	5.0%	5.0%
Annual population growth 1989–2000	1.3%	1.3%
Projections:		
GNP in 2000 as multiple of GNP in 1980	3.8	4.8
GNP in 2000 as multiple of GNP in 1990	1.6	2.0
GNP in 1990 as multiple of GNP in 1980	2.4	2.4
Per capita 2000 GNP, multiple of that in 1980	3.0	3.7
Per capita GNP in 2000 in U.S. dollars	429.5	557.2
Per capita 2000 GNP, multiple of that in 1990	1.4	1.8
Per capita 1990 GNP, multiple of that in 1980	2.1	2.1
B. Projections of imports from South Korea		
Scenarios:		
Income elasticity of imports from South Korea, 1991–1995	1.85	2.30
Income elasticity of imports from South Korea, 1996–2000	1.40	1.85
Bohai's share of PRC imports	20.0%	20.0%
Projections (current $U.S. millions)		
PRC imports from South Korea in 1989	1,438.0	1,438.0
PRC imports from South Korea in 1995	2,610.9	4,051.8
PRC imports from South Korea in 2000	3,867.8	7,593.4
Bohai imports from South Korea in 1989	287.6	287.6
Bohai imports from South Korea in 1995	522.2	810.4
Bohai imports from South Korea in 2000	773.6	1,518.7

excessive demand by reducing the money supply and checking the growth of nonstate sectors. However, there is widespread concern among China observers that although they may be justifiable for the purpose of short-run stabilization, the tight fiscal and monetary policies, recentralization, and renewed price controls could jeopardize not only the course of economic reforms but also the pace of economic growth.

The pessimistic scenario in Table 8.8 projects a 5 percent annual growth rate between 1990 and 2000.[10] At this rate China will not achieve its goal of quadrupling GNP; its GNP in 2000 will be 3.8 times that in 1980. Such prolonged stagnation is not an impossible scenario. China's rapid growth in the past decade was supported by the growth of nonstate sectors and the open-door policy. If these dynamic elements are throttled, even a 5 or 6 percent growth rate may not be attained. The current policy directions place a considerable restraint on these dynamic economic actors. If China's economy grows at 6 percent per year, it would barely achieve the goal of quadrupling GNP. Even then, its per capita GNP will be merely $460 in the year 2000, provided that there is no depreciation of the yuan and population grows at 1.3 percent per annum, as in the past decade. This implies that the economic distance between China and the Asian NIEs will not be reduced. Considering that China's economy grew at less than 5 percent during periods of economic recentralization and adjustment (4.4 percent in 1981 and 3.9 percent in 1989), we find a 5 or 6 percent growth rate plausible, if a conservative and not totally reactionary growth strategy is followed.

If we combine the pessimistic scenario on GNP growth with a pessimistic assumption about the income elasticity of PRC demand for South Korean products, we get the following estimates for Chinese imports from South Korea: $2.6 billion for 1995 and $3.9 billion for 2000. This pessimistic scenario assumes that the income elasticity of PRC import demand for South Korean products for the 1991–96 period will be reduced from its 1985–88 level of 2.30 to 1.85. The latter is an arithmetic average of 2.30 and 1.40 (the income elasticity of PRC demand for non–South Korean products during the 1981–88 period). The pessimistic scenario also assumes that the income elasticity of PRC import demand for South Korean products for the 1995–2000 period will be the same as the income elasticity of PRC import demand for non–South Korean products of 1.40. In this scenario, Bohai imports from South Korea will be $500 million for 1995 and $800 million for the year 2000.

A more optimistic scenario is possible if China's future economy replicates its trend for the past decade. That decade was characterized by the initiation of reform in 1979, adjustment in 1981 and 1982, and then six boom years until 1988. Thus, the optimistic scenario assumes that after three years of adjustment to 1991, the economy would resume its 9 percent growth rate in 1992, followed by six boom years. Then there would be another three-year adjustment in 1998 with a 5 percent annual growth rate. According to this scenario, China's GNP in 2000 would be 4.8 times bigger than that in 1980, and per capita GNP would exceed $550.

The optimistic scenario also assumes that the income elasticity of PRC import demand for South Korean products for the 1991–96 period will be 2.30, the same as that for the 1985–88 period, and that the elasticity for the 1995–2000 period will be 1.85, which is an arithmetic average of 2.30 and 1.40 (the income elasticity of PRC demand for non–South Korean products for the 1981–88 period). According to this scenario, PRC and Bohai imports from South Korea in 1995 will be $4.1 billion and $0.8 billion, respectively. In 2000 the figures will go up to $7.6 billion and $1.5 billion, respectively.

Conclusion

Although it is difficult to predict precisely by how much, the opening of formal trade relations between the PRC and South Korea will undoubtedly expand trade between Bohai and South Korea. Here we have made some projections for such trade expansion on the basis of historical data and what we regard as prospects for economic growth for both China and South Korea. Making such projections as we have done here, however, is full of hazards, especially because we have not taken into account various structural changes that take place in the course of economic development.

At low- and even middle-income levels, countries with an especially rich endowment of natural resources tend to rely heavily on these for export revenues. China's exports of petroleum, coal, and "other crude materials" reflects such a resource-endowed pattern at present. But China will not continue with this pattern of trade as its economy develops. Although China is abundantly endowed with many natural resources, its large population and ambitious development goals will undoubtedly increase the domestic demand for these resources, and little will be available for export markets.

In contrast, low-income countries, where capital is scarce relative to labor, tend to export light manufactured products or in some cases labor-intensive agricultural products. Given severe land constraints and the PRC's emphasis on grain self-sufficiency, expansion of agricultural exports is likely to be limited despite the current importance of such export products as raw fibers and fruit and vegetables. Thus, it seems that the PRC's best prospects for future export growth lie in labor-intensive light manufactured products. But for there to be a significant increase in the export of these manufactured products their quality must improve, and this can happen at least for now only with imported technology and capital goods. It is in this area where the strongest complementarity may lie between Bohai and South Korea in the years to come.

Notes

1. See Kwon (1987) on Sino–South Korean indirect trade through Hong Kong.

2. See Finger and Kreinin (1979) for the index of export similarity. The index was also applied in Bayard et al. (1982).

3. Y. Zhang (1988) investigated complementarity in trade between Taiwan and China and between China and South Korea.

4. This statement assumes that without the South Korea–Bohai trade opening, South Korean import elasticity remains the same. In this case, substitution of Bohai products for domestic products is reflected in the increase of income elasticity of total South Korean import demand.

5. For the price elasticity approach used to analyze the effect of U.S.-China trade normalization, see Bayard et al. (1982).

6. We would normally expect trade diversion to take more time to go into effect than pure trade-creation effects, which might be more immediate.

7. See Won Bae Kim (1990) on several scenarios for the two economies.

8. Some factors can increase intraindustry specialization in Sino–South Korean trade. For instance, if the trend is such that China's pattern of exports to Korea is becoming more similar to that of ASEAN–4, we can expect greater diversion of South Korean imports under the optimistic scenario of Sino–South Korean direct trade and tariff reductions. Cumulated foreign investment in the past will also stimulate intraindustry trade through vertical integration. More knowledge about domestic markets in partner countries might stimulate horizontal integration through greater product differentiation.

9. This document was published in the overseas edition of *Renmin ribao* (*RMRB*) on January 17, 1990, two months after the committee plenum. Other documents include a report by the new minister of the State Planning Commission, Zou Jiahua (*RMRB*, March 23, 1990), a report by Premier Li Peng (*RMRB*, March 21, 1990), and a report by Minister of Finance Wang Bingqian (*RMRB*, March 23, 1990), in the People's Congress held in the spring of 1990.

10. For additional scenarios, see Lee and Mark (1990), which provides four different growth patterns for the PRC economy.

Chapter 9

Competitive Advantage, Two-Way Foreign Investment, and Capital Accumulation in South Korea

Since the late 1980s, increasing amounts of direct foreign investment (DFI) flowing from newly industrializing economies (NIEs) have raised questions regarding the theoretical explanation and empirical analysis of this phenomenon (Kumar and McLeod 1981; Lall 1983; C. Lee 1990a; Taniguchi 1990; Wells 1983). A recent review by Lall (1990) of DFI behavior in four Asian NIEs, South Korea, Taiwan, Hong Kong, and Singapore, indicates somewhat varying patterns and motivations. This diversity relates to divergent economic structures and differing structural adjustment patterns.

Some theoretical efforts to explain the so-called emergence of Third World multinationals have been from the perspective of the investment development cycle or path, as first set out by Dunning (1981) and subsequently modified in Dunning (1988). Dunning's theoretical explanations of outward DFI by developing countries involve modification and extension of the so-called general eclectic paradigm of DFI (Dunning 1988), which states that a firm will engage in international production if and when the following three conditions are satisfied: first, that the firm possess certain economic advantages over their competitors (so-called *ownership advantages*); second, that the firm find it in its best interest to engage in productive activities based on ownership advantages, rather than sell the rights to do so to other firms (so-called *internalization advantages*); and third, that the firm find it in its global interest to utilize these advantages in conjunction with at least some factor inputs from outside its base country (so-called *locational advantages*).

Investment development theory divides phases of economic development into several stages, from receiving inward DFI to generating net outward DFI. Throughout the development process, a country generates its own ownership-specific advantages and eventually starts to initiate its own outward DFI.[1] Chung Lee (1990b) and Lee and Lee (1991) relate outward DFI to changing comparative advantages and declining profitability. Kasai (1990) and Chen (1990) also analyze, from the point of view of development stages, South Korean and Taiwanese outward DFI behavior, although their focus was more on recent macroeconomic changes such as trade surpluses, rising wages, and protectionism as the factors driving outward DFI in both countries.

Although Dunning's paradigm is a grand conceptual framework, it does not provide much help in empirical analysis. This chapter aims to develop a relatively simple but focused model, specifically designed for empirical analysis of two-way DFI and its relationship to domestic capital accumulation, with application to South Korea.

The following section on a simple theoretical framework will derive several empirically testable hypotheses. Subsequent sections test these hypotheses empirically. This chapter will look at competitive advantages and outward DFI behavior in South Korea, focus on inward DFI, and consider the relationship between domestic capital accumulation and DFI. With rich, updated data on South Korean outward DFI and detailed industrial subsectors, a more advanced and updated analysis of Korean DFI and industries will be done here than has been attempted in the past, for instance in Kasai (1990) and Jo (1981). Finally, some concluding remarks will be made.

Theoretical Framework and Hypotheses

International production is a mix of factors of production originating in different countries. However, factor inputs from different countries cannot be combined or substituted without additional transaction cost. So why does international production ever happen despite the additional costs associated with it? Aside from marketing-related reasons, the production basis of international production is the existence of differences in productivity or factor prices across countries.

What are the conditions under which international production occurs? First, domestic capital is more likely to launch international production when the profit rate in international production is at least higher than that in domestic production (*profit advantage*), although the profit rate difference is not a sufficient condition for outward DFI.

The point can be more clearly demonstrated with the help of a simple formula, which defines profit as follows:

$$PR = Y - wL - C \qquad\qquad (A)$$

where PR is profit, Y is net output or value added, w is wage rate, L is labor input, and C is the sum of rents, taxes, and other miscellaneous costs. Then the profit rate, defined as profit per unit of capital (K), can be decomposed into two elements as follows:

$$PR/K = (Y/K)(PR/Y)$$
$$= (u)(1 - m) \qquad\qquad (B)$$

where PR/K is the profit rate, u is the average capital productivity (Y/K), and (1 minus m) is per unit profit (PR/Y). Unit profit is 1 minus the unit wage and other costs, m = (wL + C)/Y. In other words, this formula defines the profit rate as average capital productivity times per unit profit, or average capital productivity times 1 minus total unit costs.

Expression (B) suggests that to increase the profit rates, one must either increase capital productivity (u) or reduce unit costs (m). If productive capital (high u) is transferred to a foreign country to be combined with cheap labor (low m), the profit rate will be higher than in domestic production. Or, if there is more than one type of capital (let's say, types X and Y) required in the production process, domestic capital of type X can be combined with foreign capital of type Y, which is more productive than domestic capital, with a view to increasing average capital productivity. However, to offset any additional transaction costs from international production, per unit wages and other cost margins in a foreign country should be large enough in the former case, and the productivity difference between domestic and foreign capital should be large enough in the latter case.

Next, the investor should have certain owner-specific competitive advantages over his potential competitor in foreign local or world markets (*competitive advantages*). Otherwise, the venture cannot survive even if potential profit rates from international production are higher than those of domestic production. The owner-specific competitive advantages embodied in the products of international combinations can be expected to be a reflection of those of domestic production run by the parent firm in its home country. Accepting Balassa's index of the revealed comparative advantage (RCA) as a good measure of international competitive advantage,[2] we can thus hypothesize that a country's outward DFI is more likely to flow from those sectors that show high RCA in world export markets, regardless of whether DFI is targeted at a less developed country or a more developed country.

In sum, international production is more likely to occur when it results in profit advantages and competitive advantages. Even if international capital has some competitive advantages, there will be no international production if the profit advantage is not high enough to offset additional costs. If additional transaction costs involved in international production are too high, then the potential investing firms might find it in their interest to sell or lease them to foreign firms (international licensing).[3]

To augment its international competitive advantages, a developing country can try to invite inward DFI, preferably through joint ventures, and thereby domestic firms can obtain some technology transfer. This has been an important goal of all NIEs in their respective industrial policies. Various investment incentive schemes are often instituted to attract inward DFI, although the importance of these incentives is generally estimated to be far less significant than macroeconomic factors such as robust aggregate demand growth, price stability, and so forth (Ramstetter and Plummer 1990). To the extent that this strategy is successfully pursued and competitive advantages are developed, outward DFI flows from countries like the NIEs are more likely to come from the sectors in which the NIEs themselves received more inward DFI from more developed countries. Alternatively, a developing country can try to increase additional transaction costs for potential international investors by installing various types of artificial barriers and regulations, so that they may decide to license their advanced technologies to local firms rather than initiate DFI. The strategy of promoting DFI in some firms, in particular, joint ventures, can be effective in a dynamic sense, when a country envisions strong potential for its own firms to develop international competitiveness both indigenously and by absorbing and modifying imported technology. This strategy appeared to be pursued by Japan in its phenomenal postwar performance (Dunning 1988, 58).

Inward and outward DFI also have important implications for domestic capital accumulation. The rate of capital accumulation basically depends on the profit rate, since higher profit rates make more investment funds available for the sector and induce more investment from other sectors. On the relationship between DFI and capital accumulation, we test the following hypotheses: (1) given a certain rate of profit, a sector generating a large flow of outward DFI is more likely to show a relatively low rate of capital accumulation, since available investment funds go abroad and repatriated profit from outward DFI is not necessarily reinvested in its original sector; and (2) a sector inviting more inward DFI flows is also likely to show a relatively low rate of capital accumulation to the extent that profits are repatriated abroad. Of course, the exact size of the effect of inward and outward DFI on domestic capital accumulation in a sector depends on the relative importance of such financial flows compared with the size of the total net investment in the sector.

Competitive Advantages and Outward DFI

Outward DFI from South Korea has increased rapidly since the late 1980s, much faster than inward DFI. During the year 1989, the amount of outward DFI (U.S.$492 million) reached more than half of realized inward DFI (U.S.$812 million).[4] Out of a total 329 cases of outward DFI conducted by the end of 1989, approximately three-fourths (252 cases) were established since 1986, with 136 cases in 1989 alone. Among various types of DFI, the rapid increase of outward manufacturing DFI in the past several years was most remarkable.

Table 9.1 presents a sectoral picture of both inward and outward manufacturing DFI in South Korea. It divides manufacturing into 28 subsectors and lists the number of all types of firms hiring more than five employees, the number of outward DFI cases, and the number of

Table 9.1

Sectoral Composition of Inward and Outward DFI in South Korea

Sector codes (A)		All firms (B)	Outward DFI cases (C)	(C/B)	Inward DFI cases Joint venture (D)	(D/B)	Wholly owned (E)
11	Food	3,825	31	0.008	49	0.013	8
13	Beverage	873	3	0.003	3	0.003	1
14	Tobacco	22	0	0	3	0.136	0
21	Textile	7,199	26	0.004	36	0.005	3
22	Apparel	5,111	157	0.031	30	0.006	8
23	Leather and fur	1,105	43	0.039	8	0.007	0
24	Footwear	638	35	0.055	5	0.008	1
31	Wood Prd.	1,756	27	0.015	1	0.001	0
32	Furniture	1,251	5	0.004	4	0.003	1
41	Paper	1,535	5	0.003	14	0.009	1
42	Printing	2,389	4	0.002	2	0.001	1
51	Indust. chemical	839	31	0.037	56	0.066	0
52	Other chemical	877	21	0.024	66	0.075	3
53	Petro. refinery	13	1	0.077	3	0.231	3
54	Miscel. products of petro. and gas	330	1	0.003	7	0.021	0
55	Rubber product	1,189	18	0.015	13	0.011	2
56	Plastic product	2,726	28	0.010	29	0.011	7
61	Pottery and china	381	5	0.013	6	0.016	0
62	Glass product	281	2	0.007	12	0.043	0
69	Other nonmetal	2,469	14	0.006	19	0.008	3
71	Basic metal	667	11	0.016	15	0.022	5
72	Nonferrous metal	515	9	0.017	10	0.019	0
81	Fabricated metal	4,294	18	0.004	46	0.011	6
82	Non-elec. machine	4,333	11	0.003	88	0.020	19

		B	C/B	C	D	D/B	E
83	Electric and electronics	4,514	0.022	101	169	0.037	38
84	Transport equipment	1,832	0.002	4	59	0.032	2
85	Medical and scientific	807	0.014	11	46	0.057	10
90	Other manufacturing	2,618	0.030	79	38	0.015	4
	Sum	59,928		701	837		123
	Average	1,942.46	0.017	25.0	29.9	0.032	4.39

Notes: See the Appendix on the data sources and usage.

(A): Twenty-eight manufacturing subsector codes classifed according to three-digit Korea Industrial Standard Classification (KISC).

(B): Total number of existing firms at the beginning of 1988, including South Korea–foreign joint ventures and wholly foreign-owned firms.

(C): Number of approved cases of outward DFI by the end of 1990, classified into 28 subsectors.

(C/B): A measure of outward DFI propensity of each subsector; figures are rounded and thus not exactly the same as the actual figures used in regression analysis (the same is true of D/B).

(D): Number of outstanding South Korea–foreign joint venture firms at the end of 1988.

(D/B): A measure of inward DFI propensity of each sector.

(E): Number of outstanding wholly foreign-owned firms at the end of 1988.

foreign joint ventures and wholly foreign-owned firms in each sector. It shows that the apparel sector has generated the highest number (157) of firms engaging in outward DFI, followed by the electrical and electronic machinery and equipment sector, which includes consumer electronics goods. The propensity to go abroad, measured by the ratio of the number of outward DFI cases to the number of all existing firms in the sector, was highest in the footwear sector (0.055), followed by the leather goods and industrial chemicals sectors (excluding the special sector of petroleum refinery, with 1 case of outward DFI observed out of 13 existing firms).

Table 9.2 presents results of regression analysis of the determinants of outward DFI from South Korea.[5] In the analysis, the outward DFI propensity measured as the ratio of the outward DFI cases to the outstanding number of firms was run against various independent variables, such as Balassa's index of revealed comparative advantage (RCA), the degree of inward DFI presence (the ratio of the number of foreign joint ventures to that of all firms), the profit rate, the capital–labor ratio, and per unit gross profit (i.e., 1 minus unit wage and other costs). It is shown that the dominant explanatory variable is the RCA index, which alone accounts for 48 percent of the variance of the outward DFI propensity. Together with the variable representing the degree of inward DFI presence, it accounts for 57 percent of the variance of the dependent variable.

The estimated coefficients of all other variables, when added as regressors in addition to the two strong variables, are not shown to be significantly different from zero, thus not increasing the adjusted R^2 ratio at all. Thus, the results imply that when we control for the RCA index and inward DFI, these capital–labor ratio, profitability, and unit wage cost variables do not provide any additional explanations.[6] The result might appear counterintuitive in terms of the common impression that the recent South Korean outward DFI was motivated by skyrocketing wage rates. In fact, the three labor-intensive sectors of apparel, leather, and footwear show high outward DFI propensities. This paradox can be explained in two ways.

First, the above sectoral analysis is inadequate to capture the wage rate increase effect on sectoral distribution of outward DFI. Those sectors that went abroad for DFI compared their unit wage costs not with those of other sectors in South Korea but with those in foreign countries. Unless the outward DFI–prone sectors were more seriously

Table 9.2

Determinants of Outward DFI in South Korea

Dependent variable: OUTDFI
Estimated parameters of independent variables

	INT	RCA	JOINT	K/L	PR/K	PR/Y	R^2	F
(2–1)	0.009 $(3.9)^{**}$	0.003 $(4.8)^{**}$					0.46	22.6**
(2–2)	0.004 (1.2)	0.004 $(5.7)^{**}$	0.244 $(2.7)^{**}$				0.573	17.8**
(2–3)	0.002 (0.6)	0.004 $(5.7)^{**}$	0.223 $(2.3)^{*}$	0.098 (0.62)			0.56	11.7**
(2–4)	0.001 (0.2)	0.003 $(5.0)^{**}$	0.243 $(2.6)^{*}$		0.003 (0.4)		0.558	11.5**
(2–5)	0.003 (0.2)	0.004 $(5.4)^{**}$	0.243 $(2.4)^{*}$			0.001 (0.0)	0.554	11.4**

Notes: See notes to Table 9.1. Number of observation is 26 manufacturing subsectors. In other words, the two special sectors of tobacco and petroleum refinery are not included. More detailed information about the data source and variables are in the Appendix: Data Sources and Usage (page 177).

**, *, and $^{+}$: significant at 1%, 5%, and 10% levels, respectively.

Variables:

OUTDFI = (cases of outward DFI)/(total number of firms) in the sector

INT = intercept term in regresssions

RCA = Balassa's index of revealed comparative advantage

JOINT = (number of South Korean–foreign joint ventures in South Korea) (total number of firms) in the sector

K/L = capital–labor ratio = (value of tangible fixed assets at the beginning of 1988 in billion won)/(average number of workers in 1988)

PR/K = (value of annual profit)/(value of tangible fixed asset)

PR/Y = (value of gross profit)/(value-added), where gross profit is defined as value added minus total employee compensation

R^2 = Adjusted R-square ratio

F = F-statistics

affected by the wage increase than other sectors, it follows that the regression analysis would not indicate that the per unit gross profit variable was significantly different from zero. Second, a direct examination of the data has revealed that some of the labor-intensive sectors with high unit wage costs did not generate many outward DFI cases relative to the total number of existing firms in the sectors, while some outward DFI–prone sectors are capital intensive (Table 9.1). The former group includes furniture, printing, rubber products, and the pottery and china industries, and the latter group includes industrial chemicals and other chemical industries (the South Korean electrical and electronic goods industry is not particularly capital intensive; its capital-labor ratio is below average). Furthermore, gross profitability measured as value added minus wage cost per fixed assets is much higher in the labor-intensive, outward DFI industries of apparel, leather, and footwear. It should also be noted that some of the sectors with a high RCA index are not necessarily labor-intensive sectors.

The results support the argument that South Korean outward DFI is from those sectors in which the country has had strong competitive advantages, as evidenced by high RCA indices,[7] and that the sectors that received more inward DFI tend to generate more outward DFI, *ceteris paribus*. In other words, it seems that accumulation of inward DFI contributed to building up competitive advantages of certain sectors.

If the sectoral regression analysis turned out to be inappropriate to confirm the wage rate increase as a cause of outward DFI, the area decomposition of South Korean outward DFI in Table 9.3 on pages 168 and 169 is consistent with the observation that South Korea's labor-intensive industries went to other Asian countries for cheap labor. In terms of numbers, almost half of South Korean DFI in developing Asia is in textiles, apparel, and footwear, although some cases are in the capital-intensive sector of chemicals. This pattern of DFI might be called *development spreading* according to Kasai (1990, 36), which is similar to early Japanese DFI in Southeast Asia as studied and regarded as *pro-trade* by Kojima (1978).

However, another pattern of South Korean outward DFI can also be discerned from Table 9.3, namely, that more than half of South Korean DFI in OECD countries is in the machinery and equipment sector. Definitely not seeking cheap labor in these countries, such DFI appears to seek mainly two things. First, it is seeking advanced technology from developed countries, as evidenced by some South Korean and

Taiwanese investment and acquisitions in Silicon Valley. This type of DFI, in Kasai's (1990, 34–37) terminology, can be called *development absorbing*.

Second, a much larger amount of South Korean DFI in OECD countries is purported to defend South Korea's export market shares and cope with import restrictions (Jun 1987). The increase in trade barriers in OECD markets tended to raise internalization advantages sufficiently to more than compensate for locational disadvantages or lack of locational advantages in OECD economies and thus induce South Korean firms to invest in OECD countries (Lee and Lee 1991). Kasai uses the term *development promoting* for this type of DFI. Many South Korean DFI cases in electrical and electronic goods produce intermediate goods, which would increase the local content of South Korean products in foreign markets. If we also include nonmanufacturing DFI in our analysis, the largest number of South Korean DFI projects in OECD countries set up foreign trading companies (284 companies as of the end of 1989). The combination of locally made intermediate goods and expanded marketing channels is expected to contribute to defend or increase South Korean products' shares in OECD markets.

In sum, South Korean outward DFI shows a clear dichotomy between "top-down" DFI in developing countries and "bottom-up" DFI in developed countries, namely, combining early Japanese-style DFI by small- and medium-scale enterprises and American-style DFI by large corporations. Nevertheless, both types of outward DFI originate in those sectors in which South Korea has achieved a certain level of competitive advantage, as evidenced by active export performance in world markets, although their advantage might be declining currently or in the near future.

The importance of the latter type is critical for the future of the South Korean economy as the weight of it is shifting into these sectors of electrical and electronic goods and transportation equipment, the main objects of South Korean investment in the developed countries. In terms of amounts, metal products and machinery and equipment accounted for about half of total DFI, while textiles, apparel, and footwear together accounted for only 20 percent, much less than its share in numbers. The bulk of non–labor-intensive DFI is conducted by the *chaebol*s (conglomerates), whose position in the domestic economy is dominant in every aspect (Lee and Lee 1991). Of all the

Table 9.3

Area and Sectoral Composition of Outward DFI from South Korea
(outstanding as of the end of 1989)

	World	Asia	% share	OECD	% share
Number of cases					
Manufacturing subtotal	295	132	100.0	82	100.0
Food and beverages	12	1	0.8	5	7.7
Textiles and clothing, toys, footwear, and leather	114	62	47.0	13	20.0
Textiles and clothing	34		25.8	10	15.4
Toys	12		9.1	1	1.5
Footwear and leather	16		12.1	1	1.5
Wood and wood products	9	7	5.3	1	1.5
Paper and paper products	7	0	0	7	10.8
Chemicals and petroleum products	33	16	12.1	9	13.8
Nonmetal mineral products	13	6	4.5	4	6.2
Basic metals	8	2	1.5	2	3.1
Machinery and equipment	62	23	17.4	35	53.8
Other manufacturing	37	14	10.6	6	9.2
Mining	15	2		6	
Forestry	10	6		1	
Fishing	34	5		8	
Construction	56	15		17	
Transportation and storage	28	5		20	
Foreign trade	377	68		284	
Other	68	7		36	
Real estate	16	3		11	
Total	899	249		465	
Amount (U.S.$1,000)					
Manufacturing subtotal	530,955	125,113	100.0	330,607	100.0
Food and beverages	14,601	3,185	2.5	7,068	2.1
Textiles and clothing, toys, footwear, and leather	90,264	44,093	35.2	14,317	4.3
Textiles and clothing	17,264	6,326	13.8	13,551	4.1
Toys			5.1	255	0.1

Footwear and leather	20,503		16.4	511	0.2
Wood and wood products	9,344	7,844	6.3	1,000	0.3
Paper and paper products	15,303	0	0	15,303	4.6
Chemicals and petroleum products	53,143	17,185	13.7	12,616	3.8
Nonmetal mineral products	25,488	30,795	24.6	1,850	0.6
Basic metals	155,624	1,379	1.1	151,844	46.0
Machinery and equipment	138,870	13,069	10.4	123,397	37.4
Other manufacturing	18,318	7,563	6.0	2,912	0.9
Mining	400,974	171,927		92,751	
Forestry	68,859	31,545		1,050	
Fishing	64,717	2,253		18,074	
Construction	49,128	5,315		21,053	
Transportation and storage	5,010	513		3,940	
Foreign trade	191,137	15,328		167,546	
Other	99,302	5,095		73,880	
Real estate	34,062	5,371		28,075	
Total	1,444,144	362,460		736,976	

Source: Calculation based on data reported in *Yearly Statistics of Overseas Investment* (Bank of Korea 1990).

Note: Asia includes all Asian countries except Japan and China. Here, OECD includes Canada, the United States, Western Europe, and Japan. Thus, it includes some West European countries that are not actually OECD members.

South Korean DFI approved for the ASEAN–4 countries and North America in 1989, the 48 largest chaebol groups accounted for about two thirds (U.S.$188 billion) of the total amount, although they accounted for only one-fourth (37 cases) in terms of numbers.[8] Thus, as Lall (1990) expects, after a relatively short-lived spurt of DFI by small- and medium-scale enterprises in labor-intensive industries, sustained growth in South Korean DFI comes from the chaebols, thereby reflecting their growing industrial strength rather than industrial decline or deindustrialization.

Inward Direct Foreign Investment

Japanese and U.S. investment dominate inward DFI in South Korea, accounting for more than 70 percent in the 1970s (Lee 1980). This DFI has been attracted by the combination of South Korea's locational advantages with their respective firms' ownership advantages and higher profit rates. But if cheap labor attracted foreign capital in the 1970s, what were the locational advantages of South Korea in the 1980s, which saw rising wages but continuing inward DFI flows? We can reasonably expect a shift in sectoral composition of inward DFI from labor-intensive to capital-intensive sectors. As South Korea attains some ownership advantages in the production process requiring middle-level technology, foreign capital must have found it in its interest to combine it with their advantages in more high-technology–oriented production processes.

The regression results in Table 9.4 attempt to verify the pattern of inward DFI in South Korea. It is not appropriate to capture the trend over time since it uses the number of DFI firms outstanding at the end of 1988 as the dependent variable. As expected, since the situation is in flux, it turned out to be difficult to find any significant explanatory variable. Most of the candidate variables were not statistically significant, except the following three, which do show a marginal significance: the capital–labor ratio, labor productivity, and per unit profit variables. Although the adjusted R^2 ratios are all low at around 12 percent, these variables turn out to differ from zero at 5.3 percent, 6.1 percent, and 4 percent, respectively.

All three variables are highly correlated, with a Pearson correlation coefficient of over 0.75. Thus, regressions incorporating more than two of them cannot be run for reliable estimates because of the

Table 9.4

Pattern of Inward DFI in South Korea

Dependent variable: JOINT
Estimated parameters of independent variables

	INT	K/L	Y/L	PR/Y	PR/K	R^2	F
(4–1)	0.011 (1.8)[+]	0.604 (2.0)*				0.112	4.2*
(4–2)	0.007 (0.8)		0.854 (1.9)[+]			0.103	3.9[+]
(4–3)	–0.044 (–1.5)			0.093 (2.2)*		0.13	4.7**
(4–4)	0 (0)	0.708 (2.1)*			0.010 (0.7)	0.09	2.3
(4–5)	–0.042 (–1.3)			0.092 (2.1)*	–0.001 (–0.1)	0.09	2.2

Notes: See notes to Tables 9.1 and 9.2.

Y/L = average labor productivity = (value added in 1988 in billion won)/(average number of workers in 1988).

collinearity problem. In other words, high capital–labor ratios would support high labor productivity, which would in turn lead to low per unit wage costs and hence high per unit profit. All the results are consistent with the interpretation that inward DFI tends to be concentrated in those sectors with a high capital–labor ratio, low unit wage costs, and high labor productivity.

In fact, the extent of inward DFI presence, measured by the ratio of the number of joint ventures to that of all types of firms in a given sector, was highest in the chemical products (0.075), followed by industrial chemicals (0.067) (excluding the two special sectors of petroleum refinery and tobacco).[9] Interestingly, as of the end of 1988, there were fewer foreign joint ventures in labor-intensive sectors in terms of both absolute numbers and relative proportions.

The pattern of inward DFI described above can imply several things. First, it reflects the changing locational advantage of South Korea associated with rising labor costs and corresponding changes in the nature of incoming DFI flows. The adjusted R^2 ratios in the regressions are relatively low partly because of the transitional nature of inward DFI in South Korea. Second, given the relatively tight government restrictions imposed on inward DFI, the pattern reflects, to a certain extent, the preference of the South Korean government and business regarding the nature of invited DFI. Third, the results imply that cheap labor is no longer a locational advantage for South Korea when compared with other countries, in terms of both quality and price of labor. Sectoral analysis of a given country's inward DFI is not adequate to capture the locational advantage effect of a country vis-à-vis other countries. Foreign investors choose certain sectors in South Korea as targets of DFI, not because those sectors guarantee low unit wage costs compared with other sectors in South Korea, but rather because they compare South Korea's locational advantage vis-à-vis other countries in given sectors in which they do business. The choice of sector is to a substantial extent predetermined by the sectoral origin of the foreign investors. Moreover, when a firm chooses to invest in South Korea, the country's locational advantage may still be more productive labor at the same level of wage rates, possibly together with efficient infrastructure and low additional transaction costs.

Now, after the review of all three alternative but complementary interpretations, it is important to interpret the above regression results as *ex post* descriptive, rather than *ex ante* explanatory, of the inward DFI pattern in South Korea. Inward DFI in South Korea has concentrated in capital-intensive sectors because this is where foreign capital has competitive advantages over local firms. Following this interpretation, the causality runs more strongly from inward DFI to high labor productivity than vice versa. Such interpretation and findings are consistent with the findings in the preceding section that outward South Korean DFI is not necessarily from those sectors with high per unit wage costs or low per unit profit.

However, those sectors with inward DFI concentrations are not necessarily those with high profit rates (see results [4–4] and [4–5] in Table 9.4). This does not mean that foreign joint ventures in South Korea ended up with low profit rates. Even when foreign joint ventures face the same unit costs (m in equation [B]) as local South Korean firms, multiplication of their intrinsic high capital productivity (u) with the same per unit profit rates $(1 - m)$ makes the profit rates higher in foreign joint ventures than in local firms with relatively low capital productivity. Actually, the measured average sectoral profit rates largely reflect those of local firms, given their absolute dominance in numbers over foreign ventures.

International capital in South Korea compares its profit rates not necessarily with those of their local counterparts in that country but more meaningfully with their expected profit rates in a third country. South Korea's losing relative attraction as a cheap labor site has resulted in the withdrawal of foreign capital in labor-intensive product lines, and some of that, especially Japanese capital, has relocated to Southeast Asia.

Domestic Capital Accumulation and DFI

The preceding sections showed that profit rates alone are not sufficient to explain DFI patterns. In contrast, the rate of domestic capital accumulation is largely determined by the changes over time of the profit rate. Regression analysis in Table 9.5 (5–1) below shows that the profit rate and its percentage change over the previous period together account for 56 percent of the variance of the capital accumulation rate.

First, the positive sign of the profit rate variable implies that the sectors with higher profit rates attract more investment. Second, particularly interesting is the highly significant coefficient of the variable denoting percentage change in the profit rate. Its negative sign implies that given the same rate of profit, those sectors experiencing increasing profit rates tend to attract less investment. The opposite signs of these two coefficients suggest positive but diminishing marginal investment from additional profit, which is reminiscent of the law of diminishing marginal utility in consumer theory. Such a tendency or behavioral pattern can be rationalized.

Consider investors like chaebols, which are regarded as excessively diversified into numerous business areas (K.T. Lee 1991). Of course, a chaebol will invest more in sectors with higher rates of return. However, among those sectors with high rates of return, if only one sector shows an additional increase in profit rates, the chaebol would find it less necessary to invest more in the sector; rather, it would transfer extra profit out of that sector into those sectors that need additional investment in view of its current or potential business conditions.[10] Financial transfer among affiliated member firms is typical behavior for chaebols, and they have used it to support newly emerging businesses, which often do not make any profit for the first several years.[11] Even if a potential investor is not

Table 9.5

Domestic Capital Accumulation and DFI in South Korea

Dependent variable: Rate of capital accumulation
Estimated parameters of independent variables

	INT	PR/K	CHG(PR/K)	INDFI	DFI	R^2	F
(5–1)	0.030	0.080	–0.207			0.556	16.7**
	(0.65)	$(1.7)^+$	$(-5.5)^{**}$				
(5–2)	0.049	0.080	–0.203	–0.793		0.562	11.7**
	(1.0)	$(1.7)^+$	$(-5.4)^{**}$	(–1.1)			
(5–3)	0.050	0.091	–0.200		–0.745	0.57	12.2**
	(1.04)	$(1.9)^+$	$(-5.4)^{**}$		(–1.4)?		

Notes: See notes to Tables 9.1 and 9.2.

New variables:

   CHG(PR/K) = percentage change in the profit rate.

   INDFI = ratio of inward DFI cases to total number of firms in the sector.

   DFI = ratio of the sum of inward and outward DFI cases to total number of firms in the sector.

   "?" mark means "significant at 20%."

running a multisectoral business, he might think the marginal rate of return from additional investment would be lower in those sectors already exhibiting high profit rates.

Next, to investigate the relationship between sectoral distribution of inward DFI and the rate of capital accumulation, a regression was run with an additional variable (INDFI) indicating the ratio of the inward DFI (both joint and wholly owned ventures) cases to the total number of firms. Estimated coefficients of the INDFI variable are shown to be negative, but are not significant in line (5–2) in Table 9.5. The result suggests that those sectors that received more foreign investment are not necessarily rapidly growing sectors in terms of fixed capital accumulation. To the extent that the amount of inward DFI is small relative to the total amount of investment in the sectors, the above methodology does not sensitively capture the sectoral accumulation effect of inward DFI. However, there is a somewhat intuitive reason to believe that the effect of inward DFI firms on the sectoral accumulation rate would be negative. Although inward DFI itself immediately implies more investment, it ultimately sends profit

Table 9.6

Foreign Investment–Related Financial Flow in South Korea
(U.S.$ million)

Year	Inward DFI		Outward DFI	Investment income	
	Direct investment	Portfolio investment	Direct investment	Incoming	Outgoing
1980	96.2	45.7	12.7	552.5	2,655.4
1981	105.4	103.6	25.7	712.8	3,650.5
1982	100.6	43.9	127.4	680.9	3,831.3
1983	101.4	195.9	126.3	581.2	3,420.9
1984	170.7	410.5	37.1	719.1	3,948.4
1985	250.3	988.0	33.6	793.9	3,977.4
1986	477.5	403.0	110.4	812.4	4,020.2
1987	624.8	339.0	182.9	765.4	3,552.7
1988	919.7	180.0	151.3	1,028.5	3,048.2
1989	931.4	265.0	305.3	1,680.0	2,944.5

Source: Balance of payments figures from *Korea Statistical Yearbook*, 1989 and 1990. Only outward DFI flows are from long-term capital balance figures in Bank of Korea, *Economic Statistics Yearbook*, 1989 and 1990.

Notes: Investment income refers to profit repatriation and other incomes related to foreign investment including portfolio investment.

abroad. Thus, it is easily expected that sooner or later outward financial flows will be greater than incoming initial investment flows plus any reinvested profits.

As of the end of 1988, South Korea had approved 2,764 cases of inward DFI during the previous decades, and 342 cases of new inward DFI were approved in the year 1988 alone.[12] Although not all the formally approved DFI firms were in operation in 1988, the amount of profit and other income repatriation in 1988 must be greater than newly arrived investment in the same year.

Table 9.6 confirms a large volume of financial outflow related to foreign investment in South Korea, although the figures include not only those directly related to DFI but all other forms of foreign business or property incomes. It also shows that, corresponding to the recent rapid increase of South Korean outward DFI, South Korean receipts of foreign investment–related income from abroad are catching up. However, since those incoming financial flows are not necessarily reinvested in their sector of origin, the net effect of outward DFI on capital accumulation in its sector of origin must be negative.

In sum, we can hypothesize that those sectors with active inward and outward DFI will accumulate more slowly than other sectors, given the same profit rates. Regression results in line 5–3 of Table 9.5 support this hypothesis. The DFI variable here is the ratio of the sum of inward and outward DFI cases to the number of all existing firms in the sector. Although still marginal, this variable turns out to be significant at 18 percent.

Conclusion

This chapter began with a simple theoretical exposition of the relationship among competitive advantage, inward and outward DFI, and domestic capital accumulation, which was subsequently applied to analysis of the South Korean case. Empirical analysis has verified the following hypotheses derived from the theory.

First, outward DFI in South Korea is largely from those sectors in which the country has had competitive advantages in world markets, and the profit rates in these sectors are not necessarily low. Second, inward DFI has contributed to enhancing competitive advantages of South Korean manufacturing and thereby enabled it to undertake its own outward DFI. Third, more and more inward DFI in South Korea is flowing to capital-intensive sectors where foreign capital has its own competitive advantages. Fourth, those sectors with active inward and outward DFI movements tend to show a low rate of capital accumulation, receiving a smaller amount of investment given the same profit rate. Fifth, the relationship between domestic capital accumulation and the movement of profit rates can be summed up as the tendency of the positive but diminishing marginal investment from additional profit; the level of the profit rates and its rate of change are the most important determinants of domestic capital accumulation.

Although the framework developed in this chapter is simple and omits many important complexities of DFI and capital accumulation, it seems to be effective with respect to the pertinent empirical questions. Room still remains for further extension. However, utilization of a more complicated theory also requires more detailed data, such as country, subsector, and annual composition of DFI. Moreover, even before attempting its extension, the theory and same empirical analysis should be applied to other countries, possibly Taiwan, to see if the results can be replicated and the findings generalized.[13]

Appendix: Data Sources and Usage

1. Estimation of the RCA indices. We used the 1988 Korean SITC two-digit trade data from the *Korea Statistical Yearbook 1990* published by the National Bureau of Statistics (NBS), supplemented, when necessary, by three-digit data reported in the *Statistical Yearbook of Foreign Trade 1988* (Korean Customs Administration). World export data were retrieved from the United Nations data base. All export data were reclassified according to the Korean Standard Industrial Classification (KSIC). South Korean exports' shares of world exports for each industrial subgroup were calculated to estimate RCA indices for each subgroup.

2. Outward DFI data. *Yearly Statistics of Overseas Investment 1990* (in Korean), by the Bank of Korea, provides aggregate data of approved and actual outward DFI, classified into ten manufacturing subsectors and other nonmanufacturing sectors and countries, outstanding as of the end of 1989. Data on individual cases of outward DFI, which are required for detailed manufacturing DFI analysis, are available in the *Current State of Overseas Establishments by DFI: as of the end of 1990* (in Korean) by the Bank of Korea. We classified 701 cases of approved DFI at of the end of 1990 into 28 manufacturing subsectors according to the KSIC classification.

3. Korean manufacturing and inward DFI data. The two main sources are the 1987 Report on Mining and Manufacturing Survey, published in 1989 by the National Bureau of Statistics (NBS) of South Korea, and vol. 1 of the 1988 Report on Industrial Census published in 1990 by the NBS. The appendix of this volume provides a detailed explanation of the KSIC method. These two books provide the most complete information, including the number of foreign joint and wholly owned ventures in each subsector, about South Korean manufacturing classified up to 522 subsectors (five-digit KSIC). We used the data classified into 28 subsectors (three-digit KSIC) since available information about outward DFI cases does not allow more detailed classification.

Table A.1

Data Used in Regression Analysis in Chapter 9

Sector	RCA	(K/L)	(PR/K)	(PR/Y)	(Y/K)	ACCUM
11	0.657	0.01642	0.75014	0.74404	1.00820	0.14541
13	0.125	0.02970	1.46140	0.86058	1.69815	0.21802
14	0.431	0.03906	5.44607	0.95588	5.69743	0.23347
21	2.764	0.01170	0.69766	0.66738	1.04537	0.15542
22	7.541	0.00247	1.42216	0.54860	2.59233	0.08107
23	3.028	0.00675	1.27581	0.67992	1.87641	0.11006
24	14.498	0.00400	1.37474	0.61319	2.24195	0.08005
31	0.232	0.01001	0.51840	0.57416	0.90288	0.11532
32	0.641	0.00559	0.91276	0.58650	1.55629	0.11530
41	0.311	0.01915	0.71445	0.73482	0.97228	0.13211
42	0.021	0.00998	0.89211	0.64974	1.37303	0.00474
51	0.425	0.05735	0.54931	0.82714	0.66411	0.11253
52	0.439	0.01948	1.18351	0.81774	1.44730	0.04203
53	0.333	0.23567	1.54243	0.95802	1.61002	0.63857
54	0.003	0.01623	1.38419	0.78245	1.76905	0.13974
55	1.563	0.00536	1.09301	0.56184	1.94542	0.34601
56	0.262	0.01340	0.80857	0.71145	1.13652	0.21228
61	1.017	0.00759	0.63113	0.56350	1.12002	0.10300
62	0.768	0.01526	0.71493	0.68152	1.04903	0.12128
69	1.613	0.02798	0.54819	0.75062	0.73031	0.06543
71	1.962	0.04701	0.47882	0.79831	0.59980	0.01907
72	0.380	0.02041	0.62941	0.74781	0.84167	0.05057
81	2.131	0.01302	0.88479	0.64394	1.37402	0.51407
82	0.622	0.01048	0.97641	0.69336	1.40824	0.08966
83	2.727	0.01059	0.89619	0.71330	1.25639	0.01848
84	1.015	0.01798	0.52651	0.65393	0.80514	−0.08110
85	0.579	0.00596	1.23982	0.64420	1.92458	0.15784
90	2.194	0.00498	1.24141	0.60953	2.03666	0.16543

Note: For variable explanations, see notes to Tables 9.2, 9.4, and 9.5.

Notes

1. Dunning (1988, 25–35) illustrated numerous determinants of the three advantages of ownership, internalization, and location in country-, industry- and firm-specific terms.

2. Balassa's (1965) index of a country's RCA in a commodity is defined as the ratio of a commodity exports' share of the country's total exports to the country's share of world exports. Because the RCA is calculated with actual trade flows, using the RCA as a proxy for comparative advantage is problematic. However, alternatives are difficult to find, and the RCA is an accepted and convenient measure; hence, we use it here.

3. We can also say that regardless of the size of profit advantages, an international firm opts for international licensing when it sees that its competitive advantage over local firms is relatively small or when that of local firms is rapidly growing. Japanese firms often sell technology to a South Korean firm when a rival South Korean firm almost succeeds in developing that technology on its own.

4. The amount of inward DFI arrived at is from *Major Statistics of Korean Economy, 1990* (Seoul National Bureau of Statistics, Economic Planning Board

of Korea) p. 230. All figures in this paragraph regarding outward DFI are from *Yearly Statistics of Overseas Investment 1990* (in Korean) by the Bank of Korea.

5. The following regression analysis excludes tobacco and petroleum refinery, which comprise an extremely small number of firms.

6. The following regression analysis excludes tobacco and petroleum refinery, which comprise an extremely small number of firms. The possible multi-collinearity problem between these variables and the RCA or JOINT variable was checked and turned out to be negligible.

7. Although those sectors with active outward DFI currently show high RCA values, their RCAs might be declining, especially those of labor-intensive sectors, because of rising domestic wages. However, that does not mean that outward DFI happens only when the RCA is declining (*defensive DFI*). Even if the RCA is not declining and still high, outward DFI can seek higher profit rates in foreign countries (*aggressive DFI*).

8. Authors' estimate from the raw data provided by the Bank of Korea. See also the Appendix (page 177) on the data sources and table 4 of Lee and Lee (1991) for more.

9. In terms of absolute numbers, the electrical and electronic machinery and equipment sector has experienced the largest number of foreign joint ventures (169), followed by the non-electrical machinery sector (88) by the end of 1988, net of withdrawn cases.

10. We do not intend to generalize our results here to other economies, such as Taiwan. Taiwanese firms are smaller and much less diversified, compared to South Korean firms. Preliminary results with the same regression model show that in Taiwan, the positive sign of the profit rate variable is significant, but the negative sign of the profit rate change variable is not.

11. See K. Lee and C. Lee (1992) on the recent government measures to induce chaebols to specialize in only a few business areas, and some resistance by chaebols against such measures.

12. From *Major Statistics of Korean Economy 1990* (Seoul National Bureau of Statistics, Economic Planning Board of Korea), p. 230..

13. Chen and Lee (1991) is an attempt to provide a similar analysis of Taiwan, finding basically similar results.

Chapter 10

Taiwan's Economy and Taiwan Investment in China

Since China started to interact actively with other Asian-Pacific economies beginning in the late 1970s, many studies have appeared on its trade relations with its Asian neighbors. However, China's interaction with Taiwan in terms of direct foreign investment (DFI) is a recent but rapidly developing phenomenon, on which no serious study exists. Available information and data remain scanty on this issue.

After the Tiananmen crisis in June 1989 and the subsequent economic sanctions imposed by the West, new DFI abruptly declined and was even withdrawn from China. The prompt negative responses of the Western economic powers contrasted with ever-expanding DFI from Taiwan. While the initial shock of the Tiananmen incident has been slow to wear off for many foreign investors, Taiwan soon resumed, and indeed scaled up, its DFI in China.

The rapid growth of Taiwanese DFI has been remarkable, especially since 1989. While the cumulative amount of Taiwanese capital invested in China was only about U.S.$1 million at the end of 1987, it reached $1 billion by the end of 1989, and doubled to $2 billion by the end of 1990. Taiwan has now surpassed the United States and Japan to become the second largest investor in China, surpassed only by Hong Kong. Compared to Taiwanese investment, South Korean investment in China started late and its cumulative amount is still small; however, it has been rapidly growing. As of June 1991, South Korean DFI in China had reached $179 million disbursed over 179 projects, mostly in relatively bigger projects (*Han-kuk il-bo*, December 14, 1991).

Detailed examination of the rapid increase in Taiwanese investment is important, timely, and interesting. First, because the investment environment in China is still regarded as risky and Taiwanese investment is considered unofficial (i.e., lacking a solid legal basis), the rapid growth of Taiwanese DFI poses challenging questions. Second, if the trend is not a short-run but rather a long-term, sustainable phenomenon, it implies an important change in terms of economic interdependence and structural changes in East Asia. This is because Taiwanese DFI in China is occurring partly as a result of structural changes in the Taiwanese economy—one of the most successful Asian NIEs (newly industrializing economies).

The next section provides an overview of Taiwanese investment in China. This chapter will then assess Chinese policy toward Taiwanese capital and investment climates in China compared with Southeast Asia. The assessment focuses on the question of what the best model of DFI in China would be for Taiwanese businessmen. Then, the chapter attempts to verify the arguments in the preceding section through case studies of several foreign companies in China. The next section will discuss the impacts on the economies of both countries of DFI in China. Concluding remarks follow.

Recent Trends in Taiwan Investment in Mainland China

Unlike American and Japanese investment, Taiwanese investment in China has proceeded without government-to-government relations. Facing a wide range of economic, political, and cultural imperatives to attract DFI from Taiwan, China seems to be more than willing to bridge the political and ideological schism with Taiwan through improved economic relations. From China's point of view, Taiwanese DFI provides mid-level technology and management, both of which seem to be more suited to China, than, say, DFI from Japan. Further, Taiwanese capital counterbalances that of Japan and gives China more bargaining power. For political reasons, the Taiwanese government has not been supportive of Taiwan businessmen expanding their economic transactions with China. Although Taiwan's government has tried to impose limitations on trade and investment with China, such limitations are being officially and practically phased out. Numerous Taiwanese firms have set up facilities in China unofficially or used subsidiaries in Hong Kong and other parts of Asia.

Overseas investment by Taiwanese businessmen started with Taiwan's liberalization of its foreign exchange controls in July 1986, which reflected the growing foreign exchange reserves in the economy. Even before this specific measure, Taiwanese businessmen felt the increasing need for overseas investment because of worsening labor shortages, rising wage rates, and continuing appreciation of the New Taiwan dollar.

The Taiwanese economy passed the so-called Lewisian turning point as early as the mid-1960s, and in 1987 about 65 percent of manufacturing firms were experiencing labor shortages (Zhang and Shi 1989). The continuing rise of wage rates has led to a situation in which seeking cheap labor constitutes the primary motivation of Taiwanese overseas investment (Chen 1988, 49).[1] Moreover, because of the cumulating trade surplus, the Taiwanese economy needed an outlet for its foreign exchange surplus in the 1980s, as domestic savings were far greater than domestic investments; in 1988, the savings rate was 34.89 percent, whereas the investment rate was only 23.34 percent (Table 2.2 in Zhang and Shi 1989, 5).

Taiwanese investment in China has been a part of its outward investment surge since 1988, and it grew at the same speed as Taiwanese investment in Southeast Asia. The impetus came when, in 1987, the Taiwanese government gave Taiwanese permission to visit their relatives in China. From China's perspective, Taiwanese capital was more than welcome as the Chinese economy was facing an increasing need for capital for its modernization and reform program, as well as a serious labor surplus in rural areas; in 1983, the average labor surplus rate in mainland China was estimated at 35.02 percent (Gao 1983, 48–49). In other words, a strong economic rationale exists for capital to flow from Taiwan to China to employ mainland labor or for labor migration from China to Taiwan.

Table 10.1 provides aggregate figures for Taiwanese investment in China since 1987. The agreed investment amount was only $100 million in 80 cases in 1987, but by 1989 the amount increased ten times, to about $1 billion. By the end of 1990, the agreed investment amount reached $2 billion, spread over more than 2,000 projects.

Table 10.2 on page 184 shows the regional distribution of Taiwanese investment in China. It shows that more than 90 percent of investment is concentrated in Guangdong and Fujian provinces in the southeastern coastal area, which makes sense considering that three of the four special economic zones (SEZ) designated in 1979 are located in Guangdong,

Table 10.1

Direct Investment Trends by Taiwanese Businessmen in China
(cumulative amounts in U.S.$ million and number of cases)

	1987	1988	1989	1990
Total				
Contract amount	100	600	1,000	over 2,000
Actual amount of investment	N.A.	294	N.A.	N.A.
Number of cases	80	430	N.A.	over 2,000
Fujian Province				
Contract amount	39	115	226	1,182
Actual amount of investment	N.A.	N.A.	N.A.	500
Number of cases	58	230	302	877

Sources: Renmin ribao Overseas Edition, June 25, 1991, and April 25, 1990. Also, Zhang and Shi (1989, 122) and Economic Ministry of ROC on Taiwan (1990, report 4, p. 6).

Note: N.A. means "not available."

and one is in Xiamen in Fujian. Because the Shenzhen SEZ already faces high wage rates, Taiwanese investment is spreading to other coastal regions where wage rates are lower.[2]

For the time being, the Xiamen SEZ will attract a large share of Taiwanese capital. Fujian is the ancestral province of many overseas Chinese, including those in Taiwan; according to Chinese statistics, over 70 percent of the total population in Taiwan is of southern Fujianese origin (Xiamen City 1991, 4). Because of the common dialect and the same cultural background, people from Fujian and Taiwan feel close to one another. Moreover, the investment climate in Xiamen is regarded as better than that in other regions in terms of electricity and industrial water supplies and the quality of labor, owing to the high educational standard of the Xiamen area. In 1990, the SEZ was expanded to cover the whole city area, whereas before it was restricted to Huli Industrial Park. Furthermore, the city government designated Xinlin and Haichang as Special Taiwanese Investment Districts.

In the Xiamen SEZ, 1,034 foreign-funded projects had been approved by April 1991, with a total contractual investment of U.S.$2.997 billion, of which $2.175 billion represents foreign capital (Xiamen City 1991). Out of these, DFI projects with Taiwanese capital constitute 434 cases with a total contractual investment of U.S.$1.099 billion, of which U.S. $1.014 billion comes from Taiwanese businessmen.

Table 10.2

Regional Distribution of Taiwanese Investment in China

Province	Period	Cases	Amount (U.S.$ million)
Total	end 1990	over 2,000	over 2,000
Total	mid-1991		2,500
Guangdong	mid-1991	1,200	N.A.
Shenzhen		530	500 (agreement)
			400 (actual)
Baoan	mid-1991	over 100	over 50
Hainan	mid-1991	35	23.8
Fujian	Jan–Jun 1991	877	1,182 (agreement)
	end 1990		500 (actual)
Dongshan	mid-1991	28	N.A.
	end 1990	N.A.	35
Xiamen	Apr 1991	434	1,099
Shandong			
Qingdao	mid-1991	40	300
Jinan	mid-1991	45	44.8
Yantai	mid-1991	over 40	41.7
Hebei			
Tangshan	mid-1991	22	47
Heilongjiang			
Mudanjiang	Jan–Jul 1991	10	6.5
Liaoning			
Shenyang	mid-1991	18	28
Dalin	mid-1991	65	N.A.
Jilin	mid-1991	100	29
Sichuan	mid-1991	55	N.A.

Source: Renmin ribao, various issues, 1991.

Note: N.A. means "not available."

China's Policies Regarding Taiwanese Capital

In 1983, the PRC government passed its first central-level legislation encouraging Taiwanese businessmen to invest in China. However, since the Taiwanese government did not allow any contact across the Taiwan Strait, the legislation did not have any actual impact. Nevertheless, ever since investment by Taiwanese businessmen began in 1987, much local-level legislation regarding Taiwanese investment has appeared. The specific treatment of Taiwanese capital varied from locality to locality, and, in general, local-level provisions were more generous toward Taiwanese investors than toward other foreign investors. Only with the July 1988 Provisions on Encouraging Investment by Taiwanese Businessmen did the Chinese State Council provide unified policy concerning DFI from Taiwan. However, in this latest central-level provision, there was no great difference between treatment of investors from Taiwan and that of other foreign investors.

In other words, direct investment by Taiwanese businessmen is now subject to the same income tax regulations as that of other foreigners, whereas in the past many local provisions gave preferential treatment to Taiwanese capital. Currently, all types of foreign investment, including Taiwanese capital, are exempted from income taxes for the first two years with positive profits, and their income tax rates are reduced to half the regular rate for the next three years. Thus, only from the fifth year with positive profits do they pay according to the regular 15 percent tax rate.

Regardless of the 1988 change, investment by Taiwanese businessmen receives several unique benefits, although these benefits derive from the fact that the PRC government regards Taiwanese as Chinese citizens. For instance, unlike foreigners, Taiwanese businessmen are allowed to enter the stock market and engage in real estate, are allowed more generous heritage and asset transfer rights, and may appoint their mainland relatives or friends as their legal agents. However, since the Chinese government considers Taiwan's government a local government, investment projects by Taiwanese businessmen cannot enjoy any international or third-party protection in case of legal disputes. In sum, Taiwanese investors in China do not seem to be particularly attracted by specific policy measures by the Chinese government. Rather, they are attracted by the existence of cheap labor, given the same cultural and linguistic background.

However, a survey of Taiwanese businessmen considering overseas investment indicated that the main factors making them hesitant about overseas investment are political instability in host countries, the communication gap associated with language differences, and the lack of supportive infrastructure (Chen 1988, 49). Comparing China with Southeast Asia as an investment site for Taiwanese capital, language difference is not a problem in either area because overseas Chinese are widespread in Southeast Asia; for instance, about 30 percent of the total population in Malaysia are overseas Chinese. Most Taiwanese investment in Southeast Asia is linked with local overseas Chinese. Therefore, whether China can attract Taiwanese capital depends on its attraction power in terms of supporting infrastructure and various economic incentives, such as tax rates and wage rates.

Table 10.3 provides a simple comparison of the investment climates in China and Southeast Asia. China beats Southeast Asian countries only in wage cost. In other aspects, such as material supplies, tax incentives, and soft infrastructure, Malaysia, Thailand, and Indonesia are perceived as better, except that China is more generous in allowing dominant foreign ownership, up to 100 percent.

As has been pointed out by many studies, the investment climate in China suffers from several problems (see Chapter 7). One is unreliable input supplies associated with uncertainty in production schedules; a second is restricted convertibility of the renminbi into foreign currency, which often causes difficulties in balancing foreign exchange supply and demand for foreign companies in China. A third problem is conflict with Chinese partners.

The above considerations suggest that the most suitable form of Taiwanese investment in China would be export-oriented processing arrangements or wholly foreign-owned investments combining foreign-imported inputs with cheap local labor. This type of investment avoids possible conflict with Chinese partners, does not have to rely on Chinese inputs, and is less hampered by foreign exchange restrictions. The next section offers case studies of several foreign companies in China to test this argument.

Typical Models of Taiwanese Investment in China

Relying on case studies and field work, this section investigates Taiwanese DFI in China, including two wholly Taiwanese-owned compa-

Table 10.3

Investment Climate in China and Southeast Asia (from best to worst)

Supply of energy and other inputs
(1)   Malaysia
(2)   Thailand
(3)   Philippines, Indonesia, and China (Guangdong)

Labor costs
(1)   Export processing in China's coastal areas
(2)   Philippines
(3)   Malaysia
(4)   Non-SEZ areas in China
(5)   Thailand
(6)   Indonesia
(7)   SEZs in China

Preferential treatments in tax holidays and rates
(1)   Thailand
(2)   Malaysia, Indonesia
(3)   China
(4)   Philippines

Financial institutions and credit availability
(1)   Thailand
(2)   Indonesia
(3)   Malaysia
(4)   Philippines, China

Investment-related legislation and its enforcement
(1)   Thailand
(2)   Malaysia
(3)   Indonesia
(4)   Philippines
(5)   China

Source: Zhang and Shi (1989, 81).

nies and one wholly South Korean–owned company in the Xiamen SEZ and one South Korean–Chinese joint venture in Beijing.[3] I visited these companies as a part of extensive interview work in China during November 1991.

The first of the four sample companies is the Xiamen Guishi Industrial Company, Ltd. (hereafter, XGC), in Xiamen, which is wholly owned by its parent company in Taiwan, the Taiwan Pureone Development Company. XGC produces kitchenware for export to world markets. The second company is the Xiamen Foda Industrial Company, Ltd. (hereafter, XFC), which is located in the Xinlin Taiwan Investment Zone in Xiamen and is also wholly owned by Taiwanese capital. XFC produces plastic goods, including plastic carrying bags, for export. The wholly South Korean–owned company I visited is the Jinwoong China Company, Ltd. (hereafter, JCC), which is located in the Huli Industrial Park (the original Xiamen SEZ) in Xiamen. JCC produces tents for export. Last, the South Korean–Chinese joint venture is called the Beijing King-Luck Enterprise Company, Ltd. (hereafter, BKLC), in the city of Beijing, which is a 50–50 joint venture between the Lucky-Goldstar Business Group in South Korea and the Beijing Xuehua Electrical Appliance Corporation (40 percent) and China National Electronics Import and Export Corporation (10 percent). BKLC produces stuffed toys for export. Although two of the case study companies are South Korean companies, the nature of their business is the same as that of the Taiwanese companies in that all engage in labor-intensive production.

Investigation of these cases shows that there are good reasons why DFI in China should be wholly foreign owned, and that this is a recent trend. As indicated in Chapter 7 of this volume, one cause for the trend toward wholly foreign ownership has been that Chinese domestic funds are insufficient to match foreign funds in joint venture investments. However, more important, the recent increase of wholly foreign-owned DFI is also because foreign investors prefer 100 percent ownership. In the case of joint ventures, the most serious problem was conflicting opinion between foreign and Chinese partners in management matters.

The Taiwan Pureone Development Company, the parent company of XGC, used to run a joint venture with a Chinese partner. However, after one year of uneasy relations, Taiwan Pureone broke up with the Chinese partner and set up XGC as a separate company with 100 percent ownership. The top foreign management of BKLC also complained that middle-level Chinese managers were not cooperating with foreign managerial initiatives, unlike rank-and-file workers. Middle-level Chinese managers are dispatched from the Chinese parent company, and are not under the control of the foreign management. Since they are accustomed to the old, socialist-style company management, they are less willing to adjust themselves to new management styles.

While the managers in BKLC complained that productivity of local Chinese workers was only about 65–70 percent of workers in South Korea, the wholly foreign-owned XGC, XFC, and JCC in Xiamen indicate that productivity of Chinese workers can be as high as, or even higher than, their counterparts in Taiwan or South Korea. This high productivity, at the wage rates of about one-fifth of those in South Korea or Taiwan, allows these companies to maintain stable profits. Since direct production has low profitability, BKLC in Beijing now has to produce more and more of its output through subcontracting arrangements with local Chinese factories. Because in this arrangement the foreign side provides intermediate materials to Chinese subcontractors and pays processing fees only for qualified final products, the foreign side need not worry about supervisory management and possible conflict with the Chinese partners as in joint ventures.

All these examples suggest that 100 percent foreign ownership or export processing is the best model for Taiwanese investment in China, and that has been the actual trend. By April 1991, U.S.$1.099 billion worth of Taiwanese investment projects, including both joint venture and wholly foreign ownership, had been approved (Xiamen City 1991, 6). Out of the $1.099 billion, contributions by Taiwanese businessmen amounted to $1.014 billion. In other words, in those Taiwanese-capital–related investment projects, little mainland capital was involved, since the absolute majority of invested capital is from Taiwanese businessmen in the form of 100 percent foreign ownership. Moreover, in the case of South Korean DFI in China, wholly South Korean–owned DFI is increasing relative to South Korean–Chinese joint ventures (*Han-kuk il-bo*, December 12, 1991). As of June 1991, 100 percent South Korean–owned DFI cases numbered 108, with investments amounting to $112 million, whereas joint venture DFI cases numbered only 71, with investments amounting to $670 million (*Han-kuk il-bo*, December 14, 1991).

In the case of wholly foreign ownership, one possible disadvantage would be the lack of a Chinese partner who could deal with various state authorities and other Chinese companies in facilitating stable supplies of raw materials, energy, water, and other inputs; taxes and various administrative fee matters; and customs clearance and related transportation matters. Especially for those firms with substantial reliance on Chinese domestic human and physical resources for their business, having a Chinese partner can be critical. However, most Taiwanese companies in China import almost all of their intermediate inputs from Taiwan and other foreign countries because Chinese products are either not available or unreliable in terms of quality and delivery schedule. In other words, 100 percent foreign ownership should be combined with 100 percent importation of intermediate inputs or with self-production of inputs within China.

In general, the importance of Chinese partners in DFI in China seems to be declining. Above all, over the last decade, the investment climate in China has been improving in many respects.[4] This is especially so when foreign companies are located in the SEZs or other specially designated industrial parks, where physical and legal infrastructure are much better.

Profitable Taiwanese DFI projects on the mainland should not require the presence of many foreign managers or skilled laborers, and they should involve production processes based on simple technology. The living costs for foreigners are extremely high. For instance, apartment rents for foreigners in mainland China are often two to three times as expensive as in the United States. Especially in Beijing, foreign businessmen pay about $4,000 in monthly rent for two-bedroom apartments. In the case of BKLC, these rents are paid by the parent firm in Seoul. If these rents costs were included as costs of the BKLC joint venture, its losses would be greater.

All four companies I visited in China are operated by only a few foreigners. The two wholly Taiwanese-owned companies in Xiamen have only one factory director or manager from Taiwan resident in the companies, although the total employment size is about 120 in XGC and 450 in XFC. In other words, the factories are run well by local Chinese managers under the supervision of the top Taiwanese management. In the case of XFC, the deputy general manager is a local Chinese (the highest position attainable by a local Chinese). My impression during his interview was that he was fully in charge of management matters in the factory. In the case of XGC, the general manager is Taiwanese, but he stays mostly in Taipei or Hong Kong. The only resident Taiwanese was the factory director. The highest position for local Chinese there was assistant manager, a position that seems to have broad management responsibilities.

Another condition for successful DFI in China is high export share in product marketing because of restrictions on foreign exchange. If companies have heavy domestic sales, they will have difficulty converting their sales receipts from Chinese renminbi to foreign currency to pay for import bills. Although recently there has been expansion of "foreign exchange centers" around the country, they are insufficient to meet the demands of foreign businessmen in China. Both XFC and XGC export almost 100 percent of their products.

In sum, successful Taiwanese DFI in China should be able to transform local cheap labor into high productivity, and, for this purpose, foreign management should be able to exercise fully its managerial initiatives and supervise Chinese workers, which implies the necessity of 100 percent ownership. Alternatively, export-processing arrangements would be suitable since they avoid direct involvement in management and supervision matters and are based on simpler relationships with Chinese partners.

Impacts on the Taiwanese and Chinese Economies

Typical Taiwanese investment in China currently takes the form of export processing or wholly foreign ownership in labor-intensive production for export. This pattern is similar to previous Japanese investment in export-processing zones in South Korea and Taiwan, when they were well endowed with cheap labor. The main benefits to the Chinese economy are employment creation, foreign exchange earnings as processing fees or wages, and worker training under foreign management. However, the technology transfer effect is limited, especially in the case of wholly foreign-owned DFI, although encouragement of high-tech–oriented DFI, rather than simple labor-intensive production, is high on the policy agenda in China.

If foreign companies that import intermediate inputs for processing in China move their input-producing factories to China, China can expect more technology transfer than it can from labor-intensive production. For example, in 1991, JCC in Xiamen initiated construction of a factory in Xiamen that will locally produce intermediate materials for tents. This company used to import all tent materials from South Korea and combined Chinese labor with South Korean–imported tent material to produce tents as final products for export. The construction of a tent material production factory in China means the complete relocation of all production processes from South Korea to China.

As this example indicates, with the intermediate input production factory in China, foreign companies can save on the cost of transporting intermediate materials. Although saving transportation costs is an obvious incentive for most foreign companies, it is too early to say whether actual relocation of intermediate material production factories to China will become a trend. Greater uncertainty exists with this type of DFI than with simple processing DFI, because the production process will entail higher technical complexities, more skilled laborers will be needed, and the factory relocation itself may cost more.

From the point of view of the Taiwanese economy, there is an important difference between processing-type DFI and relocation of intermediate input production factories to a foreign country. Processing-type DFI is a form of intrafirm international division of labor, which means relocation of only a part of the production process to a foreign country. However, relocation of factories producing intermediate inputs touches on the more sensitive issue of deindustrialization and the erosion of the industrial base of the Taiwanese economy. So long as outward DFI is based on intrafirm international subcontracting, the Taiwanese economy loses only a relatively small number of jobs for simple labor.[5] Since Taiwan is facing a shortage of simple labor, this can be considered good. The Taiwanese economy also benefits from relocating those production processes that have lost international competitiveness because of rising wage rates.[6] The machines used in these production processes would become useless if they stayed in Taiwan. However, transported to China and combined with cheap labor there, they continue to produce goods that are internationally competitive. Furthermore, since Taiwanese-owned processing factories in China import intermediate materials from Taiwan, it generates Taiwanese exports to the mainland. According to one estimate, this export creation effect of Taiwanese DFI in China amounted to about 17.4 percent ($398.66 million) of total Taiwanese exports ($2.240 billion) to the mainland in 1988 (Zhang and Shi 1989, 106).

Conclusion

The flow of capital investment into China has brought technology, capital, managerial and marketing know-how, employment creation, and trade growth, and thus eventually it can lead to changes in the comparative advantages of China's industries. Yet outward direct foreign investment from Taiwan also facilitates structural adjustment in Taiwan's economy, which is demanded by changing domestic and international economic conditions (e.g., loss of competitiveness of labor-intensive industries in Taiwan because of the increase in domestic labor costs and the emergence of new producers in other regions with cheaper labor).

Given the current investment climate in China, investment by Taiwanese businessmen will continue to take the form of wholly foreign ownership in labor-intensive, simple processing-type production for export with imported inputs. In this case, the technology transfer effect will be limited. Although some recent investment projects seem to include relocation of factories producing intermediate materials and some capital-intensive production lines (*Renmin ribao*, July 26, 1991), the future of this type of new investment is still uncertain. The Chinese government should try to improve the investment climate further so that it is more suitable for capital-intensive DFI projects. However, such improvement does not seem to be achievable in a short period of time, since it has to do with the level of overall economic development in China.

Notes

1. According to a survey in Chen (1988), the largest number of Taiwanese firms (21.3 percent of the sample) indicated that seeking cheap labor was the main reason for overseas investment. The second most important reason (17.3 percent) was marketing, and the third (12.1 percent) was to avoid foreign exchange losses associated with appreciation of the NT dollar.

2. According to Dao (1988, 164), average labor costs in different regions were as follows in 1986–87: If we take that of Hong Kong as 100, average labor costs in assembly subcontracting are 17 in Guangdong, 56 in joint ventures in Shenzhen, 46 in joint ventures in Beijing, and 73 in Taiwan.

3. For a survey analysis of a larger sample of Taiwanese investment in China, se Yan and Li (1990) (the survey is limited to the shoe-making industry).

4. See UNCTC (1988).

5. Zhang and Shi (1989) estimated that there would be a loss of 27 to 31.5 jobs for each million dollars invested outward.

6. On the related theoretical literature on structural adjustment and outward DFI, see Chung Lee (1990b) and Kojima (1973).

Bibliography

Amsden, Alice. 1989. *Asia's Next Giant: South Korea and Late Industrialization.* Oxford: Oxford University Press.

Andreff, Wladimir. 1989. "Economic Reforms in North Korea and Viet Nam." *Seoul Journal of Economics* 2, no. 1:87–107.

Aoki, Masahiko. 1984. *The Cooperative Game Theory of the Firm.* Oxford: Oxford University Press.

———. 1987. "The Japanese Firms in Transition." In *The Political Economy of Japan*, ed. Kozo Yamamura and Yasukichi Yasuda. Stanford: Stanford University Press.

———. 1990. "Toward an Economic Model of the Japanese Firm." *Journal of Economic Literature* 28:1–27, March.

Atta, Don V. 1990. "Full Scale, Like Collectivization, But Without Collectivization's Excesses: The Campaign to Introduce the Family and Lease Contract in Soviet Agriculture." *Comparative Economic Studies* 32, no. 2:109–43.

Bachman, D. 1987. "Implementing Chinese Tax Policy." In *Policy Implementation in Post-Mao China*, ed. D. Lampton. Berkeley: University of California Press.

Balassa, Bella. 1974. "Trade Creation and Trade Diversion in the European Common Market: An Appraisal of the Evidence." *Manchester School of Economic and Social Studies* 2:93–135.

———. 1965. "Trade Liberalization and Revealed Comparative Advantage." *Manchester School of Economic and Social Studies* 2:99–124.

Bank of Korea. 1990. *Yearly Statistics of Overseas Investment 1990* (in Korean). Seoul: Bank of Korea.

Bayard, T., J. Orr, et al. 1982. "US-PRC Trade Normalization: Effects on US Imports and Employment." In *China under the Four Modernizations, part 2*, ed. U.S. Congress, Joint Economic Committee. Washington, D.C.: GPO.

Berglof, Erik. 1989. "Capital Structure as a Mechanism of Control—A Comparison of Financial Systems." In *The Firm as a Nexus of Treaties*, ed. Masahiko Aoki, Bo Gustafsson, and Oliver E. Williamson, 237–62. London: Sage Publications.

Brun, Ellen, and Jacques Hersh. 1976. *Socialist Korea: A Case Study in the Strategy of Economic Development*. New York: Monthly Review Press.

Byrd, William. 1990. "Rural Industrialization and Ownership in China." *Comparative Economic Studies* 32, no. 1:73–107.

Byrd, William, and Gene Tidrick. 1987. "Factor Allocations and Enterprise Incentives." In *China's Industrial Reforms*, ed. G. Tidrick and J. Chen. New York: Oxford University Press for the World Bank.

Central Intelligence Agency. 1991. "The Chinese Economy in 1990 and 1991; Uncertain Recovery." Mimeo.

Chandler, Alfred D. 1962. *Strategy and Structure*. Cambridge, MA: MIT Press.

———. 1977. *The Visible Hand: The Managerial Revolution in American Business*. Cambridge: Harvard University Press.

Chen, An-Sing, and Keun Lee. 1991. "Competitive Advantages and Inward and Outward Direct Foreign Investment in Taiwan." Working Paper, East-West Center.

Chen, Chun-shun. 1990. "Economic Development and Foreign Direct Investment of Taiwan" (in Japanese). In Taniguchi, ed., 1990.

Chen, Tain-Jy. 1988. *Industrial Policy Related to Overseas Investment* (in Chinese). Taipei: Chunghua Institution for Economic Research.

Cheung, Steven N. S. 1986. "China in Transition: Where Is She Heading Now?" *Contemporary Policy Issues* 4 (October):1–11.

China News Analysis. 1989a. "Rural Enterprises in China: Too Many, Too Soon." No. 1380, March 1.

———. 1989b. "The Privately Run Enterprises." No. 1382, April 1.

Choi, Won-Cheol. 1989. "A Thorough Carrying Out of the Dae-an Model and the Independent Accounting System Is a Basic Requisite for the Improvement of Enterprise Management." *Kulloja* (in Korean) 4:6–10.

Christoffersen, Gaye. 1986. "China's Petroleum Export Strategies." Draft paper prepared for China Energy Study, Asian Energy Security Project, Resource Systems Institute, East-West Center, Honolulu, September.

Chung, Joseph S. 1983. "North Korean Industrial Policy and Trade." In *North Korea Today: Strategic and Domestic Issues*, ed. R. Scalapino and J. Kim. Berkeley: Institute of East Asian Studies, University of California.

Colander, David, ed. 1984. *Neo-Classical Political Economy*. Cambridge: Ballinger.

Dao, Tanqing. 1988. *Investment Climate in Mainland China* (in Chinese). Taipei: Shuquan Chubanshe.

Delfs, R. 1989. "Jiangsu's Dynamic Rural Industry Comes under Attack." *Far Eastern Economic Review*, September 14.

Dunning, John H. 1981. *International Production and the Multinational Enterprise*. London: Allen & Unwin.

———. 1988. *Explaining International Production*. London: Unwin Hyman.

Eads, G., and K. Yamamura. 1987. "The Future of Industrial Policy." In *The Political Economy of Japan, vol. 1: The Domestic Transformation*, ed. K. Yamamura and Y. Yasuba. Stanford: Stanford University Press.

Ebashi, Masahiko, and Masaharu Hishida. 1986. "China's Open Door Policy and Its Implication for Asia-Pacific Countries toward the Year 2000." Paper presented at the Beijing Conference on the Asia-Pacific Economy toward the Year 2000.

Economic Dictionary (in Korean). 1985. Pyongyang: Social Science Press.

Economic Ministry of ROC on Taiwan. 1990. *A Research Report on the Investment Climate in Mainland China.* Taipei: Economic Ministry of the ROC.

Ericson, Richard E. 1988. "The New Enterprise Law." *Harriman Institute Forum* 1, no. 2:1–8.

Feige, Edgar L. 1990. "Perestroika and Socialist Privatization: What Is to Be Done? And How." *Comparative Economic Studies* 32, no. 3:1–54.

Finger, J. M., and M. E. Kreinin. 1979. "A Measure of Export Similarity and Its Possible Uses." *Economic Journal* (December): 905–11.

Gao, Zhang. 1983. *An Estimation of Rural Surplus Labor in Mainland China* (in Chinese). Taipei: Chunghua Institution for Economic Research.

Gregory, Paul R. 1989. "The Soviet Bureaucracy and Perestroika." *Comparative Economic Studies* 31, no. 1:1–13.

———. 1990. *Restructuring the Soviet Economic Bureaucracy.* Cambridge: Cambridge University Press.

Grossman, Gregory. 1990. "Sub-rosa Privatization and Marketization in the USSR." *The Annals of the American Academy of Political and Social Science* 507 (January):44–52.

Gu, Renzhang. 1988. "Dangqian jiankang fazhan qiye jiduande jige wenti" (Several contemporary problems in how to develop enterprise groups in a healthy manner). *Jingji guanli* 1:24–27.

Hadley, E. 1970. *Antitrust in Japan.* Princeton: Princeton University Press.

Haggard, S. 1990. *Pathways from the Periphery: The Politics of Growth in the NICs.* Ithaca and London: Cornell University Press.

Han-kuk il-bo (Korean daily), December 10 and 14, 1991.

Hanson, Philip. 1988. "The Draft Law on Cooperatives: An Assessment." *Radio Liberty Research* RL 111/88, March 15.

———. 1990a. "Ownership Issues in Perestroika." In *Socialism, Perestroika, and the Dilemmas of Soviet Economic Reform*, ed. John E. Tedstrom. Boulder, CO: Westview Press.

———. 1990b. "Property Rights in the New Phase of Reforms." *Soviet Economy* 6, no. 2:95–124.

Hattori, Tamio. 1989. "Japanese Zaibatsu and Korean Chaebol." In *Korean Managerial Dynamics*, ed. Kae H. Chung and Hak Chong Lee. New York: Praeger.

Hewett, Ed A. 1988. *Reforming the Soviet Economy: Equality versus Efficiency.* Washington, D.C.: Brookings Institution.

Ho, Samuel. 1978. *Economic Development of Taiwan 1860–1970.* New Haven: Yale University Press.

Hofheinz, R., and K. Calder. 1982. *The Eastasia Edge.* New York: Basic Books.

Hong, Sung-Woong. 1990. "Korean Direct Foreign Investment in South-East Asia and China: Perspective and Prospect." Paper presented at the Workshop on Regional Development in the Yellow Sea Rim, Beijing, China, July.

Hyun, Myung-Han. 1989. "Several Problems Regarding the Uses of Circulating Capital" (in Korean). *Kulloja* 4:30–33.

Ignatius, A., and A. Bennett. 1989. "China's Economic Woes Pose Risk of New Unrest." *Asian Wall Street Journal*, August 7.

Institute of Developing Economies (IDE). 1986. "Provision on the Independent Accounting System in State Enterprises." In *Literature Collection on New Economic Trends in DPR Korea* (in Japanese), ed. IDE, 7–32, March.

International Monetary Fund (IMF). 1989. *Direction of Trade Statistics Yearbook.* New York: United Nations.

International Monetary Fund, World Bank, OECD, and IBRD. 1991. *A Study of the Soviet Economy,* 3 vols. Paris: Author.

Ioffe, Olimpiad S. 1989. *Gorbachev's Economic Dilemma: An Insider's View.* St. Paul: Merrill/Magnus Publishing Co.

James, William, and Rodney Young. 1987. "Can China Succeed in Economic Modernization through the Open Door." Working paper, East-West Center.

Japan Times. 1986. "China Ready to Apply for GATT Membership," July 10, p. 1.

Jo, Sung-Hwan. 1981. "Overseas Direct Investment by South Korean Firms: Direction and Pattern." In K. Kumar and M. McLeod, eds. 1981.

Johnson, Chalmers. 1982. *MITI and the Japanese Miracle.* Stanford: Stanford University Press.

———. 1987. "Political Institutions and Economic Performance: The Government-Business Relationship in Japan, South Korea, and Taiwan." In *The Political Economy of the New Asian Industrialism,* ed. F. Deyo. Ithaca and London: Cornell University Press.

Jones, Anthony, and William Moskoff. 1989. "New Cooperatives in the USSR." *Problems of Communism* 38 (November/December):27–39.

Jones, L., and I. Sakong. 1980. *Government, Business, and Entrepreneurship in Economic Development: The Korean Case.* Cambridge, MA: Harvard University Press.

Jun, Yongwook. 1987. "The Reverse Direct Investment: The Case of Korean Consumer Electronics Industry." *International Economic Journal* 1, no. 3:91–104.

Kang, Myoung-Kyu. 1987. "Industrial Management and Reforms in North Korea." Paper presented as the Conference on Economic System and Reforms in a Changing World. Seoul: Institute of Social Sciences, Seoul National University.

———. 1989. "Industrial Management and Reforms in North Korea." In *Economic Reforms in the Socialist World,* ed. S. Gomulka, Y. Ha, and C. Kim. London: Macmillan.

Kang, Myoung-Kyu, and Joon-Koo Lee. 1990. "Economic Consequences of National Division in Korea." In *Korea and Germany: Lessons in Division,* ed. M. Kang and H. Wagner. Seoul: Seoul National University Press.

Kang, Myoung-Kyu, and Keun Lee. 1992. "Industrial System and Reform in North Korea: A Comparison with the Case of China." World Development 20, no. 7: 947–58.

Kasai, Nobuyuki. 1990. "Korean Foreign Direct Investment to Southeast Asia" (in Japanese). In Taniguchi, ed., 1990.

Kim, Chul-Sik. 1986. "The Associated Enterprise in Our Country Is a New Form of the Socialist Enterprise Organization" (in Korean). *Kulloja* 2:70–76.

Kim, Eun Mee. 1988. "From Dominance to Symbiosis: State and Chaebol in Korea." *Pacific Focus* 3 (Fall):105–12.

Kim, Kwang-Jeon. 1990. "On the Industrial Management System in the DPR Korea." Paper presented at the Third International Conference on Korean Studies. Osaka: Osaka Law and Economics University.

Kim, Sookon. 1990. "Labor Management Relations: Past, Present, and Future." Paper presented at a workshop on Comparative Analysis of Development Policies in China, Japan, and Korea, Seoul, Korea, May.

Kim, Won Bae. 1990. "Scenarios for the Yellow Sea Region." Mimeo, East-West Center, Honolulu, Hawaii.

Kim, Ung-Ki. 1988. *Structure of Enterprise Ownership and Development of Capital Markets* (in Korean). Seoul: KIS Research Monograph Series.

Kiyonari, Todao, and Hideichiro Nakamura. 1980. "The Establishment of the Big Business System." In *Industry and Business in Japan*, ed. K. Sato. Armonk, NY: M. E. Sharpe.

Kojima, Kiyoshi. 1973. "A Macroeconomic Approach to Foreign Direct Investment." *Hitotsubashi Journal of Economics*, 1–21.

———. 1978. *Direct Foreign Investment: A Japanese Model of Multinational Business*. New York: Praeger.

Kojima, Reiitsu. 1987. "Economic Reforms and the Open Door Policy in China." In *Development Strategies and Productivity Issues in Asia*, ed. S. Ichimura. Tokyo: Asian Productivity Organization.

Komiya, Ryutaro. 1980. "Monopoly Capital and Income Redistribution Policy." In *Industry and Business in Japan*, ed. K. Sato. Armonk, NY: M.E. Sharpe.

———. 1987. "Japanese Firms, Chinese Firms: Problems for Economic Reform in China, part 1." *Journal of Japanese and International Economies* 1, no. 1:31–61.

Korea Labor Institute (KLI). 1990. *Survey Study on the Employee's Opinion about Labor-related Issues and Industrial Relations* (in Korean). Seoul: Author.

Kornai, Janos. 1986. "The Soft Budget Constraint." *Kyklos* 39, no. 1:3–30.

———. 1987. "The Dual Dependence of the State-Owned Firm in Hungary." In *China's Industrial Reform*, ed. G. Tidrick and J. Chen. New York: Oxford University Press for the World Bank.

Kumar, Krishna, and Maxwell McLeod. 1981. *Multinationals from Developing Countries*. Lexington, MA: Lexington Books.

Kwon, Jene K. 1987. "The Korea–China Trade: Its Potential and Prospects." Paper presented at the 16th Pacific Science Congress, Seoul, Korea, August.

Lall, Sanjaya. 1983. *The New Multinationals: The Spread of Third World Enterprises*. New York: John Wiley & Sons.

———. 1990. "Emerging Sources of FDI in Asia and the Pacific." Paper presented at the Roundtable on Foreign Direct Investment in Asia and the Pacific in the 1990s. Honolulu: East-West Center.

Lange, Oskar. 1964. *On the Economic Theory of Socialism*. New York: McGraw-Hill.

Lee, Chon Pyo, and Sang Woo Park. 1989–90. "On the Trade Structure of the Korean Economy with Reference to the Coastal Development in the Yellow Sea Rim." Paper presented at the China–Korea Workshop in Qingdao.

Lee, Chung H. 1980. "United States and Japanese Direct Investment in Korea: A Comparative Study." *Hitotsubashi Journal of Economics* 20.

———. 1990a. "Direct Foreign Investment, Structural Adjustment, and International Division of Labor: A Dynamic Macroeconomic Theory of Direct Foreign Investment." *Hitotsubashi Journal of Economics* (December).

———. 1990b. "Outward Direct Foreign Investment and Structural Adjustment in a Small Open Economy." *Kobe Economic & Business Review* 36:1–15.

———. 1992. "The Government and Financial System in the Economic Development of Korea." *World Development* 20.

Lee, Chung H., and Keun Lee. 1991. "A Transition Economy and Outward Direct Foreign Investment: The Case of Korea." Paper presented at the APO-EWC Seminar on the Role of Foreign Investment in Development, Seoul, September 16–20.

Lee, Chung, and Ippei Yamazawa, eds. 1990. *Economic Development in Japan and Korea: A Parallel with Lessons.* New York: Praeger.

Lee, Hong Yung. 1991. *From Revolutionary Cadre to Party Bureaucrats in China.* Berkeley: University of California Press.

Lee, Hy-Sang. 1990. "North Korea's August Third Program: The Hidden Reform." Proceedings of the Fourth International Conference of Korean Economists. Seoul: Korean Economics Association, pp. 1849–79.

Lee, Keun. 1990. "Chinese Model of the Socialist Enterprise: An Assessment of Its Organization and Performance." *Journal of Comparative Economics* 14, no. 3 (September): 384–400.

———. 1991. *Chinese Firms and the State in Transition: Property Rights and Agency Problems in the Reform Era.* Armonk, NY: M. E. Sharpe.

Lee, Keun, and Chung H. Lee. 1990a. "Problems and Profitability of Direct Foreign Investment in China." *Journal of Northeast Asian Studies* 9, no. 4 (Winter):36–52.

———. 1990b. "Trade between Korea and China and Its Bohai Region: An International Perspective." *Journal of Northeast Asian Studies* 9, no. 4 (Winter):15–35.

———. 1992. "Sustaining Economic Development in Korea: Lessons from Japan." *Pacific Review* 5, no. 1:13–24.

Lee, Keun, and Hong Yung Lee. 1992. "States, Markets and Economic Development in East Asian Capitalism and Socialism." *Development Policy Review* 10, no. 2:107–30.

Lee, Keun, and William James. 1991. "External Shocks, Economic Reform, and Foreign Trade Behavior of the USSR, China, and Hungary." *Economics of Planning* 24, no. 2:65–91.

Lee, Keun, and Shelley Mark. 1989. "Socialist Egalitarianism and the Agency Problems in China's Economic Reform." *Seoul Journal of Economics* 2, no. 4:383–401.

———. 1990. "China's Economy under Decentralization and Recentralization: Past Lessons and Prospects toward 2000." UNDP Symposium on Economic Cooperation in Asia and the Pacific, East-West Center, Honolulu, Hawaii, May.

———. 1991. "Privatization in China's Industry." *China Economic Review* 2, no. 2:159–73.

Lee, Keun, and Michael Plummer. 1991. "Competitive Advantages, Two-Way Foreign Investment, and Capital Accumulation in Korea: A Simple Theory and Its Application." *Asian Economic Journal* 4, no. 2 (July): 93–114.

Lee, Kyung Tae. 1991. "Policy Measures to Reduce Industrial Concentration and Concentration of Economic Power." In *Economic Development in the Republic of Korea: A Policy Perspective,* ed. L. Cho and Y. Kim. Honolulu: University of Hawaii Press for the East-West Center.

Lee, Pong S. 1987. "Interaction of Economic Reform and Political Goal: A Case of North Korea." Paper presented at the Conference on Economic System and Reforms in a Changing World. Seoul: Institute of Social Sciences, Seoul National University.

Lee, Sang-Sul. 1986. "Carrying Out the Dae-an Model and the Associated Enterprises" (in Korean). *Kulloja* 7:46–56.

Lee, Young Ki. 1990. "Conglomeration and Business Concentration in Korea." In *Korean Economic Development*, ed. J. Kwon. New York: Greenwood Press.

Li Mianchu et al. 1990. "Getidahu he siyingqiyede wupa" (Five worries of large individual and private enterprise). *Zhongguo jingji tizhi gaige* 2:49.

Lim, Hyun-jin. 1985. *Dependent Development in Korea, 1963–1979.* Seoul: Seoul National University Press.

Lim, Ungki. 1988. *Structure of Enterprise Ownership and Development of Capital Markets* (in Korean). Seoul: KIS Research Monograph Series.

Lim, Young-il. 1981. *Government Policy and Private Enterprise: Korean Experience in Industrialization.* Korean Research Monograph No. 6. Berkeley: Institute of East Asian Studies, University of California.

Liu, Jipeng, and Yuanzhi Hu. 1988. "Cong lianheti dao gufenzhi jiduan" (From an associated system to a shareholding group). *Jingji guanli* 1:11–14.

Lindblom, C. 1977. *Politics and Market.* New York: Basic Books.

Livingston, J., J. Moores, and F. Oldfather, eds. 1973. *Imperial Japan, 1800–1945.* New York: Pantheon.

Lockett, Martin. 1988. "The Urban Collective Economy." In *Transforming China's Economy in the Eighties*, vol. 2, ed. S. Feuchtwang, A. Hussain, and T. Pairault. Boulder, CO: Westview Press.

Ma Jisen. 1988. "A General Survey of the Resurgence of the Private Sector of China's Economy." *Social Sciences in China* (Autumn): 78–92.

Mardon, R. 1990. "The State and the Effective Control of Foreign Capital: The Case of South Korea." *World Politics* 43, no. 1:111–38.

Merrill, John. 1989. "North Korea's Economy Today: The Limits of Juche." Paper presented at the Fourth Korea–US Conference on North Korea, Seoul, August.

MOFERT (Ministry of Foreign Economic Relations and Trade). Various years. *Zhongguo duiwai jingii maoyi nianjian* (Almanac of foreign economic relations and trade), Beijing: MOFERT.

Moskowitz, Karl. 1989. "Ownership and Management of Korean Firms." In *Korean Managerial Dynamics*, ed. Kae H. Chung and Hak Chong Lee. New York: Praeger.

Myrdal, Gunnar. 1968. *Asian Drama: An Inquiry into the Poverty of Nations.* New York: Pantheon.

Naughton, Barry. 1986. "Finance and Planning Reforms in Industry." In *China's Economy Looks toward the Year 2000*, Vol. 1, ed. U.S. Congress, Joint Economic Committee. Washington, D.C.: GPO.

New York Times. 1991. "Soviets Vote to End State Monopoly," July 2.

Odgaard, Ole. 1988. "The Success of Rural Enterprise in China: Some Notes on its Social and Economic Effects." *China Information* 3, no. 2:63–76.

Olson, Moncur. 1982. *The Rise and Decline of Nations.* New Haven: Yale University Press.

Organization for Economic Cooperation and Development (OECD). 1989. *Financing and External Debt of Developing Countries: 1988 Survey.* Paris: Author.

Park, Young-chul. 1990. "Development Lessons from Asia: The Role of Government in South Korea and Taiwan." *American Economic Review* 80, no. 2:118–21.

Perry, Elizabeth, and Christine Wong, eds. 1985. *The Political Economy of Re-*

form in Post-Mao China. Cambridge, MA: Council of East Asian Studies, Harvard University.

Ramstetter, Eric, and Michael G. Plummer. 1990. "Motives and Policies Affecting U.S. Direct Investment in ASEAN." *Asian Economic Journal* (September).

Renmin ribao (People's daily). Overseas Edition, various dates in 1989, 1990, and 1991.

Reynolds, Bruce. 1987. *Reform in China: Challenges and Choices.* Armonk, NY: M. E. Sharpe.

Schroeder, Gertrude. 1991. "Perestroyka in the Aftermath of 1990." *Soviet Economy* 7, no. 1:3–13.

Shen, Xiaofang. 1990. "A Decade of Direct Foreign Investment in China." *Problems of Communism* 39, no. 2:61–74.

Srinivasan, T. N. 1985. "Neoclassical Political Economy, the State and Economic Development." *Asian Development Review* 3, no. 2:38–58.

State Council of China. 1988. *Zhongguo 1985 nian Gongye Pucha Ziliao* (1985 Industry census of China). Beijing: China Statistics Press.

State Statistical Bureau (SSB) of China. 1989 and various years. *Zhongguo Tongji Nianjian* (Statistical yearbook of China). Beijing: State Statistical Press.

Steers, Richard, Yoo Keun Shin, and Gerardo Ungson. 1989. *The Chaebol: Korea's New Industrial Might.* New York: Harper & Row.

Suh, Seung-Hwan. 1986. "Bonuses and Their Nature" (in Korean). *Kulloja* 3:43–47.

Taniguchi, Koji, ed. 1990. *Taiwan, Kankoku no kaigai tosi no tenkai* (Development of Taiwanese and Korean overseas investment). Tokyo: Institute of Developing Economies.

Tedstrom, John E., ed. 1990. "The Reemergence of Soviet Cooperatives." In *Socialism, Perestroika, and the Dilemmas of Soviet Economic Reform.* Boulder, CO: Westview Press.

Tedstrom, John, and Philip Hanson. 1989. "Supreme Soviet Issues Decree on Leasing." *Report on the USSR* 17:17.

Tidrick, Gene. 1987. "Planning and Supply." In Tidrick and Chen, eds., 1987.

Tidrick, Gene, and Jiyuan Chen, eds. 1987. *China's Industrial Reform.* New York: Oxford University Press for the World Bank.

Toshio, Sumiya. 1989. "The Structure and Operation of Monopoly Capital in Japan." In *Japanese Capitalism since 1945*, ed. T. Morris-Suzuki and T. Seiyama. Armonk, NY: M. E. Sharpe.

Tsou, T. 1986. "Reflections on the Formation and Foundation of the Communist Party-State in China." In *The Cultural Revolution*, ed. Tang Tsou. Chicago: University of Chicago Press.

United Nations Center on Transnational Corporations (UNCTC). 1988. *Foreign Direct Investment in the People's Republic of China.* New York: United Nations Publications.

United States Embassy in Beijing. 1986. "Problems Posed by China's Possible Admission to the GATT." Paris: U.S. OECD Trade Committee Working Party.

Wade, Robert. 1988. "The Role of Government in Overcoming Market Failure: Taiwan, Republic of Korea, and Japan." In *Achieving Industrialization in East Asia*, ed. H. Hughes. Cambridge: Cambridge University Press.

————. 1990. "Industrial Policy in East Asia: Does It Lead or Follow the Market." In *Manufacturing Miracles: Paths of Industrialization in Latin America and East Asia*, ed. G. Gereffi and D. Wyman. Princeton: Princeton University Press.

Wadekin, Karl-Eugene. 1990. "Is There a 'Privatization' of Soviet Agriculture." In *Socialism, Perestroika, and the Dilemmas of Soviet Economic Reform*, ed. John E. Tedstrom. Boulder, CO: Westview Press.

Walder, Andrew. 1987. "Wage Reform and the Web of the Factory Interests." *China Quarterly*, no. 109 (March):22–41.

Wang, N. T. 1984. "Reforms in Foreign Trade and Investment in China." *Hong Kong Economic Papers* (December).

Wang, Y. 1987. *Jingji gaige yu lishi weiwu zhuyi tizhi* (Economic reform and the system of historical materialism). Beijing: Zhonggu jingji chubanshe.

Wells, Louis, Jr. 1983. *Third World Multinationals, The Rise of Foreign Investment from Developing Countries*. Cambridge, MA: MIT Press.

Westphal, Larry E. 1984. "Fostering Technology Mastery by Means of Selective Infant Industry Protection." In *Trade, Stability, Technology and Equity in Latin America*, ed. M. Syrquin and S. Teitel. New York: Academic Press.

Wickman, Stephen B. 1981. "The Economy." In *North Korea: A Country Study*, ed. F. Bunge. Washington, DC: American University.

Williamson, Oliver E. 1975. *Markets and Hierarchies: Analysis and Anti-Trust Implications*. New York: Free Press.

Winiecki, Jan. 1990. "Why Economic Reforms Fail in the Soviet System: A Property Rights–Based Approach." *Economic Inquiry* (April 28): 195–221.

Wong, Christine. 1985. "Material Allocation and Decentralization: Impact of the Local Sector on Industrial Reform." In *The Political Economy of Reform in Post-Mao China*, ed. E. Perry and C. Wong. Cambridge, MA: Council on East Asian Studies, Harvard University.

Xiamen City, Bureau of Foreign Company Management. 1991. *A Guide to Investment in the Xiamen Special Economic Zone*. Xiamen: Xiamen City Government Press.

Xiao, Liang. 1986. "Gaige chengzhen jiti suoyouzhi jingjide jige wenti" (Several problems in reforming urban collective economy). *Jingji tizhi gaige* 2:12–17.

Yan, Zhongdai, and Huiqin Li. 1990. *Investment in Mainland China and Its Impact on Taiwan Industry* (in Chinese). Taipei: Chunghua Institution for Economic Research.

Yu, Tzong-shian. 1988. "Unofficial Trade between the Mainland and Taiwan." Paper presented at the Conference on Chinese Economic Relations held at the University of California at Berkeley.

Yun, Ken. 1989. "Crossing the Yellow Sea." *China Business Review* (January–February):38–48.

Zhang, Gangzhu. 1988. "Qiye jiduande gufenzhi gouzhao" (Shareholding structure of the enterprise group). *Jingji lilun yu jingji guanli* 3:34–39.

Zhang, Guisheng. 1988. "Qianyi zhengqu fenkaide qiben tujing" (A tentative discussion on the basic approach to the separation of the government and the enterprise). *Jingji guanli* 1:42–43.

Zhang, Yingteng. 1988. "An Analysis of Factors Influencing Indirect Trade between Taiwan and Mainland China through Hong Kong." Paper presented at China–Korea Conference on System Integration of Divided Nations, Taipei, December.

————. 1989. "An Analysis of Factors Influencing China–Taiwan Trade through Hong Kong" (in Korean). *East Asian Research* 16:645–68.6.

Zhang, Yingfeng, and Huizi Shi. 1989. *A Study of the Investment Climate in Mainland China and Investment Relations across the Strait* (in Chinese). Taipei: Chunghua Institution for Economic Research.

Zheng, Guangliang. 1987. "The Leadership System." In Tidrick and Chen, eds., 1987.

Zhou Qiren and Zhangjun Hu. 1989. "Asset Formation and Operational Features of Industrial Enterprises in Chinese Townships and Their Macro-Effects." *Social Sciences in China* (Summer):108–44.

Zou, Gang, and Jun Ma. 1989. "China's Coastal Development Strategy and Pacific Rim Free Trade Block." Paper presented at the Conference on the Pacific Asian Business, Honolulu, Hawaii.

Zysman, John. 1983. *Government, Market, and Growth: Financial Systems and the Politics of Industrial Change*. Ithaca and London: Cornell University Press.

Index

Keun Lee is an assistant professor in the Department of Economics, Seoul National University, and an associate editor for *Seoul Journal of Economics*. After receiving a Ph.D. in economics from the University of California, Berkeley, he became a research fellow at the Institute for Economic Development and Policy at the East-West Center, Hawaii, and later a lecturer in economics at the University of Aberdeen, Scotland. A specialist in economic development and comparative economic systems in East Asia, he has published articles in such journals as the *Cambridge Journal of Economics, Journal of Comparative Economics, Economics of Planning,* and *World Development,* as well as a monograph entitled *Chinese Firms and the State in Transition: Property Rights and Agency Problems in the Reform Era* (1991).